Palgrave Studie

Series Editors
Michelle Brown
Department of Sociology
University of Tennessee
Knoxville, TN, USA

Eamonn Carrabine
Department of Sociology
University of Essex
Colchester, UK

This series aims to publish high quality interdisciplinary scholarship for research into crime, media and culture. As images of crime, harm and punishment proliferate across new and old media there is a growing recognition that criminology needs to rethink its relations with the ascendant power of spectacle. This international book series aims to break down the often rigid and increasingly hardened boundaries of mainstream criminology, media and communication studies, and cultural studies. In a late modern world where reality TV takes viewers into cop cars and carceral spaces, game shows routinely feature shame and suffering, teenagers post 'happy slapping' videos on YouTube, both cyber bullying and 'justice for' campaigns are mainstays of social media, and insurrectionist groups compile footage of suicide bomb attacks for circulation on the Internet, it is clear that images of crime and control play a powerful role in shaping social practices. It is vital then that we become versed in the diverse ways that crime and punishment are represented in an era of global interconnectedness, not least since the very reach of global media networks is now unparalleled.

Palgrave Studies in Crime, Media and Culture emerges from a call to rethink the manner in which images are reshaping the world and criminology as a project. The mobility, malleability, banality, speed, and scale of images and their distribution demand that we engage both old and new theories and methods and pursue a refinement of concepts and tools, as well as innovative new ones, to tackle questions of crime, harm, culture, and control. Keywords like image, iconography, information flows, the counter-visual, and 'social' media, as well as the continuing relevance of the markers, signs, and inscriptions of gender, race, sexuality, and class in cultural contests mark the contours of the crime, media and culture nexus.

More information about this series at
http://www.palgrave.com/gp/series/15057

Rebecca M. Hayes • Kate Luther

#Crime

Social Media, Crime, and the Criminal Legal System

palgrave
macmillan

Rebecca M. Hayes
Central Michigan University
Mount Pleasant, MI, USA

Kate Luther
Pacific Lutheran University
Tacoma, WA, USA

Palgrave Studies in Crime, Media and Culture
ISBN 978-3-319-89443-0   ISBN 978-3-319-89444-7   (eBook)
https://doi.org/10.1007/978-3-319-89444-7

Library of Congress Control Number: 2018941099

Cover image © myella/Getty Images
Cover design by Tjaša Krivec

This Palgrave Macmillan imprint is published by the registered company Springer Nature Switzerland AG
The registered company address is: Gewerbestrasse 11, 6330 Cham, Switzerland

Acknowledgments

We both would like to thank some amazing colleagues for their time and care that they took in reviewing drafts of the chapters. Thank you to Dr. Gregg Barak, Dr. Raymond Surette, Dr. Emily Lenning, and Dr. Walter DeKeseredy. Thank you also to contributors Inspector Sylva Polfliet, Dr. Raymond Surette, Dr. Nicola Henry and Dr. Anastasia Powell. It is always helpful to have experts on the matter contribute their own words. Also, thank you to Chrissy Cook who went above and beyond to provide additional information on trolling. It is colleagues such as these that make this job worth doing.

Rebecca M. Hayes Writing a book was on my bucket list and was a very difficult, frustrating, and yet rewarding experience. I would like to give a special thanks to my patient coauthor, Dr. Kate Luther, who's more than a colleague, but also a wonderful friend. I would also like to thank my two favorite coffee shop owners: Thomas Vreriks (Mr. Bean in Leuven, Belgium) and Cara Nader (Strange Matter Coffee in Lansing, Michigan); if your businesses did not exist, my business would never get done. Finally, I thank my partner, Nick Garlinghouse as you had to provide all the stress reduction at the end of this project. Thank you for your patience as well.

Kate Luther Writing this book with Dr. Rebecca M. Hayes has yet again proven that she is an amazing coauthor and friend. I would like to thank my students at Pacific Lutheran University, who I kept in mind throughout the writing process as I framed arguments and wrote discussion questions. I would also like to thank my family for putting up with this project that took over our dining room table during my sabbatical.

Contents

List of Boxes

Chapter 4

Chapter 5

Introduction

We live in a digital culture. It is undeniable and unavoidable. There are few places where one can go in our society without some form of media being present. Today, media impacts all of our social institutions, and the criminal legal system is no exception. Based on the pervasiveness of media, and in particular new media, we set off in this book to explore the connections between media and crime.

We begin each chapter with a real-world example of a crime connected to media. These connections include how new media is utilized to: inform the public about incidents of crime; document criminal motivations by perpetrators; aid law enforcement investigations; and react to injustices in the criminal legal system. Throughout each chapter, we refer back to these examples to explain different concepts. As new media is quickly changing, we recognize that by the time this book is published, some of these examples may seem outdated. We tried to choose examples that address significant issues that will continue to be concerns of the criminal legal system for years to come.

Much of the research we use in this book examines crime and media in Western societies. This is due to the fact that a lot of research is focused on Western societies, primarily the Global North. Where possible, we include research on the Global South, mainly Australia. The literature referenced in these chapters is largely drawn from traditional scholarly sources, yet as a book addressing media we also utilize many media sources from around the globe and provide specific examples from social media platforms. These examples help to illustrate our arguments and provide the reader with clear connections between media and crime.

We hope this book inspires students of criminology to consider the ways new media shapes perceptions of crime, the commission of crime, and criminal legal system responses. Due to the small amount of research on new media and crime, we ask the reader to consider many questions that are yet to be answered by scholars. By doing this, we want to encourage innovative research that helps to grow the interdisciplinary study of new media and crime.

1

#Crime: The Theoretical Underpinnings

On the evening of Friday, November 13, 2015, a group of men killed 130 people and injured hundreds through a series of attacks in Paris. The so-called Islamic State (also referred to as Isis, Isil, or Daesh) claimed responsibility for the attacks at the Bataclan Concert Hall, where the American rock band Eagles of Death played; outside of the Stade de France, which was hosting an international football match; and at multiple restaurants and a bar. Following the attacks, police led raids in both France and Belgium, where many of the men lived, to arrest those associated with the planning and execution of the attacks (BBC 2015a; Reuters 2015). Throughout this chapter, we refer back to these horrific crimes and subsequent investigations to explore the role of new media, to examine the applicability of criminological theory to crimes that transcend borders, and to highlight key concepts in the study of media and crime.

Terrorism is the crime du jour in our global society of the twenty-first century. While efforts to focus on terrorism are negotiated and policies are created, there is a need to discuss the role that media, and in particular new media (e.g. social media), plays in the commission, perception, and reaction to this crime. In response to the Paris terrorist attacks, Rutledge (2015) wrote in her blog post in *Psychology Today*:

© The Author(s) 2018
R. M. Hayes, K. Luther, *#Crime*, Palgrave Studies in Crime, Media and Culture,
https://doi.org/10.1007/978-3-319-89444-7_1

Social media is the terrorist's best and worst friend. Acts of terrorism need to be public to get attention, make a statement and spread fear. Social media amplifies these events, allowing people around the world to instantaneously see and respond to the horror and to feel the sense of vulnerability and chaos. Social media is also the terrorist's worst friend. Social media shows terrorism for what it is, senseless, reprehensible violence. It unites people against their cause.

This quote highlights the importance of new media in the study of crime. The massive assault in Paris was coordinated across borders in Europe and the aftermath of the crime played out on new media platforms throughout the world. The role of new media and how it impacts the act of crime, criminal justice responses not only within a country but also across borders, and perceptions of crime need to be better understood both theoretically and empirically.

There is an extensive body of literature examining legacy media (e.g. traditional media) and crime, and over approximately the past ten years scholars have *begun* to explore the impact of new media on crime. According to Surette and Gardiner-Bess (2014), there has been little research on this relationship, but there are plenty of hypotheses. Throughout this book, we draw from cutting-edge criminological and media studies research on new media, as well as proposing and discussing hypotheses for future research. We pose questions that encourage the reader to consider how new media applies to and expands existing theoretical frameworks and research in our global world that is increasingly interconnected through new media.

As new media is an ever-changing technology, writing this book was a daunting task. Questions about whether our examples would be outdated by the time this went into print were asked, to which we responded, "Yes, of course." New examples will always present themselves as they do in all areas of justice inquiry. Even when examples are no longer fresh, the concepts and issues raised with the "outdated" examples can still be relevant. For example, criminal justice textbooks in the United States commonly discuss the O. J. Simpson trial (see box *O.J. Simpson*), which occurred over 20 years ago, but is still timely for numerous reasons. The role of race and racism in the trial, which led to much divisiveness in how the trial was viewed by white versus black Americans (Brown et al. 1997), is still relevant in today's criminal justice system. Likewise, the notion of being able to buy your innocence and America's fascination with celebrity status (especially sports celebrities) were also key issues in this case that continue to be relevant. And, most pertinent to this book from the O. J. Simpson trial is how it brought up questions about the role of the media in criminal proceedings. Judge Lance Ito allowed television cameras into the courtroom to capture the entire trial, which contributed to the fascination with the case. Even though the murders of Nicole Brown and Ron Goldman occurred in 1994, this case is part of our collective understanding of how the criminal justice system operates in America (Barak 1996; Brown et al. 1997; Dershowitz 1997). The current interest in the case is evidenced by FX's recent *The People vs. O.J. Simpson: American Crime Story* (2016) and ESPN's *O.J.: Made in America* (2016), which continue to encourage conversations about race, crime, and the media.

O. J. Simpson Orenthal James (O. J.) Simpson, a United States football star, was charged with murdering his ex-wife, Nicole Brown Simpson, and Ronald Lyle Goldman. He was acquitted of their murders in criminal court, but later found liable of battery and wrongful death in civil court. The cases, which occurred during the 1990s, were publicized in a manner that previous cases in the United States had not been. It was one of the first cases where cameras were allowed in the courtroom, which allowed the public a firsthand look at the criminal legal system that previously did not exist, and thus ushered in a new era of media involvement in the criminal legal system. Even more interesting is that these cases brought about questions and discussions about the US legal system, race, gender, and class, which provide a unique look into American society. This case (even 20 years later) is still being discussed and is still presented in many criminal justice texts. There was even an *FX* series on this case in 2016. (For further reading on this case and its impact, refer to Gregg Barak's, 2012 *Representing O.J.: Murder, Criminal Justice and Mass Culture* or Jeffrey Toobin *The Run of his Life: The People v. O.J. Simpson*.)

In the following chapter, we:

1. Define legacy media and new media with particular attention to social media
2. Discuss trends in media consumption
3. Overview a selection of key theories (Social Construction, Moral Panics, and Cultivation Theory) on media and crime, and how/if they are applicable to new media
4. Discuss new theories and concepts that directly apply to new media and crime

Defining Media and Exploring Trends

It is important to establish the distinctions between legacy and new media as even though there is overlap there are differences in the effects of each on the criminal legal system. *Legacy media* includes print media (pamphlets, novels, newspapers, etc.), visual media (television, film), and sound media (radio). *New media* includes the internet, social media, electronic games, and the smartphone. While these definitions are taken partially from Surette (2015), we acknowledge that there are competing definitions of these terms and some overlap between them. For example, traditional print media is now available through social media.

Media began with print, followed by audiovisual, and finally, the digital age emerged (University of Minnesota nd), where media is now commonly accessed through the internet. In a Ted talk, Shirky (2009), a journalism professor who specializes in global networks, discusses how social media is the next big boom that ties all previous media booms together. The printing press, the telephone, the television have all evolved with social media. Everyone has a printing press in their pocket with a smartphone, access to the internet, and a social media account. Media is now almost instantaneous. When something happens in our social world, we can tweet or post an Instagram picture immediately. Shirky provides the example of public officials in China not admitting to an earthquake until three months after it took place. More recently, an earthquake in China was reported on Twitter in real time and public officials were not able to delay their reporting of the event. This made us think about how social media is impacting crime, the criminal justice system, and the public response. One such example is the recent fatal shooting of Philando Castile by police in Minnesota, the United States, which was livestreamed on Facebook by his girlfriend. Instead of the police being able to control the narrative, Castile's girlfriend was able to shape the narrative with her real-time video (CNN 2016).

Throughout this book we use the term "new media," which encompasses social media (Surette 2013), but we need to spend some time defining social media, which itself has many definitions. The *Oxford Dictionary* defines social media as "websites and applications that enable users to create and share content or to participate in social networking." Similarly, the *Merriam-Webster Dictionary* defines social media as "forms of electronic communication (as Web sites for social networking and microblogging) through which users create online communities to share information, ideas, personal messages, and other content (as videos)" (April 26, 2016). However, in communication studies an accessible commonly used definition is: "Social media are Internet-based channels that allow users to opportunistically interact and selectively self-present, either in real time or asynchronously, with both broad and narrow audiences who derive value from user-generated content and the perception of interaction with others" (Carr and Hayes 2015, p. 50). From Carr and Hayes (2015) here are *some* examples of social media: social network sites (e.g. Facebook and Google Plus), professional network sites (e.g. LinkedIn), Tinder, and Instagram. Here are some examples of *not* social medium: online news services (e.g. NYT online, PerezHilton.com), Wikipedia, Skype, Netflix, E-Mail, Online News, SMS/Texts, Oovoo, Tumblr, and Whisper. Largely, it seems that at least according to Carr and Hayes (2015), when we discuss social media, we are often discussing social networking, which to us is a subset of social media.

According to Wikipedia, here are the top ten most popular social network sites of August 2017: Facebook, YouTube, WhatsApp, Facebook Messenger, WeChat, QQ, Instagram, QZone, Tumblr, and Twitter. Social networks are a subset of social media, and most of the time when people are talking about social media, they are discussing social networks. Blogging and microblogging are also social media, but do not seem to be nearly as popular as they once were. Here is a list of each of some of the popular and common social media:

Student Activity *Define each of these forms of new media and come up with idea of how it can be involved with the commission or control of crime. Additionally, what new media is not listed here? How could this media be involved with the commission or control of crime?*

- Facebook
- Twitter
- LinkedIn
- Pinterest
- Google Plus
- Tumblr
- Instagram
- Vkontakte
- Flickr
- Vine
- Snapchat
- Reddit
- 4chan or 8chan

We are sure that as you are reading this, this list has already changed. Ello, in 2014, for example, attempted to take on the giant moguls at Facebook by offering a minimalistic design and promising an ad-free space. Ello, as of this writing, has not gained popularity, but a change in the technological climate, such as a data breach, could change the social media landscape.

The Changing Mediascape

With legacy media, radio, newspaper, and television all had their day. Now these media are evolving in the new media space, and this comes with some decline. The newspaper business overall continues to decrease in popularity in the United States, with a recent 7% decrease in daily circulation, according to the most recent State of the News Media report (PEW 2016). Some of the other key findings comparing 2014–2015 from this report include a/an:

- 8% increase in cable television viewership, which PEW suggests may be related to interest in the presidential primary
- 5% (late night) and 2% (morning) decrease in local television viewership
- 1% (evening) increase and 2% (morning) decrease in network television viewership

These trends are also mirrored in Europe. For example, in Europe newspapers have also decreased in popularity (De Bens 2004; Lauf 2001). Market research in Belgium highlighted that it is mainly young, single, urbanized men that are not reading newspapers (De Bens 2004). This is not a new decline, as research has demonstrated that in Europe newspaper readership has been on the decline since the 1980s and this is due to age and cohort effects, mostly that young people do not read the news daily (Lauf 2001). Another place where there is a global decline is in television viewership. Media reports argue that there is a decline in overall television viewing as noted in the report by Luckerson (2014) in *Time* magazine, or a recent article on *Screen Media Daily* (2015). Though on the decline, television is still the main source for news consumption with internet being a close second in 9 out of 11 countries (exceptions were Norway and South Korea) in a study by Papthanassopoulos et al. (2013).

The State of the News Media (PEW 2016) report in the United States also highlighted the use of digital media platforms for accessing news media. Although the majority of surveyed Americans "often get news" through television (57%), 38% said that they "often get news" through digital sources. Between 2014 and 2015, the audiences for digital news sources grew and, in particular, much of the growth was due to consumers accessing their news on mobile devices versus desktops. Indeed, regarding television, in 2015 the Nielsen report stated that media usage is moving to mobile and TV-connected devices and the largest growth is among those aged 18–34 and 35–49 (Nielsen Report 2016). The Nielsen report for 2016 stated this breakdown more specifically, according to which media consumption for adults of ages 18–34 is as follows: only 29% of TV, 18% radio, 9% PC, 11% TV-connected devices, 28% smartphones, and 5% tablets (Nielsen Report 2017). Compare that with adults over 50, where 55% of their consumption is TV, 18% radio, 3% TV-connected devices, 8% PC, 14% smartphones, and 3% tablets. While television viewing is still occurring, there is a shift toward greater use of these platforms.

Another new media trend are podcasts. Coincidently, Serial, "the world's most popular podcast" (Ronson 2014), is about crime and criminal justice—or possibly injustice. Podcasts are still not listened to by the majority of Americans, but they are growing in popularity (PEW 2016). In 2016, 21% of Americans (ages 12 and older) were listening to podcasts, which is a significant increase from 9% in 2008. Although podcasts do not have the audiences of other forms of media, such as television or social media, there is increasing investment in podcasting by news organizations (PEW 2016). The "Serial Effect," referenced in the State of the News Media report (PEW 2016), refers to the growth in podcasting following the popularity of Serial.

This change in news consumption and television viewing among younger people can be broken down further. For example, in the United States, where 69% of adults use social media (PEW 2017), we do see there are some differences in social media usage based on sex, age, education, and income level. According to the Pew Research Center (2017), in the United States:

- Women (72%) use social networking sites more than men (66%)
- 86% of adults aged 18–29 use social media compared with 80% for those aged 30–49, 64% for those aged 50–64, and 34% for those aged 65 and older
- 78% of adults with college degrees use social media compared to 58% of adults with high school degrees or less
- 78% of adults with incomes $75,000 and above use social media in comparison to 60% of adults with incomes below $30,000

In the United Kingdom, according to the Office for National Statistics (2016), we see similar trends with 63% of adults (ages 16 years and older) using social networking sites such as Facebook and Twitter. Additionally,

- Women (64%) and men (62%) use social networking sites at similar rates
- 91% of individuals of ages 16–24 use social networking sites compared with 89% of individuals of ages 25–34, 75% of individuals of ages 35–44, 66% of individuals of ages 45–54, 51% of individuals of ages 55–64, and 23% of individuals aged 65 and older

Social media sites have not shown any sign of slowing, as the number of worldwide users of social networking sites is expected to reach 2.5 billion by 2018 (Statista 2016). North America has the highest concentration of social networks with 60% of the population having an account. Facebook leads the social networking scene, as the only site with over 1.5 billion active users worldwide. With social networking users logging 101.4 minutes per day on these sites, this demonstrates high and consistent exposure (Statista 2016). Access to social media sites has only increased with the use of smartphones and tablets. Again, the leader here is Facebook with 580 million users in the first quarter in 2015 accessing the site solely through mobile devices.

These numbers all clearly demonstrate that usage is on the rise and evident across the globe. With such popularity of new media, it is even more pertinent to examine the impact this has on crime, definitions of crime, and the criminal justice system.

Theoretical Perspectives for Crime and Media Research

As a field of study, media and crime can be considered a subdiscipline underneath the larger field of criminology. Greer coined the term "News Media Criminology" (2010) when referring to the main theoretical issues and debates in the media, crime, and justice landscape. We venture to call it Media Criminology (Jewkes 2015), instead of News Media Criminology, in order to embrace all media—both legacy and new—that shapes the commission, control, and perceptions of crime. Regardless of the terminology, this field is interdisciplinary with criminology, sociology, social psychology, communications, media studies, and cultural studies.

Within criminology, Media Criminology is often studied from the cultural or critical criminological perspective. "In this world the street scripts the screen and the screen scripts the street; there is no clearly linear sequence, but rather a shifting interplay between the real and the virtual, the factual and the fictional" (Ferrell et al. 2008, pp. 123–124). This quote highlights the cultural criminological perspective. Cultural criminology examines how the *culture* aids implicitly in the construction of crime and crime control (Ferrell et al. 2012). One of cultural criminology's main principle states "that cultural dynamics carry within them the meaning of crime" (Ferrell et al. 2012, p. 2). Cultural criminologists acknowledge the importance of power, hegemonic relationships, and the constant shifting of collective meaning and identity that impacts definitions, experiences, and reactions to crime. New media is a cultural tool and needs to be studied within the cultural criminological framework. Likewise, Media Criminology is also studied within critical criminology. Critical criminologists focus on the influence of power and the state in labeling what is deemed by a society as crime. Starting with Hall et al.'s (1978) pivotal work in critical criminology—*Policing the Crisis: Mugging, the State and Law and Order*—critical criminologists have focused on the media's role in defining crime (Jewkes 2010, 2015). Hall et al.'s examination of how mugging became defined as a major social issue (i.e. moral panic) in British society in the 1970s is still an important empirical piece in Media Criminology, as many scholars use this study as a theoretical basis for their research.

Drawing from criminology, and in particular cultural and critical criminology, sociology, media studies, communications, and cultural studies, we overview the major theoretical frameworks guiding Media Criminology. As these disciplines derive from multiple perspectives, there are different and sometimes conflicting theories and methods which complicate the merging of these fields. When appropriate, we bring attention to these challenges facing media criminologists, especially regarding the study of new media. The research agenda for Media Criminology is continually shaped by the theoretical concepts of newsworthiness (certain characteristics that are perceived to have public appeal

(Jewkes 2004) are explained in more detail in Chap. 2), fear of crime, and moral panics (Greer 2010). We begin by discussing three key theoretical perspectives—social construction, moral panics, and fear of crime/cultivation theory—which will be referenced throughout the book to understand media and crime.

Social Construction

At the most basic level, social constructionists argue that individuals place meaning on a certain event or object and that becomes our reality. Regarding crime, there are some acts (murder or theft) that are constructed and fixed as criminal in many cultures and through different times; in contrast, there are other acts (alcohol or marijuana usage) that are constructed as crimes, but ideas about them change throughout time and within different cultures (see Surette and Otto 2001). Therefore, these criminalized constructs are legitimized or delegitimized as actual crime and become worthy of academic research (Surette 2015). Surette and Otto (2001) argue that the media play the primary role in the (de)criminalization process.

Surette (2015, p. 33; direct quotes with our words in brackets), in *Media, Crime and Criminal Justice*, outlines how crime is socially constructed in four steps:

1. The Physical World—[is where] crimes or terrorist acts occur and are noted by individuals and organizations.
2. Competing Social Constructions—offer differing descriptions of what the physical world is like [and] differing explanations of why the physical world is as it is purported to be, [which then we] argue for a set of public and individual policies.
3. Media as Social Construction Competition Arena—[is where] the media help filter out competing constructions. [At this stage, media chooses which social constructions of crime receive the most attention. Surette writes that if those advocating for a particular construction are not skilled at working with media, their construction of crime may never be heard.]

4. Winning Social Construction—[is the] emergence of a dominant social construction, [which] directs public policy. [Surette argues that the media is extremely influential in this process because most people do not have direct knowledge of crime related issues].

Following these steps, let's walk through the social construction of sexual assault on college campuses in the United States. First, non-consensual sexual contact occurs on college campuses. This criminal behavior is recognized by individuals—victims, friends, and family members—and organizations—campus counseling centers, law enforcement, and victim advocates. Second, there have been differing social constructions of this behavior. One explanation blames victims for being intoxicated or dressing provocatively and encourages college students to avoid behaving in ways that "ask for" sexual assault. Another explanation is that certain college students are preying on fellow students and engaging in criminal behavior. This construction advocates for campus policies including processing those accused of sexual assault through the campus discipline system (and sometimes through the criminal justice system, as well) and teaching college students how to become active bystanders so they can intervene in potential sexual assaults. At the third stage, media plays a role in determining which social construction garners the most attention. Does the media portray victims as encouraging sexual assault or perpetrators as committing a crime? Last, through this process, "a dominant social construction" of campus sexual assault emerges, which in turn leads to public policy. Campus sexual assault is now viewed as a serious social problem in the United States, which is evidenced by the US Federal Government's Not Alone Program (https://www.notalone.gov/) under President Obama. As we write this book, Betsy DeVos, President Trump's secretary of education, appears to be challenging the dominant social construction of campus sexual assault and working to change Obama-era policy.

Student Activity *Work through the four steps in the social construction of crime with the Paris Bombings.*

The social construction of crime is constantly changing. "Revenge porn" is a current example of something that is being socially constructed into a crime. Briefly, "revenge porn" in colloquial terms or "image-based sexual abuse" in academic circles (DeKeseredy and Schwartz 2016) describes how sexualized images or videos that are created with consent are then distributed online without consent (Salter and Crofts 2015). This typically follows the termination of a relationship or during an attempt to terminate the relationship and is seen as an act of "revenge." This is an issue which has required some attention within countries such as the United States (Franks 2015) or New Zealand (Smith 2015) where legislation is being created in response. As mentioned by Surette (2016), criminologists think that they lead in the creation of what constitutes important crime and justice issues; instead, in the case of revenge porn, it was very clearly picked up by the media before criminologists. Not only that, but it was constructed in an online environment and spread primarily through new media such as Reddit and blogs. Only now are academics beginning to research this phenomenon and, even so, not at a rate to provide a firm understanding of the issue. The question remains as to whether revenge porn is a crime, which highlights the social construction process of defining behavior as criminal. We return to revenge porn in Chaps. 4 and 5.

When discussing the social construction of crime, we draw attention to the popular example of copycat crime. Recent case study work demonstrates how the long history of "copycat crime" has evolved into a socially constructed criminalized term worthy of research (see Surette 2016). "Copycat crime" is a term used to describe a crime that is thought to mirror the circumstances of a prior mediated representation of a fictional or nonfictional crime (Surette 2016). School shootings are one example of a crime discussed by the news media as having potential to result in a copycat crime. It is suggested that individuals will watch the reporting and discussion of a school shooting and will then, in turn, commit a similar—copycat—crime to gain similar recognition. As Surette (2013, 2015) explains, the media is the important linkage in this process, in that if it was not for the media representation of the first crime, the second crime would not exist. Some discussions regarding terrorist events suggest that it is the media coverage and recognition the terrorists are seeking, in order to create fear and recruit for their cause; but a copycat may engage in a terrorist activity, and it is the recognition itself that serves their purpose (Surette 2015). Following this logic, in the case of the Paris bombing, others may become emboldened to engage in further terrorist activity in order to receive that media coverage. Only their event needs to create more chaos and carnage in order to compete for the media spotlight.

At this point, copycat crimes are more often a tagline haphazardly applied by the media, and are rarely subjected to an empirical analysis. Surette (2016) noticed this substantial gap in the literature and created a methodological tool that includes seven indicators that can be used to assess whether a crime is a copycat. These indicators include: time order, time proximity, theme consistency, scene specificity, repetitive viewing, self-editing, offender statements, and second-party statements. Now criminological inquiry can assess with more confidence the incidences in which the media report are copycat crimes.

New media offers a place for criminologists to engage in the construction of the crime issues, called Newsmaking Criminology (Barak 1988, 2007). In the 1980s, Gregg Barak coined the term "Newsmaking Criminology" and encouraged criminologists to engage with the media and examine how it socially constructs problems. It is where criminologists aid in writing the media narrative, rather than simply being used as a "prop" to back up the already-constructed narrative (Barak 2007). Barak (1988) argued that it is important to establish relationships with journalists and contribute in a real way as a type of public intellectual. With new media, a criminologist can become the main narrative voice for issues. For example, Dr. Chris Uggen, an established criminologist and recent past president of the American Society of Criminology, has a blog http://chrisuggen.blogspot.be/ and a Twitter account (with 4786 followers at the time of writing this book, which although isn't considered a large Twitter following, he is able to educate a larger audience than just students in his classrooms) where he discusses crime-related issues. Similarly, in 2017, the leadership of the American Society of Criminology put forth the hashtag #realcrimedata and are urging criminologists to use this hashtag when posting about their research. Of course, one needs followers in order to reach the public, and this is where having an established relationship with legacy media is helpful. If the press decides to cite you, it could increase your readership and thus your impact in shaping the crime and justice narrative.

Moral Panics

Building on social construction research, the concept of *moral panic*s was first developed through sociological research and continues to be a very popular media and crime theory (e.g. Critcher 2003; Carrabine 2008; Jewkes 2004). The basis of a *moral panic* is how society will focus and react (read: panic) to a certain behavior/issue and subsequently demonize the group they see as responsible for the behavior. Moral panics were introduced by Jock Young in 1971 (Carrabine 2008), with his study of drug taking, but popularized by Cohen in 1972 with his research on the construction of deviance (Cohen 2008). Originally, this theory was primarily written and applied to deviant youth subcultures such as mods/rockers, juvenile muggers, children viewing violent videos, ravers, and ecstasy users.

The demonization of certain social behaviors over others generally includes what is termed a *folk devil* (Cohen 1972). The *folk devil* is essentially a societal scapegoat that can be blamed for any type of real or constructed social problem. The folk devils in many moral panic narratives are minority youth, especially if they are viewed as threatening to the status quo (Hall et al. 1978, 2013). In moral panics, folk devils are generally marginalized and negatively socially constructed. One of the seminal studies of moral panics is Hall et al.'s (1978, 2013) examination of the media frenzy that encouraged extreme treatment of blacks in the United Kingdom by law enforcement. This original research on mugging demonstrates how moral panics can be used as a form of social control. Although this study is almost 40 years old, its key findings are still relevant. A more recent empirical example is the Rotherham abuse scandal in the United Kingdom, where girls were sexually abused from 1997 to 2013 (Meyer 2016), but the media coverage overestimated the number of victims, used emotive language that could be fear inducing, and created "folk devils" of Asian men and the public sector for failure to protect.

We can use the moral panic framework to understand the United States' War on Drugs (see box *War on Drugs*), where the main narrative scapegoated inner-city black youth as "crack dealers and users." This moral panic led to the 100:1 sentencing disparity between crack cocaine and powder cocaine in 1986 and 1988 (this was changed to an 18:1 sentencing disparity through the Fair Sentencing Act of 2010). This moral panic led to a mass incarceration of predominantly black low-level dealers or users of marijuana, which is discrepant to the race comparison among usage statistics (Alexander 2011). During the time that this moral panic took place, in the late 1980s and today, statistics demonstrate that illicit drug use among non-Hispanic African-Americans and whites are similar, with African-American youth statistics demonstrably lower than white youth (Bachman et al. 1990; Wallace et al. 2002; Alexander 2011). This moral panic was far-reaching, and a case study of one town of Tulia, Texas, demonstrates the gravity of the issue. In Tulia, in 1999, 10% of the town's African-American population were arrested on drug charges based on the testimony of one undercover officer. In 2003, the convictions were overturned by a Dallas judge (https://www.aclu.org/racist-arrests-tulia-texas). Obviously, racial prejudice played a key role here, but initially went unnoticed. This is, at least partially, due to the moral panic that the war on drugs caused.

War on Drugs "The term war on drugs is a phrase often used but not defined" (Bush-Baskette 2010, p. 26). It is basically the political climate shift of the 1970s and 1980s regarding crime, which ushered in a focus on drugs as "the" crime problem, particularly crack cocaine. As politicians, media, and society defined drugs as a problem, legislation and penalties were increased for drug crimes and they largely targeted people of color (Alexander 2011). In order to define the War on Drugs, the policies, Anti-Drug Abuse Acts of 1986 and 1988, which resulted in mandatory minimum penalties for crimes involving crack cocaine, need to be included. The 1986 Act imposed mandatory minimum penalties for 29 felonies including crack cocaine. It also indicated a shift from treatment of drug offenders to the punishment of drug offenders by the US Federal Government. The 1988 Act amended the previous act and imposed mandatory imprisonment for individuals in possession of crack cocaine (Bush-Baskette 2010).

Recently, in the moral panic special edition of *Media, Crime & Culture*, Cohen (2011) predicted that migrants, refugees, and immigrants would end up in the moral panic narrative. An example of this in Europe is "benefit tourism" (Roberts 2015). When those who reside in the new and less-wealthy European Union (EU) countries perceive a threat to their safety and livelihood, it is assumed that they will engage in this so-called benefit tourism by moving to the wealthier countries to benefit from their social welfare system rather than working (Roberts 2015). This threat was largely lauded by politicians in the early 1990s, and there has not been much credence to this argument. The moral panic narrative of migrants/asylum seekers/refugees is also ongoing in both Europe and America through the veil of terrorism's threat and underlying Islamophobia. An Op-Ed ran in the *L.A. times* on October 13, 2015, titled *"Europe's Moral Panic about the Migrant Muslim Other."* Cottee (2015), a senior lecturer in Criminology at the University of Kent, stated:

> Muslim migrants press against sensitive nerves about the future of Europe and its cultural identity. They are a perfect target against which to redefine ever-blurring boundaries, the conjured folk devils stalking a troubled and rapidly changing landscape.

This op-ed was published just weeks before the terrorist attacks in Paris, which only added to the moral panic narrative. An example of similar othering was also demonstrated in the United States' presidential primary race in 2015. The presidential candidate and now president, Donald Trump, said regarding Muslims, "They are not coming to this country if I am president…We are not talking about isolation, we're talking about security. We're not talking about religion, we're talking about security. Our country is out of control" (Crilly 2015). Likewise, Seymour (2015) wrote an article on the "unchecked Islamaphobia" of France's far right. In this article there is a picture from a National Front party poster which shows a woman with a hat and a woman with a hijab and the statement, "Choose your Suburb: Vote Front." This campaign is clearly meant to "other" Muslim women. We will discuss this othering in more detail in Chap. 3, where we highlight how media impacts who we see as criminal. But, these anecdotal examples point in the direction of a moral panic through creation of a folk devil, and a thorough empirical analysis is needed.

When Donald Trump reacted to the attacks in Paris he "called for a database to track Muslims living in the United States," while his closest rival, Ben Carson, "suggested refugees of the Syrian conflict should be screened as they might be 'rabid dogs.'" (McCarthy and Jacobs 2015). However, even with this seemingly obvious negative rhetoric, not terming the reaction a "moral panic" is what Garland (2008) calls an ethics of attribution. An ethics of attribution is where the situation may appear to be a moral panic, but ethical considerations considering the sensitivity of the issue make it inappropriate to overtly state it as one. Calling these incidences "moral panics" might be considered innocuously inappropriate on one end and offensively insensitive on the other. After 9/11, the reaction was not described as a moral panic, even after interviews where "moral panic sociologists" acknowledged the signs while avoiding the usage of the exact term (Garland 2008). The issue is that the harm from these type of incidences is real, as is the threat of future danger and we as a society are unaware of the scope and scale, therefore making it seem insensitive (and highly political) to label them as moral panics even when the response to these incidences is often exaggerated.

Moral panics are tied to the politicalization of events (Cohen 2011; David et al. 2011), making these events and the response to them highly political. This is witnessed in the defining and response of many moral panics, such as in early work with "defining" muggers in the United Kingdom (Hall et al. 1978) or later work on climate change (Rohloff 2011). If we want to examine the ongoing terrorism situation as a moral panic, as Welch (2006) did referring to scapegoating post-9/11, this is tied to politics and impacts how the research will be received. In the same way, the response to the war on drugs was highly politicized and was part of the larger "get tough on crime" approach used by politicians in multiple parties in the United States.

Even though the study of moral panics has been traditionally associated with the field of deviance, studying moral panics is also a study of media's impact on what is labeled crime. Cohen focuses on the media in the second chapter of his book as a main driver of moral panics. Not without its critics and updates (Critcher 2003; David et al. 2011; Goode and Ben-Yehuda 1994; Garland 2008; Jewkes 2004; McRobbie and

Thornton 1995; Thompson 1998; Waddington 1986), this concept has proven to have withstood the test of time, but is it applicable to new media? Conceptualization and operationalization of moral panic theory differs according to each researcher's interpretation, which arguably means that the concept has probably been applied incorrectly (Critcher 2003; Garland 2008; Jewkes 2004). The cohesiveness of the theory is that it focuses on the definers of deviance, and those who study it seem to have a critical, humanist, interventionist, and mostly qualitative approach (David et al. 2011). Nevertheless, the commonness of the phrase has hit the media and the public, where "moral panic" is applied arbitrarily to a variety of events without careful scrutiny.

While the term "panic" itself implies an irrational reaction to something, Cohen argued that this is not necessarily the case. In order to make it easier here to understand moral panics, we adopted Jewkes' (2004) concise and straightforward formulation of the theory in her book, *Media and Crime*. According to Jewkes (2004, p. 67), there are five defining features of moral panic theory:

1. Moral panics occur when the mass media take a reasonably ordinary event and present it as an extraordinary occurrence.
2. The media sets in motion a "deviancy amplification spiral" in which a moral discourse is established by journalists and various other authorities, opinion leaders, and moral entrepreneurs, who collectively demonize the perceived wrongdoers as a source of moral decline and social disintegration.
3. Moral panics clarify the moral boundaries of the society in which they occur, creating consensus and concern.
4. Moral panics occur during periods of rapid social change, and can be said to locate and crystallize wider social anxieties about risk.
5. It is usually young people who are targeted, as they are a metaphor for the future, and their behavior is regarded as a barometer with which to test the health or sickness of a society.

Student Activity *Go back to Jewkes' five defining features of moral panic theory. Choose a "reasonably ordinary event" and discuss how it has turned into a moral panic.*

Jewkes' tenets reiterate how the media is the main driver of moral panics, but with social media there is a tipping of the control to the younger generations that was not present in legacy media. As mentioned earlier in this chapter, younger adults use significantly more social networking than older adults (Pew Research Center 2017). Moral panics typically target young people and social media might complicate this process. This means that young people can now impact the "moral panic" narrative in ways not previously possible. Therefore, we ask you to consider some questions in light of what you now know about social media usage and moral panics:

- Are moral panics by older generations against youth culture declining?
- In addition to being used more often by younger people, new media compared with legacy media is very interactive. How does the interactive new media impact the moral panic narrative, since legacy media is more passive?
- How does social media affect the moral panic narrative given its interactive *and* global reach? Will the global reach of social media make it easier to label moral panics on other societies?
- Was the original theory meant to address how one society can call moral panics on another society while ignoring the problems within their own?

Regarding the last two questions, moral panics can be declared in a particular society by another society. Garland (2008) discussed the misunderstandings, criticisms, and merits of moral panics, and used an example from the *New York Times* (NYT) of how they constructed a moral panic from the deaths of five British youth. The NYT article raised concern about the rise of drugs, firearms, and gangs, pointing out how this is indicative of a society that is losing control. An article in the *Daily Telegraph* argued that British society needed to be recivilized, and a conservative party leader also warned that this represented a breakdown of the family. According to Garland (2008, p. 15), in the United Kingdom there might be a shift from consensual moral panics to conflictual culture wars, where "the power balances between contending groups [are] much less asymmetrical." Consensual moral panics occurred when opposing viewpoints in the mass media were less common. Society was less globalized with less exposure to differing viewpoints, and it was easier to live in a "bubble," whereas conflictual culture wars are where there appears to be less societal agreement on an issue. An example in the United Kingdom (and other places in Europe) regards Muslim women wearing the hijab in school or other public places, where these countries are trying to ban or limit wearing the hijab. They appeared to start as moral panics, but quickly shifted to a political clash and subsequent debate (Garland 2008). The moral panic is about how the hijab represents a lack of integration into the mainstream culture, as aspects of Islam are seen as a threat to the manner in which the larger society chooses to live.

Social media complicates the cross-cultural moral panic narrative further as it is everywhere. Therefore, we may see more or less cultural conflict. Social media's impact on these types of arguments could shift the balance of power, by making the argument less one-sided and more accessible to multiple viewpoints. Of course, social media may not necessarily shift the power of the media but maintain it; future research will be able to shed some light on that discussion. Additionally, legacy media can be the cause (inciting it) of the moral panic, and then also turn around and criticize it as a moral panic in the same breath (Garland 2008), which could occur in social media as well.

At this point in our discussion of moral panics, you may be asking yourself if moral panics can have positive effects. Cohen (2011), one of the key scholars in this area of study, does think moral panics can be good. In this context, "good" means panicking about a situation that needs societal attention; "bad" means that moral panics overhype or misconstrue a situation and often target a group as the scapegoats, which leads to discrimination. For instance, Rohloff (2011) discusses Al Gore's *Inconvenient Truth* as an example of a "good moral panic," which drew attention and concern to climate change. Even feminists have been able to use the moral panic narrative to raise awareness about certain issues, such as violence against women (Cohen 2011). Critical of this is Critcher (2011), who argues that power matters. Some argue that extensions of moral panic theory to "good moral panics" could occur around white-collar or corporate crimes (which are largely ignored) and have impact on society, but Critcher (2011) would disagree due to the influence of power. White-collar criminals are too embedded in the power structure to really be labeled "folk devils." Time and academic research will confirm whether "good moral panics" exist.

Alternatively, what begins as a "bad moral panic" can backfire and become a "good moral panic." As we are writing this, in the United States transphobia appears to be taking hold in the political sphere. However, many Americans are not on board with this rhetoric. Recently, some states have introduced legislation or initiatives that seek to repeal non-discrimination protections or restrict transgender people's access to sex-/gender-specific facilities like restrooms. South Dakota introduced what is being called "the bathroom bill" in February 2016 and North Carolina in March 2016. Assuming these bills are actually enforceable (last time we checked, citizens do not carry their birth certificates to the restroom!), it would be legislation that is directed at people who do not neatly fit into gender expressions. What it does is allow open discrimination based on assumptions. It is difficult to ignore that this is occurring after same-sex marriage was supported in the US Supreme Court and became the law of the land. Or that this follows the "coming out" of transgendered individuals in television shows such as Laverne Cox in *Orange is the New Black* or Caitlynn Jenner, previously known as Bruce Jenner the Olympian, in *Keeping up with the Kardashians*. The political (perhaps moral panic) rhetoric is what we have seen before, where politicians are asserting that we are protecting women and children from sexual predators. While some of the public is "taking the bait," others are not, and protests against state governments have occurred. If this is a moral panic, meant to scapegoat transgendered individuals, it could end up being beneficial to the marginalized transgender population if these bills continue to be challenged by the public.

Regardless of good or bad moral panics, "A tabloid front page is often a self-fulfilling prophecy" (McRobbie and Thornton 1995, p. 485), and today it is online. Even though moral panics as a concept are still occurring, and updates to the theory have occurred (see the special edition of *Crime, Media & Culture,* 2011), the theory needs to be updated to account for new media. McRobbie and Thornton (1995) called for a restructuring of moral panic research in the 1990s as the world became more heavily multimediated. Likewise, Cohen (2011) briefly discussed how information technology and social networks are likely to impact how moral panics are created and disseminated. Thus, we call for research on *how* this will actually occur. As of this writing, it is 2018 and the globalization of the media and social media make cross-cultural influence more possible than in the past. The moral panic narrative is potentially wide-reaching. Social media is a space where anyone can report the news in real time as long as they have a smartphone. Those in power still hold some control over the media, but to what extent?

According to Critcher (2011), we are witnessing a time where media frames news issues as righteous, but yet are still contributing to the "culture of fear" (David et al. 2011). It is here that we now turn to the fear of crime discussion.

Fear of Crime and Cultivation Theory

Fear of crime, much like moral panics, has been extensively researched. Much of the fear of crime research, at least in Western democracies like the United States and the United Kingdom, proposes that people are fearful of crime to the extent that it affects their sense of safety and well-being (Hale 1996; Nalla et al. 2011; Warr 1984). In that, fear of crime makes crime appear to be a larger problem than it is in reality. The fear of crime is disproportionate to the rates of crime in society. Moral panics aid in fear of crime, and the result is reciprocal as fear of crime can make individuals more likely to react to a moral panic. For example, the moral panic narrative of immigrants, migrants, and asylum seekers turn them into scapegoats (aka folk devils) and the face of terrorism and crime. Underlying this is the fear of terrorism and crime. The fear of terrorism and crime is exacerbated by actual events, such as the Paris attacks or the sexual assault attacks in Cologne (see box *Cologne*). The people responsible for the Paris attacks are reported to have been part of IS and of North African or Arab descent in the attacks in Cologne. Then the actions of these attackers get placed on the people within a whole religion, country, and/or ethnicity. Thus, the moral panic narrative is confirmed to those who subscribe to it and it continues. One possible example of this is the recent Brexit vote in the United Kingdom to leave the EU. Although the Brexit vote was related to numerous complex factors (see Chu 2016 or Riley 2016 for further discussion), one explanation is that a moral panic through fear of the immigrant other encouraged some to vote to leave the EU.

Cologne On New Year's Eve 2015, it is reported that many (different news reports, different numbers) women were sexually assaulted (groped, robbed, intimidated) at the train station in Cologne, Germany. Many of the perpetrators were reported to be of "North African or Arab descent" (Richards 2016). After this attack, the news media did not originally report the proposed race/ethnicity of the perpetrators. Once that information was released there was a lot of attention on that aspect, and political groups have protested against the immigration of refugees.

Although aside from moral panics and fear of crime research, how the media impacts fear of crime has largely been researched through examining television viewing habits. According to cultivation theory, heavy television viewing influences people's perceptions of reality and skews it toward the mediated reality (Gerbner and Gross 1976; Gerbner et al. 1994; Shanahan and Morgan 1999). Cultivation theory, as originally studied, examined whether heavy television viewing was related to people's perceptions of violence with the belief that television viewing is fundamentally different than other forms of media (Gerbner and Gross 1976). The basic premise is that heavy television viewers will construct a worldview that resembles what they see on television more than light television viewers. As television, especially in the United States, includes a lot of violence, this will impact the heavy television viewer into constructing the world as a much more violent and scary place than it is in reality. This, in turn, would lead to a higher fear of crime.

Television viewing and fear of crime have a complex history of research (Heath and Gilbert 1996; Kort-Butler and Hartshorn 2011) with some research in support of this link (Gerbner and Gross 1976; Chiricos et al.

1997, 2000; Romer et al. 2003; Jamieson and Romer 2014) and some not supportive of this connection (Doob and MacDonald 1979; Skogan and Maxfield 1981; Ditton et al. 2004). Research on television news exposure found a relationship between fear of crime and heavy news viewing regardless of neighborhood differences, such as crime rate (Romer et al. 2003). Likewise, Jamieson and Romer (2014) found in a time series analysis that TV violence in shows from 1972 to 2010 was related to fear of crime even while controlling for crime rates and perceptions of crime. Yet another study failed to find a connection between high media exposure and fear of crime, but found that participants' perceptions and interpretations of media were important (Ditton et al. 2004).

Regarding new media, Roche, Pickett, and Gertz (2016) attempted to fill this gap in the research by examining internet news exposure's relationship to fear of crime. Although they did not find a relationship, they did, however, find a relationship between legacy media and fear of crime. The question of whether cultivation theory is applicable in a new media world was also addressed by Morgan, Shanahan, and Signorielli (2015, p. 687), arguing that, "if the messages [media] provide have not changed fundamentally, then cultivation, as an explanatory model, will be as relevant today – and tomorrow – as it was 50 years ago." They argue that clearly there are some methodological changes to the research, but the parsimonious nature of cultivation theory lends itself to being studied even in the digital age. Outside of the examination of cultivation theory/ fear of crime, how new media may be impacting fear of crime is also worth criminological inquiry.

Searching for research on new media's influence on fear of crime within criminological research yields few results. In 2012, Dr. Jez Phillip's (University of Chester, United Kingdom) blog argued that social media and fear of crime should be researched. This blog briefly discussed how information by police on Twitter can perhaps lessen fear of crime. A recent reaction of Belgian citizens on Twitter during #BrusselsLockdown, which occurred after the Paris attacks, could be demonstrative of how fear can be relieved by communication among the public and police via social media. Here Belgian Citizens and the police posted cat pictures during the lockdown using the hashtag #BrusselsLockdown (BBC 2015b).

The pictures were meant to discourage people from posting about what was going on around them in Brussels, which might tip off suspects as to the location of law enforcement. Here is an example not from Twitter (for more cat pictures look up #BrusselsLockdown on Twitter), but a cat picture from our friend Steve Boughton (2018) to provide you a visual:

Belgian and global citizens alike saw this reaction, and for those experiencing it firsthand (including one of the authors) it likely assisted in alleviating fears. Arguably, the main purpose was because citizens had been asked not to reveal the movement of police so that those in hiding would not become notified. This likely aided in a sense of community, as individual citizens were not powerless in the search. Community movement was limited during this time in Brussels, but through social media, citizens of Brussels banded together online. When the city of Brussels shut down, there was a heavy presence of police and military personnel carrying around guns. Such a time as this warrants the natural heightened levels of fear among citizens, but how does social media impact it? Giroux (2006) makes a compelling argument regarding how fear (especially fear of terrorism) and our social/political life are changing due to the constant stream of exposure to new media. Researching this topic would be timely. But, perhaps new theories, focusing on the role of social media, need to occur simultaneously. With that we turn to new theories and hypotheses of media and social media.

Moving Forward: New Theories and Hypotheses for Media, Particularly New Media

The study of the media, and specifically media theories, are in need of an update to better accommodate changing trends in media and media consumption. Ferrell, Hayward, and Young (2008) point out that media and crime research has remained stagnant with only three main areas of research—content analyses, "effects" research, and media production observation (see box *Areas of Research*). Studies also tend to focus on the passivity of the media consumer, and not the interactive model that more aptly applies to social media. Jewkes (2015) argues that media and crime research/theoretical advancement needs to be taken seriously; in particular theoretical and methodological rigor needs to be taken into consideration. Jewkes suggests that if you are studying newspapers, try to attain actual newspapers, and then supplement it with search engines and keywords. Also, she recommends that researchers pay attention to the role that images play in shaping our perceptions of crime (Jewkes 2015; Greer 2007).

Areas of Research Content Analysis is a research technique that involves a systematic examination of the content contained in a medium such as photographs, newspapers, movies, and song lyrics (Neuman 2011). This method can be conducted qualitatively (e.g. examining themes within media) and/or quantitatively (e.g. counting the number of times a word or phrase appears). A crime media example would be where a researcher interested in how murder is portrayed by news media examines the content, such as language, tone, and imagery, of multiple television news sources that cover murder.

Effects research includes inquiry into how the media may impact perceptions of crime and/or the criminal legal system. That is, the *effect* of media on crime and the system. One example is research on the *CSI* effect which examines how watching shows like *CSI* may impact actual jury trials (Hayes and Levett 2011).

Media Production Research is researching the institutions that create our media. It focuses on the cultural production aspect of the media. An example is newsroom observation research.

Within the three main areas of research (content analyses, "effects" research, and media production observation), Ferrell et al. (2008) discusses that there are some dominating theoretical and methodological approaches. First, within content analyses of media and crime, there is often a qualitative focus. Content analysis is also quite popular in the definition of moral panics. That is, media coverage is often what incites a moral panic, and it is important to analyze the incendiary language and the amount of coverage a particular construct is receiving. However, in order to ascertain whether the moral panic has an impact on people, they would also need to be queried. Research using surveys, vignettes, or experiments could shed light on the actual effect of the moral panic. Second, within effects research, the cultivation perspective (discussed in this chapter) is often used, as are psychological perspectives (as discussed in Chap. 2). Within effects research, using psychological perspectives experiments are common, but often with undergraduate samples. Third, media production research includes some interesting theoretical perspectives that are still possible for expansion within new media research (see Ferrell et al. 2008 for further reading). Most of the perspectives all have in common the notion of power, in that they are examining who has the power in knowledge creation within the media. To us these have elements of a very Foucault[1] type of perspective, and indeed his philosophy has a lot to offer media and crime theorizing. Aside from these two perspectives, there are two other concepts/theories that we came across that seemed to have some promise for social media research.

Consumerist Criminology

Consumerist Criminology (Wilkins 1984) discusses the possibilities of borrowing concepts from consumerist research and applying it to criminological inquiry. The assumptions are that if people are surveyed on their knowledge, attitudes, and assumptions regarding crime issues,

---

[1] Michael Foucault, a French philosopher, was critical of social institutions in particular prisons. His philosophy is used throughout postmodern perspectives.

then consumer-driven responses could be created to impact policies and programs. For example, using new media, people could be surveyed on their perceptions of crime issues in their geographic area and then campaigns could be created to address those concerns. They could be educational campaigns if the issue is simply a fear of crime issue or the campaign could be a program to address a pressing crime issue in a community. The premise is similar to advertising. If media is impacting the criminal justice system in the manner in which research seems to suggest, then it is worth considering using a social media platform to assess whether this could work. The social media platform would make it easier to have contact with consumers to gauge their perceptions of crime. With careful methodology this concept could be useful. This concept also addresses a major criticism of media theories, especially moral panic theory, where the focus is often on media texts and statements by those in power and less on audience reactions (David et al. 2011). On the downside, this concept is older and would need some updating as social media was not a part of the criminological landscape at the time of its inception.

Web 2.0

Web 2.0 has a specific theoretical development using social media and crime (Yar 2012). It provides new opportunities to challenge, question, and, subsequently, research social media's impact. Yar (2012) points out that the ever-changing nature of the internet is likely impacting crime and victimization. The internet should not be seen as *just technology*, but as "technologically enabled social practices" (p. 207). In other words, a manner to be and do in the social world and be part of the social construction. This puts the emphasis on the social part of social media. Therefore, changes to these environments and how people interact with these changes impact social behaviors such as crime and victimization. This theory suits Ferrell, Hayward, and Young's (2008) criticism of the linearity of current media theory, by adding in the reality of the feedback loop.

Web 2.0 points out the way that the internet might be creating new forms of vulnerability (Yar 2012). It appears to be a theory of victimization more than an explanation of crime. It also seems to fit into the routine activities perspective of criminological theory, as it describes how the internet and the manner in which people use it allow for predators to more easily exploit them. For example, *grooming* is where a sexual predator through online communication manipulates the target (usually a child or teen) to eventually engage in some kind of sex act. That is, people, through social media platforms, provide information that renders them vulnerable. Yar (2012, p. 210) argues that "central to my argument is the connection between one's *visibility* and one's *vulnerability to* criminal predation or exploitation." For example, consider kids aged 12–17 on Facebook who have public profiles; in these cases, anyone—from people living down the street to individuals from all over the world—can contact them. This theory, while trying to explain how victimization occurs, means that the prevention strategies would need to be focused on the victim. This perspective is interesting, but may garner some criticism as encouraging of victim blaming. Regardless, it could be seen as the beginning of a theory of new media and crime. At this point, it may be one of the only theories that is specifically aimed and written for the internet; however, we did find one other proposed new media focused theory that is aimed at explaining online abuse.

Critical Theory of Abuse

Drawing from the Frankfurt school and Habermas, Salter (2017) argues for a critical theory of online abuse. The argument is that abuse and harassment on the internet (particularly social media) reflect the objectifying and exploitative dimensions of the social media competitive ranking system. It is in how the system is set up that in order to be part of it there is a certain amount of self objectification and exploitation that occurs. Of course, this is often a carefully constructed image, and even though you are exploiting and objectifying yourself, it is met with increased cultural capital so it is rewarding. For example, when you post your picture (even simply to begin your Facebook page), you are objectifying yourself in a way in order to attain likes. The vulnerability of posting personal stories or pictures on Twitter, Facebook, or YouTube has an exploitative nature to it where the company makes money, but because the user posts themselves, there is a sense of control and agency by the user. They are buying into the new media system. In the social media world, you are not able to control how people will receive you but you gain cultural capital through posting personal information, pictures, videos, and so on, thus setting oneself up for abuse. Salter (2017, p. 60) argues that this "objectifying view of the self and others... frequently manifests itself in the form of online abuse." Regarding online abuse, Salter discusses the role of *Abusive Idols* who accumulate their cultural capital and online influence by providing opportunities for the collective derogation of other people. Not usually anonymous but purposefully public, they increase their profile and status through the abuse of others. It is considered somewhat acceptable by society, because we victim blame those who have chosen to exploit and/or objectify themselves through posting. Think about when girls or women post pictures of themselves online or if they send them through texts to their significant others. If these pictures are used in other ways without their consent, society often blames the girls/women for even taking the picture at all. More on this in Chap. 4.

Ray Surette Interview

To further understand the impact of new media on the study of crime, we interviewed Dr. Ray Surette. Dr. Surette is a professor of Criminal Justice at the University of Central Florida and an expert on media and crime.

Question: With the pervasiveness of new media, do you think it is necessary to develop new media criminological theories or will traditional criminological theories still apply?

Surette: Looking at criminology theories as stacking up in levels that begin at the biological/genetic and continue upward through individual-level personality concepts, small social groups rooted in family, peers, and communities up to broad societal, anthropological, and cultural comparative theories, new media will have eventual influences on each level. The influences will appear faster at the higher levels but will eventually filter down to the lower levels through a long-term influence on resource allocations and criminalization processes eventually impacting who gets the better chances to procreate and survive their childhoods. Their influence will increase and be the highest as one moves up from the biological/genetic.

The traditional criminological theories will all still apply but they will need to incorporate the additional impact of new media, in particular the impact of new media on interpersonal relationships and the conceptualization of what constitutes a "peer group."

Traditional criminological theories downgraded media until Daniel Glaser's 1956 article and since any criminological theory that relied/focused on face-to-face encounters and interactions will have to expand and recognize that face-to-face is becoming less important than "face-to-face like" encounters available through new media platforms.

In sum, new multilevel integrated theories are needed that recognize the shift in how human interaction has changed, the person physically next to you may often be irrelevant (until he or she starts hitting you on the head).

A more relevant research question is: How does a mediated society function at the individual level (participant consumer/media content relationship) and at the aggregate level (the social construction of reality process)?

Question: Which criminological theories apply to new media?

Conflict Theory: to the degree that it examines the creation of media content and the social control and access of that content. Associated is "critical criminology" with Richard Quinney's The Social Reality of Crime (1970) as the basis takes a more political perspective on the construction of media content and social knowledge in general.

Two additional criminological theory groups that focused on social organization (Strain and Control theories will need to look at virtual communities and the different and similar roles they play.

Lastly, as suggested above, theories of "differential association" in the Sutherland tradition will need to include "virtual social peers" and continue to follow the path started by Glaser in 1956.

Question: How is new media influencing the criminological landscape?

New media has introduced an entirely new arena to study, collect data, test hypotheses, and explore relationships between variables. As new media comes to more define the daily "lived" lives of people, especially youth, criminologists that ignore their existence do so at the peril of being irrelevant.

In addition to being a new study arena, the same communication and information access mechanisms and platforms that drive their social influence provide criminologists opportunities to collaborate, distribute findings, and conduct research. New media provides new information exchanges, research distribution avenues that bypass journal editors and other traditional knowledge gatekeepers, and affords the creation of new research-focused virtual communities.

Conclusion

This chapter discussed legacy media, new media, trends in media consumption, and Media Criminology theories. We ended with a selection of new theories that apply to new media, but there are more that could be explored. Interdisciplinary research from psychology, communications and sociology indicate the usefulness of different theories.

As we discussed in this chapter, Media Criminology is interdisciplinary in nature and does not fit perfectly within criminology. Whether Media Criminology will find a home within cultural, mainstream, or critical criminology only time will tell. Perhaps Media Criminology will become its own stand alone area of inquiry as media and new media continue to permeate all aspects of our lives. Current media theories (such as cultivation theory or moral panics), as discussed earlier, could hold some pertinence but it depends on the research question. The question of which theories to use within this new area of inquiry changes at a fast rate and is a difficult question to answer. Much of Media Criminology is qualitative. Qualitative research often includes more theory building, whereas quantitative research conducts theory testing. New media research could engage in qualitative and quantitative inquiry in order to build theories and test existing theories.

When Gregg Barak (2012) wrote a critique of media and crime research, he used the term "blackout" to describe the progression of research addressing the social construction of crime in online environments. He argued that there are three areas of mass media that essentially interact with crime: entertainment, news, and online. And, of these areas, only entertainment and news have been extensively studied. That was written six years ago, and there has been research and theoretical advancement, but as we found in our research for this book, more needs to be conducted. According to Surette and Gardiner-Bess (2014: 387), the following are two major research questions for new media:

1. "Whether the increased distribution of crime-related content across cultures impacts how crime and justice is now being considered across these cultures?"
2. What is the actual effect of interactive new media and the merging of legacy and new media on society's crime issues and legal system?

Using existing theories or building new theories, new media researchers could tackle these questions. Even though there is theorizing in Media Criminology, the main argument we read time and time again is how theoretical advancement is still necessary and how it has not occurred enough within this field. Throughout this book we attempt to draw from the theories mentioned in this chapter, as well as highlight where new theorizing needs to occur. Additionally, we highlight spaces where more research is needed on new media. This book asks more questions than it answers, making this an invitation for future researchers to address the large gaps in theory and research in Media Criminology. In the next chapter, we discuss how the media, and in particular new media, is impacting our criminal legal system.

Discussion Questions

1. Since the publication of this book, what new forms of media have emerged that weren't discussed in this chapter? How might these types of social media be used for the commission or control of crime?
2. In the United States, mass shootings receive significant legacy and new media coverage. Think about a recent mass shooting, such as what

happened in Las Vegas in 2017; how did new media shape the coverage, understanding, and investigation of the horrific crimes?
3. Think about the three theories—Web 2.0, Consumerist Criminology, and Critical Theory of Abuse—discussed at the end of this chapter. Develop a possible research question that could test each of these theories.

References

Media References

BBC. (2015a, December 9). Paris attacks: What happened on the night. *BBC*. Retrieved from http://www.bbc.com/news/world-europe-34818994

BBC. (2015b, November 23). Belgians tweet cat pictures during #BrusselsLockdown. *BBC*. Retrieved from http://www.bbc.com/news/world-europe-34897645

Chu, B. (2016, June 26). Why did people really vote for Brexit? If we don't face the psychological reasons, we'll never bring Britain together. *The Independent*. Retrieved from http://www.independent.co.uk/voices/brexit-eu-referendum-why-did-people-vote-leave-immigration-nhs-a7104071.html

CNN. (2016, July 7). Woman streams graphic video of boyfriend shot by police. *CNN*. Retrieved from http://www.cnn.com/videos/us/2016/07/07/graphic-video-minnesota-police-shooting-philando-castile-ryan-young-pkg-nd.cnn/video/playlists/philando-castile-shot-in-minnesota/

Cottee, S. (2015, October 13). Europe's moral panic about the migrant Muslim 'other.' *LA Times*. Retrieved from http://www.latimes.com/opinion/op-ed/la-oe-cottee-fear-of-refugees-20151013-story.html

Crilly, R. (2015, December 16). Donald Trump on Muslims: 'They're not coming to this country if I'm president.' *The Telegraph*. Retrieved from http://www.telegraph.co.uk/news/worldnews/republicans/12052760/republican-debate-donald-trump-las-vegas.html

Luckerson, V. (2014, December 2). Fewer people than ever are watching TV. *Time*. Retrieved from http://time.com/3615387/tv-viewership-declining-nielsen/

McCarthy, T., & Jacobs, B. (2015, November 20). Muslim database and rabid dogs. *The Guardian*. Retrieved from http://www.theguardian.com/us-news/2015/nov/20/muslim-databases-and-rabid-dogs-gop-in-ugly-scramble-to-vilify-syrian-refugees

Phillips, J. (2012, March 12). Social media and fear of crime. Retrieved from https://drjezphillips.wordpress.com/2012/03/12/social-media-and-fear-of-crime-the-importance-of-research-in-this-area/

Reuters. (2015, November 22). Timeline of Paris attacks and investigation. *Reuters*. Retrieved from http://www.reuters.com/article/us-france-shooting-timeline-idUSKBN0TB0XZ20151122

Richards, V. (2016, February 11). Cologne attacks. *Independent*. Retrieved from http://www.independent.co.uk/news/world/europe/cologne-attacks-what-happened-after-1000-women-were-sexually-assaulted-a6867071.html

Ronson, J. (2014, December 7). Serial: The Syed family on their pain and the five million detectives trying to work out of Adnan is a psychopath. *The Guardian*. Retrieved from https://www.theguardian.com/tv-and-radio/2014/dec/07/serial-adnan-syed-family-podcast-interview

Rutledge, P. (2015, November 17). Why social media matters in the Paris terrorist attacks. *Psychology Today*. Retrieved from https://www.psychologytoday.com/blog/positively-media/201511/why-social-media-matters-in-the-paris-terrorist-attacks

Screen Media Daily. (2015). *TV Viewership sees Double Digit decline, according to Accenture*. Retrieved from http://www.digitaltveurope.net/352122/decline-of-tv-viewing-accelerating-says-accenture/

Seymour, R. (2015, December 16). Far-right feasts on France's unchecked Islamophobia. *Aljazeera*. Retrieved from http://www.aljazeera.com/indepth/opinion/2015/12/feasts-france-unchecked-islamophobia-151215122050269.html

Shirky, C. (2009). *How social media can make history* [Video file]. Retrieved from https://www.ted.com/talks/clay_shirky_how_cellphones_twitter_facebook_can_make_history

Academic References

Alexander, M. (2011). *The new Jim Crow: Mass incarceration in the age of colorblindness*. New York: New Press.

Bachman, J. G., Wallace, J. M., Jr., Kurth, C. L., Johnston, L. D., & O'Malley, P. M. (1990). *Drug use among Black, White, Hispanic, Native American, and Asian American high school seniors (1976–1989): Prevalence, trends and correlates, Monitoring the Future Occasional Paper, 30* (pp. 1–57). Ann Arbor: Institute for Social Research.

Barak, G. (1988). Newsmaking criminology: Reflections on the media, intellectuals, and crime. *Justice Quarterly, 5*(4), 565–587.

Barak, G. (1996). *Representing O.J.: Murder, criminal justice and mass culture.* Albany: Harrow and Heston.

Barak, G. (2007). *Doing newsmaking criminology from the academy.* Retrieved from http://www.greggbarak.com/custom4_2.html

Barak, G. (2012). *Mass media and the social construction of crime: A critique and implications for the future.* Retrieved from http://www.greggbarak.com/whats_new_6.html

Brown, W. J., Duane, J. J., & Fraser, B. P. (1997). Media coverage and public opinion of the O.J. Simpson trial: Implications for the criminal justice system. *Communication Law and Policy, 2*(2), 261–287.

Bush-Baskette, S. (2010). *Misguided justice.* Bloomington: iUniverse.

Carr, C. T., & Hayes, R. A. (2015). Social media: Defining, developing, and divining. *Atlantic Journal of Communication, 23*(1). https://doi.org/10.1080/15456870.2015.972282.

Carrabine, E. (2008). *Crime, culture and the media.* Hoboken: Wiley-Blackwell Publishing.

Chiricos, T., Escholz, S., & Gertz, M. (1997). Crime, news, and fear of crime: Toward an identification of audience effects. *Social Problems, 44*(3), 342–357.

Chiricos, T., Padgett, K., & Gertz, M. (2000). Fear, TV news, and the reality of crime. *Criminology, 38*(3), 755–786.

Cohen, S. (1972). *Folk devils and moral panics: The creation of the mods and the rockers.* London: MacGibbon and Kee Ltd.

Cohen, S. (2008). *Folk devils and moral panics: The creation of the mods and the rockers* (3rd ed.). Oxford: Basil Blackwell.

Cohen, S. (2011). Whose side were we on? The undeclared politics of moral panic theory. *Crime, Media, Culture: An International Journal, 7*(3), 237–243.

Critcher, C. (2003). *Moral panics and the media.* Buckingham: Open University.

Critcher, C. (2011). For a political economy of moral panics. *Crime, Media, Culture: An International Journal, 7*(3), 259–275.

David, M., Rohloff, A., Petley, J., & Hughes, J. (2011). The idea of moral panic – Ten dimensions of dispute. *Crime, Media & Culture, 7*(3), 215–228.

De Bens, E. (2004). Belgium. In M. Kelly, G. Mazzoleni, & D. McQuail (Eds.), *The media in Europe: The euromedia handbook* (pp. 145–157). London: Sage.

DeKeseredy, W. S. & Schwartz, M. D. (2016). Thinking sociologically about image-based sexual abuse: The contribution of male peer support theory.

Sexualization, Media & Society. Retrieved from http://journals.sagepub.com/doi/full/10.1177/2374623816684692

Dershowitz, A. M. (1997). *Reasonable doubts: The criminal justice system and the O.J. Simpson case*. New York: Touchstone.

Ditton, J., Chadee, D., Farrail, S., Gilchrist, E., & Bannister, J. (2004). From imitation to intimidation: A note on the curious and changing relationship between the media, crime and fear of crime. *British Journal of Criminology, 44*(4), 595–610.

Doob, A. N., & Macdonald, G. E. (1979). Television viewing and fear of victimization: Is the relationship causal? *Journal of Personality and Social Psychology, 32*(2), 170–179.

Ferrell, J., Hayward, K., & Young, J. (2008). *Cultural criminology: An invitation* (1st ed.). London: Sage.

Ferrell, J., Hayward, K., & Young, J. (2012). *Cultural criminology: An Invitation* (1st ed.). London: Sage.

Franks, M. A. (2015, August 17). Drafting an effective 'revenge porn' law: A guide for legislators. *SSRN*. Retrieved from https://ssrn.com/abstract=2468823

Garland, D. (2008). On the concept of moral panic. *Crime, Media & Culture, 4*(1), 9–30.

Gauntlett, D. (2001). *The worrying influence of 'media effects' studies*. Retrieved from http://www.theory.org.uk/tenthings.htm

Gerbner, G., & Gross, L. (1976). Living with television: The violence profile. *Journal of Communication, 26*(2), 172–194.

Gerbner, G., Gross, L., Morgan, M., & Signorielli, N. (1994). Growing up with television: The dynamics of the cultivation perspective. In J. Bryant & D. Zillman (Eds.), *Perspectives of media effects* (pp. 17–40). Hillsdale: Lawrence Erlbaum.

Giroux, H. A. (2006). *Beyond the spectacle of terrorism: Global uncertainty and the challenge of new media*. Boulder: Paradigm Publishers.

Glaser, D. (1956). Criminality theories and behavioral images. *American Journal of Sociology, 61*(5), 433–444.

Goode, E., & Ben-Yehuda, N. (1994). *Moral panics: The social construction of deviance*. Malden: Blackwell.

Greer, C. (2007). News media, victims and crime. In P. Davies, P. Francis, & C. Greer (Eds.), *Victims, crime and society* (pp. 20–49). London: Sage.

Greer, C. (2010). News media criminology. In E. McLaughlin & T. Newburn (Eds.), *The Sage handbook of criminological theory* (pp. 490–513). London: Sage.

Hale, C. (1996). Fear of crime: A review of the literature. *International Review of Victimology, 4*(2), 79–150.

Hall, S., Critcher, C., Jefferson, T., Clarke, J., & Roberts, B. (1978). *Policing the crisis: Mugging, the state, and law and order.* London: Macmillan.

Hall, S., Critcher, C., Jefferson, T., Clarke, J., & Roberts, B. (2013). *Policing the crisis: Mugging, the state, and law and order.* New York: Palgrave Macmillan.

Hayes, R. M., & Levett, L. M. (2011). Jury's still out: How television and crime show viewing influences jurors' evaluations of evidence. *Applied Psychology in Criminal Justice, 7*(1), 29–46.

Heath, L., & Gilbert, K. (1996). Mass media and fear of crime. *American Behavioral Scientist, 39*(4), 379–386.

Jamieson, P. E., & Romer, D. (2014). Violence in popular U.S. prime time TV dramas and the cultivation of fear: A time series analysis. *Media and Communication, 2*(2), 31–41.

Jewkes, Y. (2004). *Media & crime.* London: Sage.

Jewkes, Y. (2010). *Media & crime* (2nd ed.). London: Sage.

Jewkes, Y. (2015). *Media & crime* (3rd ed.). London: Sage.

Kort-Butler, L. A., & Hartshorn, S. (2011). Watching the detectives: Crime programming, fear of crime, and attitudes about the criminal justice system. *Sociology Quarterly, 52*(1), 36–55.

Lauf, E. (2001). Research note: The vanishing young reader. Sociodemographic determinants of newspaper use as a source of political information in Europe, 1980–98. *European Journal of Communication, 16*(2), 233–243.

McRobbie, A., & Thornton, S. (1995). Rethinking moral panic for a multi-mediated social world. *British Journal of Sociology, 46*, 559–574.

Meyer, A. (2016). The Rotherham abuse scandal. In V. E. Cree, G. Clapton, & M. Smith (Eds.), *Revisiting moral panics* (pp. 324–367). Bristol: Policy Press.

Morgan, M., Shanahan, J., & Signorielli, N. (2015). Yesterday's new cultivation, tomorrow. *Mass Communication & Society, 18*, 674–699.

Nalla, M., Johnson, J. D., & Hayes, R. M. (2011). Prior victimization, region, and neighborhood affects on fear of crime in Mumbai, India. *Asian Journal of Criminology, 6*, 141–159.

Neuman, W. L. (2011). *Social research methods: Qualitative and quantitative approaches.* Boston: Allyn & Bacon.

Nielsen Report. (2016). *The comparable metrics report: Q3 2015.* Retrieved from http://www.nielsen.com/us/en/insights/reports/2016/the-comparable-metrics-report-q3-2015.html

Nielsen Report. (2017). *The Nielsen comparable metrics report: Q3 2016.* Retrieved from http://www.nielsen.com/us/en/insights/reports/2017/the-comparable-metricsreport-q3-2016.html

Office for National Statistics. (2016). *Internet access-Households and individuals: 2016.* Retrieved from https://www.ons.gov.uk/peoplepopulationandcommunity/householdcharacteristics/homeinternetandsocialmediausage/bulletins/internetaccesshouseholdsandindividuals/2016

Oxford Dictionary. (2017). *Social media.* Retrieved from http://www.oxforddictionaries.com/definition/english/social-media

Papthanassopoulos, S., Coen, S., Curran, J., Aalberg, T., Rowe, D., & Jones, P. (2013). Online threat, but television is still dominant: A comparative study of 11 nations' news consumption. *Journalism Practice, (6),* 690–704.

Pew Research Center. (2016). *State of the news media 2016.* Retrieved from http://www.journalism.org/2016/06/15/state-of-the-news-media-2016/

Pew Research Center. (2017). *Social media fact sheet.* Retrieved from http://www.pewinternet.org/fact-sheet/social-media/

Riley, A. (2016). Brexit: Causes and consequences. *Barcelona Center for International Affairs.* Retrieved from http://www.cidob.org/publicaciones/serie_de_publicacion/notes_internacionals/n1_159/brexit_causes_and_consequences

Roberts, S. (2015). *Benefit tourism: A moral panic.* Conference Free Movement of Workers and Social Security Coordination. Conference Paper.

Roche, S. P., Pickett, J. T., & Gertz, M. (2016). The scary world of online news? Internet news exposure and public attitudes towards crime and justice. *Journal of Quantitative Criminology, 32*(2), 215–236.

Rohloff, A. (2011). Extending the concept of moral panic: Elias, climate change and civilization. *Sociology, 45*(4), 634–649.

Romer, D., Jamieson, K. H., & Aday, S. (2003). Television news and the cultivation of fear of crime. *Journal of Communication, 53*(1), 88–104.

Salter, M. (2017). *Crime, justice and social media.* Oxon: Routledge.

Salter, M., & Crofts, T. (2015). Responding to revenge porn: Challenging online legal impunity. In L. Comella & S. Tarrant (Eds.), *New views on pornography: Sexuality, politics and the law* (pp. 233–253). Santa Barbara: Praeger Publisher.

Shanahan, J., & Morgan, M. (1999). *Television and its viewers: Cultivation theory and research.* Cambridge: Cambridge University Press.

Skogan, W. G., & Maxfield, M. G. (1981). *Coping with crime: Individual and neighborhood reactions.* Beverly Hills: Sage.

Smith, C. (2015). Revenge porn or consent and privacy: An analysis of the harmful digital communications act 2015. *Student Research Paper.* Retrieved from http://hdl.handle.net/10063/5393

Statista. (2016). *Statistics and facts about social media usage.* Retrieved from http://www.statista.com/topics/1164/social-networks/

Surette, R. (2013). Pathways to copycat crime. In J. B. Helfgott (Ed.), *Criminal psychology* (pp. 251–273). Santa Barbara: Praeger.

Surette, R. (2015). *Media, crime, & criminal justice: Images, realities, and policies* (5th ed.). Stamford: Cengage Learning.

Surette, R. (2016). Measuring copycat crime. *Crime, Media, Culture, 12*, 37–64.

Surette, R., & Gardiner-Bess, R. (2014). Media, entertainment, and crime: Prospects and concerns. In B. A. Arrigo & H. Y. Bersot (Eds.), *Routledge handbook of international of crime and justice studies* (pp. 373–396). Abingdon/Oxon: Routledge.

Surette, R., & Otto, C. (2001). The media's role in the definition of crime. In M. Lanier & S. Henry (Eds.), *What is crime controversies of crime and what to do about it* (pp. 139–154). New York: Rowman & Littlefield.

Thompson, K. (1998). *Moral panics*. London: Routledge.

University of Minnesota. (nd). *Technological advances: From the printing press to the iPhone*. Retrieved from https://open.lib.umn.edu/communication/chapter/15-1-technological-advances-from-the-printing-press-to-the-iphone

Waddington, P. A. J. (1986). Mugging as a moral panic: A question of proportion. *British Journal of Sociology, 37*(2), 245–259.

Wallace, J. M., Jr., Bachman, J. G., O'Malley, P. M., Schulenberg, J.E., Cooper, S. M., Johnston, L.D. (2002). *Gender and ethnic differences in smoking, drinking, and illicit drug use among American 8th, 10th, and 12th grade students, 1976–2000*. Research Report. Retrieved from http://www.monitoringthefuture.org/pubs/text/jmwjgb03.pdf

Warr, M. (1984). Fear of victimization: Why are women and the elderly more afraid? *Social Science Quarterly, 65*, 681–702.

Welch, M. (2006). *Scapegoats of September 11th: Hate crimes and state crimes in the war on terror*. New Brunswick: Rutgers University Press.

Wikipedia. (2017). *Social media*. Retrieved from https://en.wikipedia.org/wiki/Social_media

Wilkins, L. T. (1984). *Consumerist criminology*. London: Hienmann. RI Inactive Titles.

Yar, M. (2012). E-Crime 2.0: The criminological landscape of new social media. *Information & Communications Technology Law, 21*(3), 207–219.

2

#*CSI* Effect: How Media Impacts the Criminal Legal System

On June 15th, 2011, the Boston Bruins beat the Vancouver Canucks in the Stanley Cup Hockey Finals. Occurring after this event was a riot in downtown Vancouver that left over 100 people injured, including police officers. People posted photos and videos on Facebook during and after the riots. There were also Facebook pages dedicated to the event meant to solicit photo images and/or videos. People's names, photographs, and descriptions of the events were all available through social media. Police investigations included the use of social media, and this ushered in a change of the manner in which investigations occur in Canada (Trottier 2012; Salter 2017).

Legacy media impacts how the criminal legal system operates, and as we write this text, new media is also changing the system. With so many people walking around with smartphones in their pockets, the criminal legal system is directly and indirectly impacted by this new reality. Whether it is through individuals recording and posting videos of law-breaking behavior on social media, such as in the case of the Vancouver riots, or live tweeting trial proceedings, we argue that due to social media's accessibility and interactive nature, it has the potential to significantly impact the functioning of the criminal legal system. The combination of

© The Author(s) 2018
R. M. Hayes, K. Luther, *#Crime*, Palgrave Studies in Crime, Media and Culture,
https://doi.org/10.1007/978-3-319-89444-7_2

legacy and new media through the ever-present accessibility of movies, television, and all things popular culture provide people with a constant stream of (mis)information.

Scholars (Barak 2012; Newman 1990) have called on criminologists to analyze the content and media of popular culture in order to ascertain the portrayal of the criminal legal system. Examining this imagery assists in understanding people's perceptions of the system and its impact on policing, courtroom proceedings, and corrections. Exploring the content and reach of new media can aid in understanding how it can shape perceptions and even the functioning of the system. For instance, think about the popular Netflix documentary *Making a Murderer*, which follows Steven Avery (who was exonerated after 18 years in prison for a sexual assault that he did not commit) and his nephew Brendan Dassey, as they are accused, arrested, convicted, and incarcerated for the murder of Teresa Halbach. Not only has *Making a Murderer* made some people question the fairness of the criminal legal system, but it has generated public outcry—including a petition on Change.org (see https://www. change.org/p/president-of-the-united-states-free-steven-avery)—regarding the injustices of the criminal legal system. From an interview with one of Avery's defense attorneys, Dean Strang, Ramaswamy (The Guardian 2016) writes:

> Could its [*Making a Murderer*] influence actually lead to the case being reopened? "I hope so," says Strang. "Maybe someone who saw something or has kept a secret for 10 years will come forward. And judges read online news sources just like everybody else. More broadly, I think the series will foster a larger conversation about the systemic weaknesses in the way we administer criminal justice. That would be a very good outcome of this documentary."

According to some, *Making a Murderer* has contributed to developments in the legal proceedings for Avery and Dassey (McDonnell-Parry 2016). Since the release of the series, Avery's case has been taken on by a well-known defense lawyer who has successfully exonerated previous clients and Dassey's conviction was overturned in 2016. At the time of this writing, we do not know where the attention generated from *Making a Murderer* will lead, but this show, on a new media platform, has drawn attention to a case that was not previously in the public eye.

> ***Making a Murderer*** Part of the true crime genre, *Making a Murderer* is the story of Steven Avery, who in 1985 was convicted of sexual assault and attempted homicide. He was exonerated in 2003 and then accused in 2005 of murdering Teresa Halbach. Media critics have praised the show, and the implications for criminology are in the matter that it provides an in-depth look at law and society (Visco 2016).

Media has a wide-reaching impact on the criminal legal system and isolating the effects would be impossible. However, there is a body of research that we brought together for this chapter to highlight the effects of media on the criminal legal system. In each of the sections, we draw from research examining how media shapes *perceptions* of the criminal legal system and research exploring how media changes the *functioning* of the criminal legal system. In the following chapter, we discuss:

1. The impact of media on law enforcement
2. The impact of media on juries and trial outcomes
3. The impact of media on lawyers and judges
4. The impact of media on corrections

Research on the Impact of Media on the Criminal Legal System

Media Effects on Law Enforcement

Media impacts perceptions of law enforcement. Not only do we see crime shows and news media shaping perceptions, we also see how perceptions may even influence the way officers perform their jobs. New media expands the impact on law enforcement through innovations in policing and citizen accountability of police.

Legacy Media's Influence on Law Enforcement

Media and law enforcement have a complicated relationship. With crime news making up a large portion of news media content and crime shows as popular entertainment, law enforcement are concerned with their portrayal as they are aware that positive portrayals might increase public support which aids in enforcement of the law (Marsh and Melville 2009). Additionally, law enforcement can use media to inform the public about crime and justice issues, but the media would need to cooperate and accurately portray the message as intended. As many people do not have direct contact with the criminal legal system, the social construction of law enforcement largely occurs through the media. The social construction of the police is impacted by *experiential reality* (experiences) and *symbolic reality* (media exposure) (see box Experiential and Symbolic Reality).

Experiential and Symbolic Reality *Experiential reality* (first source of knowledge) is the reality constructed by a person's experiences. It is all the events that have happened directly to you, and the knowledge and perception of those events that you have attained. *Symbolic reality* (next three sources of knowledge) is the reality where a person constructs their reality from others (people, institutions, and the media). It is the knowledge gained from these other sources. You may not personally have experienced something but believe it exists because your friend told you about it or you heard it through the news media.

There are seemingly endless media representations of law enforcement—turn on the television, Netflix, or Hulu, and you'll see *Law and Order*, *Criminal Minds*, or *NCIS*, to name a few. Whether it is through films, television shows, or local news programming, the general public can easily view media presenting fictional or nonfictional law enforcement. According to Surette (2015), the media commonly portrays "crime fighters" in problematic ways, which leads many people to subscribe to incorrect views of the work of law enforcement. Generally, law enforcement officers are portrayed through the frame of either "good cops" or "bad cops" (Surette 2015). In the case of "good cops," law enforcement officers are shown as effective agents in the criminal legal system. In contrast, in the case of "bad cops," law enforcement is presented as being so ineffective that many times "citizen crime fighters" are needed to do the job.

Legacy media research on law enforcement focuses on public perceptions based on media viewing. This research is complicated and mixed; it is more complicated than examining media usage on public opinion as other social factors need to be taken into consideration. Some research does not find a relationship between television, crime, and news viewing and attitudes toward police (Chermak et al. 2006; Dowler 2003; Kääriäinen et al. 2016), but when broken down by race, media does relate to attitudes toward police (Weitzer and Tuch 2004a, 2005). In a study examining whether local media of a highly publicized case affected specific attitudes toward police, the researchers found no effect (Chermak et al. 2006). In Finland, Kääriäinen et al. (2016) examined the impact of a 2013 news media uproar on the public's trust in the police and found that trust did not decrease. Regarding not finding a relationship between media and attitudes, it could be that even when law enforcement officers are portrayed as bad, such as corrupt or bending the rules, as long as they solve the crime this is overlooked. That is, they are still good because they solved the crime, and justice was done. Therefore, the portrayal of police on television is complicated and often conflicting, where they are shown as professional crime fighters, but also incompetent and ineffective (Surette 1998, 2013). With conflicting imagery, it could be what one chooses to watch that impacts one's perception or one's perception could impact what one chooses to watch.

Research on perceptions of police highlights racial differences (Escholz et al. 2002; Lundman and Kaufman 2003; Weitzer and Tuch 2004a, b, 2005), class differences (Weitzer and Tuch 1999), and even neighborhood contextual differences (Weitzer 1999; Weitzer and Tuch 2005). In the United States, researchers find that an individual's race impacts their perceptions of law enforcement. Blacks and Hispanics are more likely than whites to report negative interactions with police (Lundman and Kaufman 2003; Weitzer and Tuch 2004a) along with viewing negative media exposure of police misconduct that negatively impacts their perceptions (Weitzer and Tuch 2004a, 2005). This means that blacks and Hispanics view negative experiences through media compared with whites, but are also more likely than whites to experience or witness negative police interactions with citizens. Indeed, blacks and Hispanics more than whites report wanting police reform as they believe that police corruption, unwarranted stops, and verbal/physical abuse of citizens are common events (Weitzer and Tuch 2004b). Even when watching reality television crime shows, such as *COPS*, research has demonstrated that effects of viewer satisfaction only increases for whites but not for blacks (Escholz et al. 2002). Therefore, negative media exposure could be impacting certain groups more than others, and how this impacts police and community relations is complicated. It supports the notion of the experiential reality and symbolic reality we mentioned earlier, as certain races have disproportionately more contact with the police than other races. This may have something to do with the social construction of who is criminal. We will further discuss the racialized aspect of who is constructed as a criminal in Chap. 3.

Law enforcement officers, due to negative media coverage and public perception, may be less motivated to do their jobs. They may view their job as more dangerous due to the media coverage of incidences, such as riots (Nix and Wolfe 2017). Nix and Wolfe (2017) examined negative publicity of officers association with reported levels of self-legitimacy. Officers were less motivated to do their job as a result of negative publicity and were less likely to view themselves as legitimate authority figures. This is only one study, and more research needs to be conducted on the impact of negative publicity on police officers particularly in how it impacts job performance. While this study examined negative publicity, they measured it by asking officers their own perceptions of publicity without discerning between legacy and new media. Legacy and new media are likely impacting perceptions of law enforcement and law enforcement perceptions of their job.

New Media's Influence on Law Enforcement

New media is impacting the way law enforcement does their job. Police have been turning to social media for crime prevention and response (LexisNexis 2014). In 2010, an International Association of Chiefs of Police survey found 81% of law enforcement agencies in their sample used social media. In the United States, over 75% of the largest departments have a social media presence on at least one of the following sites: Facebook, Twitter, or MySpace (Lieberman et al. 2013). According to LexisNexis (2014), law enforcement social media usage has increased, and it is believed that this rise shall continue. Social media is used to anticipate crime, to solve crimes, and to notify the public.

The *anticipation of crime* occurs when law enforcement officers use social media information to anticipate public gatherings (or other criminal/deviant activities). Social media's impact on policing is the increased amount of surveillance that we as a society are subjected to, and are somewhat implicit in (Surette 2015; Trottier 2012). As we subject ourselves to surveillance by posting on social media, we are more accepting of the increased amount of surveillance of our activities (Surette 2015). The impact of law enforcement is that they can track our activities more easily, in the name of public safety. Trottier (2012) discusses how police and other institutions take advantage of social media, and it is not the technological sophistication of it, but is the sheer volume of information that is present. Social media aids in *solving crimes* by using it for crime investigations. Law enforcement can track Facebook check-ins (LexisNexis 2014) or find evidence of criminal activity posted on social media sites. In the Vancouver example, which was presented at the beginning of the chapter, police investigated through social media. Another example of this is Sergeant Andy Green in Lima, Ohio, who uses Facebook to post pictures of wanted criminals and unsolved crimes (Sowinski 2013). *Notification of the public* occurs when law enforcement agencies provide real-time information about suspects (LexisNexis 2014) or instructions to the public. During the Brussels Lockdown, police asked the public to not post their whereabouts on social media while there was an ongoing investigation (http://newsmonkey.be/article/61023).

In the *Stokes Croft Riot* (see box *Stokes Croft Riot*), law enforcement agencies used Twitter to refute claims. Procter et al. (2011) of *The Guardian* examined tweets and how seven different riot rumors spread, finding that someone (not a news source) posts and, then, others repost, and legacy news eventually posts as well. This occurs even in the case that the rumor is false or unsubstantiated. Therefore, law enforcement using Twitter to refute claims swiftly could assist with stopping the spread of misinformation.

Stokes Croft Riot Crowd violence occurred in the Stokes Croft area in Bristol, United Kingdom, on April 21, 2011. Legacy and new media had conflicting accounts of what began the riot. Legacy media coverage suggested that it was caused by the protestors against the opening of a Tesco supermarket. New media coverage on YouTube suggested that it was not residents but police officers who were using heavy-handed police tactics toward the protestors that escalated the violence (Reilly 2013).

Law enforcement agencies have also used messages (such as tweets) as evidence of a social disturbance, with the individual then being prosecuted (Bowcott et al. 2011). However, these examples may be rare. One study in the United States examined the content of police postings on social media and found that posts typically focus on crimes occurring/ have occurred (e.g. arrest of a suspect) or on public relations announcements (e.g. police department hiring) (Lieberman et al. 2013). That is, the postings resembled more of a police blotter (think crime resolution) than seeking citizen participation or informing them about potential risks of crime in their area (think crime prevention). However, there are places that use social media in new and interesting manners. In Belgium, Inspector Sylva Polfliet uses Facebook to assist victims of cyberbullying. Officer Polfliet works in the Asse, Merchtem, Opwijk and Wemmel (AMOW; Belgium) office and focuses on social investigations, largely involving complaints for child abuse and neglect. She also provides victim support after a crime in an advocate-type role. The role of NetCop is only a small portion of her job. We called her for an interview and she agreed. Following is a summary of our interview.

Question: What is NetCop?

NetCop, she said, was brought to her and she implemented it last year. Since then, she is often referred to as "The NetCop." The idea derived from school visits where students liked the idea of an officer on Facebook. Officer Polfliet began the campaign by visiting schools and introducing herself, and providing them the information of how to contact her on Facebook. First, she had a

Facebook profile, but now it is a Facebook page: https://www.facebook.com/ Netflik-Amow-990605580981012/?fref=ts.

The basic idea is that students who are experiencing cyberbullying can contact her through Facebook. Through this messaging she can provide them information and resources on what to do. She mentioned that often she asks the student who they have talked to about the situation, such as a parent or a teacher. Commonly, she encourages them to tell someone and/or report it. She often also provides them resources, such as a referral to the Jongen Advies Centrum or Youth Advice Center.

Question: What are the benefits and disadvantages of using Facebook for policing?

She discussed the benefit that students can contact her somewhat confidentially through this medium. Students can have a different screen name instead of their real name, and she does not investigate the student after they contact her. Therefore, it is not possible to file an official complaint through Facebook. Therein, she mentions, lies also the disadvantage of this initiative: if the student does not choose to take her advice, then nothing beyond this conversation will occur. Students have the freedom to use the information she provides to them or they can choose not to.

Another benefit of using Facebook is that students are also using Facebook. She talked about how bullying used to be limited within the school walls, but now it follows them home. Students have computers and smartphones where bullies can reach them 24/7. With bullying occurring around the clock, it is a benefit to have the social media presence of an officer that students can turn to and request assistance. At this time, however, the Facebook NetCop is not a 24-hour online presence.

Question: What is the future of NetCop?

At this point, she is not aware of any other police organizations engaging in this initiative. This initiative is not used for investigating cyberbullying; instead, it is only used for responding to the victims. She does not consider herself a social media expert and, therefore, is limited in her capacity to expand. However, other police organizations could be using social media in different ways.

Student Activity *Contact your local law enforcement to see if they have a version of NetCop. If they do, see what the position entails. If not, ask them how they police social media.*

In addition to new media impacting how law enforcement agencies do their jobs, new media can also change the public's relationship with law enforcement. Camera phones and social media sites have given rise to what is known as *citizen journalism*. Citizen journalism is where an individual can email, text, phone, or send in live footage of the events (Radsch 2016). Citizen journalism is arguably impacting how law enforcement agencies do their jobs, such as in the Vancouver riots case mentioned in the beginning of this chapter. In that case, citizen journalists posted videos, photos, and names online of people supposedly involved in the rioting. These were essentially witnesses to the event that were providing information, but citizen journalism can go beyond traditional witness roles. Citizen journalism has also been called citizen-led or participatory justice (Powell 2014) and includes user-generated publications such as those on social networking sites (i.e. YouTube, Facebook, or Twitter). There are scholars who promote this type of behavior, where others denigrate it as threatening to the democratic structure (Powell 2014). Powell (2014) discusses *technology mediated justice* in which new media users are active participants in the justice process and can either facilitate and/or disrupt. People post and repost information about a crime event and these reach extensive online networks not only locally, but globally. The information as it is may not necessarily be vetted as factual or not. According to Powell (2014, p. 6), there are three outcomes of technology-mediated justice: "tools to assist *conventional justice responses* (such as in police investigations and as evidence in court); mechanisms that facilitate citizen-led, non-State sanctioned, or *informal justice responses;* and social practices that, whether intentionally or incidentally, *disrupt formal justice processes* and threaten the rights and/or due process protections of accused persons."

Conventional justice responses: This outcome refers to how social media is used to essentially facilitate justice, but through formal institutions such as law enforcement. An example of this facilitation of justice is in the Vancouver, Canada, example mentioned at the beginning of the chapter, in which law enforcement used the evidence that had been posted on new media. Individuals present at the event had recorded videos and uploaded them, there were Facebook pages dedicated to the Vancouver riot, and law enforcement used these to identify people suspected of causing harm at the riot. The community participation in identifying suspects is evident, and this event highlighted how law enforcement and community members can work together via social media (Salter 2017). Had the police not engaged in interaction with the community and used their information as part of their investigation, this could have been viewed as *informal justice responses*, especially if there were reactions by the public to individuals involved.

Informal justice responses: This outcome occurs when after citizen journalists have posted the activities/stories, the people (not law enforcement, at least initially) react to them by collectively gathering in response. One example is from 2016, when first across the United States and then internationally there was a "clown scare," in which people were posting on social media about individuals in clown suits attempting to harm others (McGann and Said-Moorhouse 2016). The mainstream media ran stories about clown sightings (Chan 2016; McGann and Said-Moorhouse 2016), but the social media reaction and response was different. The social media reaction was to post sightings (often unfounded), and students on a few college campuses, such as at Central Michigan University (Yanak-Jonaitis 2016), gathered and went out looking for the clowns. The reactions seem to be an example of a social-mediated moral panic, yet research will need to confirm that. What is important to note is that during these reactions, police were urging citizens to let them do the investigating, and not to react. The response of citizens in these cases also could have led to the disruption of justice that Powell (2014) discusses.

Disruption of formal justice processes: For example, if there are clowns going around attacking people, then it is assault, and there would likely be a police investigation. However, in a case of citizens gathering and hunting for clowns this could not only disrupt the investigation, but might result in an assault on someone who is dressed as a clown but has done nothing wrong. Another example of the disruption of formal justice processes is the revealing of police officers' location during an investigation via social media.

Student Activity *Identify and discuss examples of technology-mediated justice in your communities.*

The examples described earlier are all somewhat straightforward, and it can become rather complicated as to whether justice is being disrupted or facilitated through citizen journalism. Scholarly work on police response to citizen journalism discusses the role of power, and how there have been hundreds of cases where police have smashed/confiscated cameras and/or threatened the users (Wall and Linnemann 2014). Citizen journalism is challenging the role of the state and the power of institutions in directing the justice narrative. As stated above in the Stokes Croft Riot, the mainstream media was reporting that the law enforcements raid was a positive action by police to protect citizens, which means they would likely view the citizens as being disruptive. Whereas Twitter feeds on #stokescroft suggested that the police were the initiators of the violence. YouTube videos posted by eyewitnesses also attempted to corroborate the side of the story where police were to be blamed for "heavy-handed" police tactics (Reilly 2013).

We also see new media playing a potential role drawing attention to law enforcement when people believe they or their communities have been treated unjustly. While legacy media reports on some incidences of police brutality, it does not allow for the open public discussion that new media does. New media provides a place for the postings of any alleged incident of police brutality and open discussion of these incidences. In 2011 in Bristol, United Kingdom, citizens posted on YouTube about the Stokes Croft Riot (Reilly 2013). Legacy media suggested that it was a riot based on the opening of a Tesco and new media accounts suggested that it was "heavy-handed" police tactics that caused the rioting. While new media postings may have raised awareness, commenters on the YouTube videos still tended to support legacy media's account of the riots that protestors were the ones who caused the issues (Reilly 2013). New media, at least according to this study, did not end up disrupting the legacy media narrative.

In the United States, we also see new media drawing attention to policing practices with the Black Lives Matter movement. Criminologists discussed these issues—racial profiling and police brutality—within academia for many years and it is considered common knowledge in communities with people of color. Now, however, with help from Black Lives Matter, the discussion has moved to the mainstream. The Black Lives Matter campaign may (or could have already) change the nature of police work in the United States. Research needs to be conducted on whether police organizations have changed their rules on proper gun usage or, more importantly, whether police have started to respond differently to perceived threats; each of these would demonstrate that Black Lives Matter had an effect. Of course, the effect on perceptions could also be negative, as legacy media often called rioters "thugs" which reinforces stereotypes of black men as criminals (more on that in Chap. 3).

Media Effects on Juries and Trial Outcomes

Along with the impact of media on law enforcement, there is a substantial body of research examining legacy media effects on the courts. Much of the research in the United States is in the area of psychology and law and is focused on juries (and not all countries use juries) (see box *Adversarial Systems*), particularly the *CSI* Effect and the impact of pretrial publicity (see box *Pretrial Publicity*). These concepts are argued to impact the jury, thus threatening the notion of justice because jurors may use information of the criminal legal system—gained from television shows or pretrial media news coverage—to understand real cases. Jury research may also include examining new media's impact on juries and trial outcomes. Particularly, pretrial publicity is not limited to legacy media, as people gain information on the criminal legal system from social media such as Twitter as well. New media (as opposed to legacy media) also poses additional challenges for courtrooms, some of which are impacting juries and potentially trial outcomes. This section covers the research on legacy media effects on juries and trial outcomes followed by the new challenges posed by new media and the potential effects.

Adversarial System *Adversarial system* is used by the United States and Australia. The criminal justice system in the United States is an adversarial system, where two opposing parties present their sides to a neutral party. All three parties work together in order to determine the outcome of a case. American and Australian law is derived from European (mostly English) law, and the outcomes of court cases become legal precedent (Lab et al. 2011). *Inquisitorial or nonadversarial system* (used by France, the Netherlands, Germany, and Japan) is also developed and adopted in Europe; but, unlike the adversarial system, here the judge is the state's representative. The attorneys in this system provide additional questions for the judge to ask witnesses (Strier 1992–1993). The adversarial system is seen as opposing sides where one side will emerge as the victor, whereas inquisitorial system is seen as a truth-seeking system.

Pretrial Publicity PTP research is a popular area of research within the psychological field, particularly the subsection of psychology and law. This research is derived from the conflict between the right to a fair trial and the freedom of the press (Hayes-Smith 2009). PTP research is interested in assessing to the extent with which jurors who are exposed to media coverage of an event before trial are impacted with that information (i.e. biasing their perspective). Jurors could find the defendant guilty or not guilty depending on the biased information. There are also two different types of pretrial publicity: general and specific. General PTP argues that any media exposure, not specific to the case the juror is deciding, may have a biasing effect on their decision (Greene and Wade 1988). However, case-specific PTP refers to media exposure that relates directly to the case that jurors are deciding (Hayes-Smith 2009). General PTP is the umbrella under which the *CSI* Effect research rests.

Legacy Media's Impact on Juries and Trial Outcomes

According to Wikipedia[1] (2016), the Nielsen Report demonstrated that *CSI* came in with a 20.8 million viewers and ranked #10, and over the next ten years it stayed in the top 10 with between 14.92 and 26.26 million

---

[1] We used the Wikipedia for this citation because Nielsen does not compile data in this manner.

viewers annually. The popularity of *CSI* (its spinoff shows – *CSI Miami, CSI New York, CSI Las Vegas,* and *CSI Cyber*) and other shows like it has led to concern over the "The CSI Effect." The "CSI Effect" is believed to ultimately affect jurors' verdicts (Tyler 2006). If forensic evidence (see box *Information on Use of Forensic DNA (deoxyribonucleic acid)*) is absent, this may cause the jury to be skeptical of testimony or other common trial evidence. Alternatively, when forensic evidence is present, the focus is on the forensic evidence, even if it is not particularly strong evidence, disregarding all other pieces of evidence (Tyler 2006). This leads to two possibilities of affecting juror decisions: (1) *Pro-defense*: If forensic evidence is absent, the jury will be more likely to render a not-guilty verdict, regardless of other evidence. (2) *Pro-Prosecution*: If forensic evidence is present, this increases the likelihood that jurors will render a guilty verdict, regardless of other evidence (Tyler 2006). Therefore, the *CSI* Effect encourages jurors to believe that they are experts on forensic evidence and that forensic evidence is the most important evidence in a trial.

Information on Use of Forensic DNA (deoxyribonucleic acid) In a survey of DNA crime laboratories in 2001, they demonstrated an increase in cases that were being analyzed along with how most labs (81%) have backlogs (Steadman 2002). However, DNA usage in criminal cases in trial is relatively low. Where DNA is extremely useful is in the exoneration of those who are wrongfully convicted (www.InnocenceProject.org). Media has had a hand in the perceived popularity of DNA evidence to solve crimes as they cover when it occurs in the news (Justice.gov), and there are numerous shows which use forensics as the major plotline. Still though, some DNA research has issues and there are arguments in the scientific community about "junk science." "Junk science" refers to research that is not methodologically sound being used in court proceedings, and because it is seen as science, jurors are swayed toward the research without a full understanding. "Junk science" is often admitted into courtrooms because neither lawyers nor judges are trained in the scientific method; they only receive legal training. There is a push for all criminal legal system actors to have some training in forensic collection and presentation in order to understand the rapidly evolving technique that is useful for the system (Justice.gov).

Arguably, the media constructed this phenomenon (Hayes and Levett 2012); in 2003, the CSI Effect began to appear in the press as something that impacted the criminal justice system (Houck 2006). The research and support on this concept is limited. In one mock jury study, participants who watched *CSI* rendered the same verdicts as the participants who did not (Podlas 2006). Two other web-based mock jury studies did not find a direct *CSI* Effect on juries (Reardon et al. 2007; O'Neil 2007). While Hayes-Smith and Levett (2011) did find an effect, it was not a direct effect of crime show viewing on verdict. Instead, perceptions of the defense were impacted by the interaction between the amount of forensic evidence available at trial and participants' number of crime show viewings. Participants who viewed crime shows were more likely to have favorable perceptions of the defense than participants who did not view crime shows. This study, unlike the ones mentioned earlier, used actual jurors, with mock cases to ascertain the validity of the *CSI* Effect concept. Mancini (2013), also using jurors, found an impact of heavy crime fiction show viewing on the likelihood to acquit the defendant in a murder trial. Yet, another study using actual jurors did not find much of an effect (Shelton et al. 2006).

The earlier-mentioned studies all directly examined whether crime show viewing had an "effect" on juror verdict, and other studies have found support for crime show viewing impacts on perceptions of forensic evidence. Participants who viewed many (four to eight) episodes of *CSI* rated evidence differently from non- or light viewers (Smith et al. 2007). Research has also demonstrated that heavier *CSI* viewers infer more confidence in their judgments about the reliability of the evidence (Patry et al. 2008; Smith et al. 2007). Beyond the show *CSI*, studies have found that crime show viewers rate the shows to be an accurate representation of the justice system (Shelton et al. 2006) or even educational (Hayes and Levett 2012). All of this research, not without its criticisms, points out that the *CSI* Effect is more complicated than simply a direct effect of a person watching crime television and then rendering a verdict based on the viewership.

Pretrial publicity is another way that the media reportedly impacts the criminal legal system. Here it is easy to see how legacy media was initially concerning, but social media with its wide-reaching accessibility might be of even more concern. PTP is information disseminated through the media about a particular trial (Studebaker and Penrod 1997). PTP is thought to influence jurors' pretrial attitudes and subsequent decisions regarding the case, such as whether to acquit the defendant (Tyler 2006). That is, jurors could find a defendant guilty or not guilty because of the information they learned before the trial. Studies of the effects of PTP (all using legacy media) on juror verdicts have ranged from how it affects pretrial judgments of the defendant's guilt to how it can influence the final verdict (Studebaker et al. 2000). Research has also examined whether PTP has a positive or negative impact on trial outcomes (Ruva et al. 2011). Case law in the United States has been delving into the the concern of biased PTP since the 1950s, the first being *Stroble v. California* (1952) (Hardaway and Tumminello 1996).[2] Other actions that have been taken in response to PTP are motions for mistrial, changes of venue, continuances, "gag orders," and more detailed *Voir Dire* (aka Jury Selection) (Otto et al. 1994). The research on whether these actions are working to unbias the effects from PTP is mixed (Fulero 2002).

The Impact of New Media on Juries and Trial Outcomes

The concept of case-specific PTP is perhaps easier than general PTP to examine for assessing the effects of social media or online usage. Recent jury research by Daftary-Kapur et al. (2014) examined case-specific PTP for a trial in New York and when inquiring about exposure to pretrial information participants were asked about online usage. Daftary-Kapur et al. (2014) pointed to the fact that with blogs and other polarized media sources, the influence of PTP has even more potential to bias jurors. In *State v. Komisarjevsky* 2011 (United States), Lofink and Mullaney (2013) described that while counsel were under a gag order during this trial, reporters were live tweeting from the courtroom. Additionally, they mentioned that there were over 600 "hate" groups on Facebook prior to this

---

[2] This was followed up by *Irvin v. Dowd* (1961), *Rideau v. Louisiana* (1963), *Estes v. Texas* (1965), and *Sheppard v. Maxwell* (1966). Later case precedent indicated a hesitancy for case reversal in *Murphy v. Florida* (1975) and *Patton v. Yount* (1984) (with the exception of *Mu'Min v. Virginia* (1991), where the case was reversed).

trial among 10,000 news articles, Twitter feeds, blogs, and other social media exposure. Lofink and Mullaney (2013), as litigation technology support specialists, created a database of all this coverage to attempt to change the venue of the trial to which the motion was denied. The rest of their article provides tips on how to assess and manipulate the potential impact of PTP from their years of work on this topic.

While the Lofink and Mullaney (2013) article tends to focus on high-profile cases, rightfully so, the impact of new media shows how high-profile cases can be made out of low-profile cases. We see this in the case of Adnan Masud Syed, who was found guilty of murdering Hae Min Lee in 1999, and was not a household name at the time of his trial. Fast forward to 2014 and the release of *Serial Season 1*—this podcast reached five million downloads faster than any previous podcast on iTunes (Dredge 2014). In 2016, Syed was granted a new trial, and, at the time of this writing, whether or not he should receive a new trial is being decided in the Maryland, United States, court system. If Syed does receive a new trial, the role of PTP generated from the podcast will need to be considered in jury selection. PTP through new media and the impact on trials needs to be researched further.

PTP research examines *general pretrial publicity* and *case-specific pretrial publicity*. Case-specific PTP refers to information that jurors are exposed to through the media for the trial where they will decide the outcome. An example of case-specific PTP using social media is where a jurist reads Facebook posts about that specific trial. General PTP refers to general information in the news media that is not directly related to the case that the jurors will be adjudicating, but still may have a biasing effect on jurors' decisions or perceptions of evidence (Greene and Wade 1988). Again using Facebook as an example of general PTP would be reading or viewing information on a trial or general phenomenon, and then participating in an unrelated case in which that information affects the juror's decision. General PTP is more difficult to isolate as people are exposed to all types of information throughout their daily lives that could bias their decisions.

Another way that new media may impact courts is through local people connecting to each other through Facebook, Twitter, Snapchat, and

YouTube. Here they can share information with each other expeditiously, and to a wider audience. Facebook "friends" often include many acquaintances, even people who they have met only once; Twitter includes followers that are strangers; and YouTube includes a global audience, especially if a video is trending. This is where the social media "problem" can impact juries. Jurors utilizing social media can challenge the fairness of the trial.

Jurors receive instructions not to speak with anyone about the facts of the case that are outside of the jury. However, there have been incidences where jurors have gone on social media to report. According to Eve et al. (2014), Facebook is the favored platform for juror misconduct. Recently, in Tennessee (United States) in the case of *State v. Smith* (2013), a juror engaged in a Facebook exchange with a witness. The Tennessee state court here concluded, in the digital age, that courts should take additional precautions to make sure jurors understand the instructions. The additional precautions include instructions regarding social media and forbidding the use of it to discuss trial information. In another case, *Sluss v. Commonwealth* (2014), an exchange never took place, but because jurors had undisclosed friendships on Facebook with the victim's mother, this was used as one of the reasons to call for a mistrial in the State of Kentucky (United States) (Eve et al. 2014). This reason was unsuccessful as the court decided that a connection through Facebook does not equate to an actual friendship. However, the Kentucky State Supreme Court reversed and remanded because neither the nature of the relationship was investigated nor did the jurors admit to having a Facebook connection during the jury questioning process.

These cases bring up the question of how commonly jurors use social media to discuss cases. Eve et al. (2014) surveyed 583 jurors post service in Illinois (the United States) and found that only 8% (47) were tempted to use social media to communicate about the case. Of those tempted, when asked what prevented them, they responded that they were swayed by the judge's instructions not to engage in discussions on social media. Thus, in this era of social media, courts need to be diligent in their up-to-date education of jurors about the rules of social media use.

Media Effects on Lawyers and Judges

Unlike juries, which are made up of laypeople, the rest of the courtroom system is largely made up of individuals who are educated on the criminal legal system. Judges and lawyers (aka advocates or barristers) are impacted differently by legacy media's characterization of the criminal legal system than the general population. The impact of legacy media on lawyers and judges has also been researched, and one of the findings is that lawyers and judges *think* that jurors and the general population become biased and that this perception impacts the outcomes of the criminal legal system (Houck 2006; Maricopa County 2005; Stinson et al. 2007; Stevens 2008; Tyler 2006; Watkins 2004). With new media the impact on lawyers and judges is a bit more complicated, as the impact is more direct than with legacy media. Lawyers and judges are active on social media and there is concern about this usage and the content that these individuals are putting forth to the public (as all social media is public to an extent). The current section includes a discussion regarding legacy media's impact on lawyers and judges, followed by the proposed impact of new media as much more research is needed.

Legacy Media Impacts on Lawyers and Judges

Surveying attorneys regarding perceptions of the *CSI* Effect has found that they do believe that it exists, meaning that they think jurors have distorted views of the legal system due to crime show viewership (Maricopa County 2005; Watkins 2004; Patry et al. 2008). Prosecutors and defense attorneys have reported changing the types of questions they ask jurors during *voir dire* based on their belief that a *CSI* Effect exists (Watkins 2004). Depending on attorneys' perceptions and the use of *voir dire* questions, certain jurors may be (have been) excluded based on their viewing behavior; this occurred without strong research that shows that there is an effect of watching *CSI* on juror decision-making. The impact these changes have on jurors could also influence the case, such as York et al. (2006) found that an anti-*CSI* warning decreased jurors' beliefs/confidences in the prosecution. There are already negative public perceptions of lawyers that are at least in part due to media portrayals, and how new media impacts these perceptions can impact "the integrity of our justice system" (Boothe-Perry 2014, p. 74) and requires regulation in order to protect it.

New Media Impacts on Lawyers and Judges

The view on the usage of social media in the legal community is mixed. Courts have argued that it will interfere with the trial process, while attorneys argue its usage is important for jury selection and evidence needed for trial (Janoski-Haehlen 2011–2012). Social media/internet was the cause of approximately 90 verdicts challenged between 1999 and 2010 in the United States (Grow 2010). Twenty-eight cases resulted in overturned verdicts or new trials with the majority happening in 2009 and 2010; this suggests that there is at least some impact of the internet on the courts (Grow 2010). According to Johnston et al. (2011), they report that the Law Commission in the United Kingdom identified at least 18 appeals related to juror misconduct and some of these related to social media. Examples are where jurors: discuss the trial with each other through Facebook, comment about a trial on social media after it is complete, use social media to seek advice, or search the internet for information (Johnston et al. 2011). This has in an impact on lawyers and judges through social media policies. One such example is in Australia:

> An adjournment of a trial or a stay of the prosecution may be granted because of adverse media publicity. The court proceeds on the basis that the jurors will act in accordance with their oaths and directions given against being prejudiced by media publicity and opinions disseminated in social media. A stay will only be granted where no action can be taken by the judge to overcome any unfairness due to publicity taking into account the public interest in the trial of persons charged with serious offences. (Judicial Commission of NSW, Criminal Trial Courts Bench Book 2011, pp. 1–450)

Although, as evidenced earlier, there is a lack of research on the prevalence of social media usage by jurors. According to the US Courts (2014), a survey of US district judges reported that social media use by jurors is infrequent and so are the problems from it.

Regardless of the *actual* impact of media and social media on juries, lawyers and judges *think* there is an impact. Courts in the United States (Seguin 2011) and Australia (Johnston et al. 2011) have created instructions for jurors regarding social media. In Australia, states and territories have developed model directions that include a warning to jurors to not use the internet (Johnston et al. 2011). The jury instructions in the United States written by the Judicial Conference Committee on Court Administration and Case Management (2012) indicate that the instructions should be provided to the jurors prior to and at the end of the trial, but also at the end of each day and other times when appropriate. In the instructions it states:

> You may not communicate with anyone about the case on your cell phone, through e-mail, Blackberry, iPhone, text messaging, or on Twitter, through any blog or website, including Facebook, Google+, My Space, LinkedIn, or YouTube. You may not use any similar technology of social media, even if I have not specifically mentioned it here. (Judicial Conference 2012, p. 1)

There are also courtroom social media policies aimed at lawyers, judges, and courtroom workers. See, for example, in the United States: the Michigan Trial Court Standards and Guidelines for Websites and Social Media (see courts.mi.gov/socmediaguide). These standards draw attention to possible concerns facing trial court employees' use of social media, including the following:

- "User entries on blogs, wikis, or any other form of user-generated media can never truly be erased or deleted. The ability to preserve and replicate an Internet message or image for many years exacerbates the potential risks."
- "Due to perceived anonymity, a trial court employee may engage in conduct online that the employee might refrain from in person, without understanding that online communications may be traced to a particular user."

Social media is impacting day-to-day actions in the courts; it is used to provide information to the public and to individuals proceeding within the criminal legal system (Bladow and Raby 2011; Gibson 2016;). Social networking sites (e.g. Facebook) and micro-blogging sites are being used by courts to provide information (Bladow and Raby 2010). Of these two types, they argue that micro-blogging is being used the least. Courts are using social media and there are examples of using Twitter to report court judgments. The US Supreme Court has a Twitter account (see: @USSupremeCourt), as does the International Criminal Court in the Hague, the Netherlands (see: @IntlCrimCourt). As of this writing, in Australia three states use social media; an example is the Supreme Court of Victoria @SCVSupremeCourt (Gibson 2016). Social media has also been used to help self-represented litigants (Bladow and Raby 2011) who are individuals representing themselves during their court proceedings. As one can imagine, they lack the qualifications and knowledge of a lawyer and providing information about legal proceedings can be valuable. However, the information provided to them must be legal information, but not legal advice. Videos and documents that are created to aid them must be carefully scrutinized and clearly understandable to the layperson. Indiana's (United States) court posted videos on YouTube on how to represent oneself in court (see https://www.youtube.com/user/incourts).

Of course, there are potential issues associated with using new media in the court system. For example, it could be problematic if courts do not create an official public Facebook profile (Bladow and Raby 2011). With Facebook's "check in" feature, anyone can check into a place. If the place does not yet exist on Facebook, they can create it. Anyone can create a false public profile, and courts creating an official page will not change that, but it will at least allow for the proper information to be available. Additionally, as discussed earlier, the use of social media to educate individuals who are representing themselves in court is potentially problematic if the materials are not properly developed and reviewed.

There are ethical concerns for the use of social media by judges (Gibson 2016; Krawitz 2013; Janoski-Haehlen 2011–2012) and attorneys (Janoski-Haehlen 2011–2012). There are questions of whether the rule of law, which judges and lawyers are obliged to uphold, is being challenged by social media use (Gibson 2016) and this includes personal use. As Gibson (2016, p. 3) states:

whether courts "do business" with "customers" (i.e. court users) in an inter-active way, and whether the administration of justice is a process in which being "liked", responded to or re-tweeted by these court users should form any part of the courts' function.

In the United States, several states have used communication rules for judges and interpreted them to apply to social media, while others have stayed silent. Krawitz (2013) argued that for judges in Canada, Australia, and the United Kingdom there is insufficient guidance on the use of social media. Nevertheless, there have been a couple of incidences where judges have been recused due to social media usage where they have posted about their cases (Janoski-Haehlen 2011). Courts, as any social institution, need to progress along with society. However, they must do so in a manner that maintains the integrity of the institution. The American Bar Association has also acknowledged that there are ethical issues surrounding social media, and the recommendations and changes are ongoing (Harvey et al. 2014). This is a very complicated matter. A lawyer in 2011 was charged by the Virginia (United States) State Bar for professional misconduct, as he had discussed his completed cases on his blog and did not add an advertisement disclaimer (Poll 2012). Judges in the state of Florida are not allowed to be Facebook "friends" with prac-ticing attorneys (Janoski-Haehlen 2011–2012). The issues here surround the blurring of the professional and personal in these cases, and as courts navigate these lines it becomes increasingly difficult as technology con-tinues to change.

Media Effects on Corrections

Unlike the other areas of the justice system, corrections are a less-public institution. The manner in which legacy media impacts corrections is less through an impact on the actual system and more often on perceptions of corrections (Surette 2013). In the following section, we discuss the role of media in shaping our understanding of both corrections and punish-ment. We also briefly mention how due to the restrictions on media use inside correctional institutions, there is limited research on social media and corrections.

Legacy Media's Impact on Corrections

Through legacy media, especially movies, correctional institutions are portrayed unrealistically often with a focus on prisoners and demonization of correctional officers (Surette 2015). In movies, real prison problems are not highlighted, and if they are (such as prison rape), they are grossly misrepresented. In the news, journalists do not have the same kind of access to prisons as they do other aspects of the justice system. Therefore, they are limited in what they cover and the coverage largely casts a negative light. Overall, Surette (2013, 2015) argues that corrections are portrayed unrealistically and negatively. Regardless of the way corrections is portrayed, media representations of corrections can shape viewers' perceptions of the correctional system. Surette (2015) argues that because most people lack firsthand knowledge of the correctional system, the media's portrayal of corrections plays an important role in the public's construction of their understanding of jail and prison.

Most recently, we've seen the correctional system front and center in the award-winning popular Netflix show *Orange is the New Black*. Premiering in 2013, *Orange is the New Black* is based on Piper Kerman's (2011) memoir detailing her incarceration in a federal prison. The show highlights the stories—both what led to their incarceration and their experience of incarceration—of a diverse group of incarcerated women. Although *Orange is the New Black* does not always accurately portray women's incarceration experiences, it does bring issues of incarceration into the living rooms of people who have never stepped foot into a prison. As Seth Abramson (2013), a former public defender, wrote in the *Washington Post*:

> In a nation whose justice system often offers little more than one-size-fits-all injustice, a television series that inspires viewers to see convicts as fellow human beings can help us better understand and perhaps have a bit more empathy toward them. We should not confuse a TV program with a criminology course, but "Orange Is the New Black" goes a long way toward narrowing the gap between our perceptions of convicts and the sometimes surprising reality.

Schwan (2016) also suggests that *Orange is the New Black* presents to the viewer a critical assessment of mass incarceration and even advocates for prison reform. Whether *Orange is the New Black* has an impact on perceptions of prisons or prison reform could be studied.

Another and related manner in which media might be impacting correctional institutions is through punishments. Media consumption is reported to impact the public's fear of crime (Surette 1998). However, the research on this is decidedly mixed. Dowler (2003) found that viewing crime shows is related to fear of crime. But, they did not find an impact of media consumption on punitive attitudes. Sotirovic (2001) has suggested that media does have an impact on justice policy preferences, and that it has to do with the type of media exposure that one receives. That is, infotainment (Surette 2015) or the sensationalized, overly simplified crime news content that Jewkes (2010) discusses would likely increase punitive attitudes. While content that is more nuanced and complicated has an impact, the impact is less likely to be punitive. Britto and Noga-Styron (2014) found that controlling for other factors, television and talk radio consumption had an impact on support for capital punishment while newspapers and the internet did not. Regarding specific television genres, police-reality, news, and crime drama programs were all associated with favorable support for capital punishment. There are also anecdotal or a few extreme cases in which we witness media having an impact on punishment, but not necessarily through fear of crime. In 1986, Len Bias, who had been drafted two days before to play basketball for the Boston Celtics (Massachusetts, United States) as the second overall National Basketball Association draft pick, died from a supposed crack cocaine overdose. In Baum's book *Smoke and Mirrors: The War on Drugs and the Politics of Failure* (1997, p. 225), he wrote:

> Immediately upon returning from the July 4 recess, Tip O'Neill (then the Speaker of the House from Massachusetts) called an emergency meeting of the crime-related committee chairmen. Write me some goddamn legislation, he thundered. All anybody up in Boston is talking about is Len Bias. The papers are screaming for blood. We need to get out front on this now. This week. Today. The Republicans beat us to it in 1984 and I don't want that to happen again. I want dramatic new initiatives for dealing with crack and other drugs.

Although it was later determined that Bias died from a powder cocaine overdose (Bush-Baskette 2010), the coverage of his alleged crack cocaine overdose might have aided in the continuation of the War on Drugs in the United States. This example is demonstrative of cultivation theory (Gerbner et al. 1980) and social construction (Berger and Luckmann 1967; Surette 2015), as discussed in Chap. 1.

New Media's Impact on Corrections

As far as social media's reach within corrections, Surette (2013) argues that the focus has been on keeping inmates away from social media. Unlike with law enforcement, citizen journalism using social media or, in this case, "prisoner journalism" has not yet taken hold. Imagine the implications if prisoners were allowed to use Facebook, tweet, or post about their experiences! There are instances of inmates using smuggled smartphones to access social media illegally behind prison walls. For instance, in Tennessee (United States) a local news station investigation found that approximately 100 inmates were using Facebook from prison to correspond with both those on the outside and other inmates (Finely 2013). It would likely change the public consciousness about prisoners, which could be negative or positive.

As far as our knowledge goes, social media's role in views of punishment has not yet been researched. However, social media impacts public outrage and could therefore impact public policy and punishment. As citizen journalism continues to occur, it is possible that these postings on social media sites are impacting people's punitive perspectives.

Conclusion

While there is an impact of legacy media and new media on the criminal legal system, current research does not adequately demonstrate the scope of that effect. It is difficult for researchers to isolate the effect of media on the criminal legal system; therefore, this research receives a fair amount of criticism. The research on the criminal legal system is called effects research (introduced in Chap. 1), and Gauntlett (2001) clearly laid out ten criticisms with this research in the *Worrying Influence of Media Effects Studies*. Some of the criticisms are that it lacks theory and it oversimplifies children as victims, and perhaps the most important issue is that of causality. Media effects research highlights correlations, but not causation. For example, we see that crime show viewing is correlated to viewing those shows as educational (Hayes and Levett 2012). However, we cannot say that crime show viewing causes that viewpoint; viewers could have had that viewpoint prior to watching those shows. And with new media being essentially everywhere, how does one isolate the effect of one medium over another?

These criticisms are not meant to assert that media does not have an impact on the criminal legal system or perceptions of crime. It is that the direct effects model is too simple for the complicated nature of media, especially today with new media (Barak 2012; Ferrell et al. 2008). There needs to be more theoretical development with focus on indirect methodological studies, in order to successfully advance the narrative of Media Criminology. Future research in this area must extend to include new media. Thus far, policing is probably changing the most due to new media influence compared with other parts of the criminal legal system. The main aspect of that is regarding surveillance (think: your social media accounts are being read and followed regardless of privacy settings), and the debate continues as to the role surveillance has in our society and whether "Big Brother" is going too far. Opinion research on surveillance with the public can ascertain whether there is a consensus regarding the impact. Research on whether surveillance is impacting criminal investigations in a positive manner, along with cost effectiveness, needs to be conducted. Also regarding surveillance, will prisons be subjected to increased surveillance? Prisons which have historically been closed to outside observers and constructed very negatively by legacy media could be affected by leaked surveillance. If prisoners start to gain access to new media more easily, will this change our view of prisoners? Regarding juries and the courtroom, new media is influencing the manner in which courts need to do their job. There are ethical and research-oriented questions. The boundaries for judges and lawyers regarding the personal and professional lives are being blurred with new media. How much control should the government have over government actors? Similarly, with so much social media information in the public domain, should we allow attorneys to access that information on potential jurors?

Discussion Questions

1. How does law enforcement use social media in your community? How could law enforcement use social media more effectively?
2. Currently, social media use is not allowed in correctional facilities. What would be the pros and cons of allowing the use of social media by inmates?
3. What role should new media play in the courtroom? How can forms of new media be used to positively or negatively impact the courtroom?

References

Media References

Abramson, S. (2013). How orange is new black humanizes inmates. *Washington Post*. Retrieved from https://www.washingtonpost.com/opinions/how-orange-is-the-new-black-humanizes-inmates/2013/07/26/d1559bac-f3e5-11e2-9434-60440856fadf_story.html?utm_term=.9d0c57ca64ef

Bowcott, O., Carter, H., & Clifton, H. (2011, August). Facebook riot calls earn men four-year jail terms amid sentencing outcry. *The Guardian*. Retrieved from https://www.theguardian.com/uk/2011/aug/16/facebook-riot-calls-men-jailed

Chan, M. (2016, October). Everything you need to know about the 'clown attack' craze. *Time*. Retrieved from http://time.com/4518456/scary-clown-sighting-attack-craze/

Change.org. https://www.change.org/p/president-of-the-united-states-free-steven-avery

Dredge, S. (2014). Serial podcast breaks ITunes records as it passes 5m downloads and streams. *The Guardian*. Retrieved from https://www.theguardian.com/technology/2014/nov/18/serial-podcast-itunes-apple-downloads-streams

Finely, J. (2013). Inmates party, display drugs & cash in Facebook posts and video. *WSMV.* Retrieved from http://www.wsmv.com/story/22080698/inmates-party-display-drugs-and-cash-in-facebook-posts-and-video

Grow, B. (2010, December). As jurors go online, US trials go off track. *Reuters.* Retrieved from http://www.reuters.com/article/2010/12/08/internetInternet-jurors-idUSN0816547120101208

Lofink, C. R., & Mullaney, M. (2013). Pretrial publicity and courtroom Umami. *The Jury Expert.* Retrieved from http://www.thejuryexpert.com/wpcontent/uploads/1305/JuryExpert_1305_Umami.pdf

McDonnell-Parry, A. (2016). Making a murderer one year later: Everything you need to know. *Rolling Stone.* Retrieved from http://www.rollingstone.com/culture/news/making-a-murderer-one-year-later-everything-to-know-w455262

McGann, H., & Said-Moorhouse, L. (2016). Creepy clown craze sweeps the globe. *CNN.* Retrieved from http://www.cnn.com/2016/10/10/world/creepy-clown-sightings-global/index.html

Orange is the New Black. Netflix Series.

Procter R., Vis, F., & Voss A. (2011). How riot rumours spread on Twitter. *The Guardian.* Retrieved from http://guardian.co.uk/uk/interactive/2011/dec/07/london-riots-twitter

Sowinski, G. (2013). Police turn to social media as a crime-fighting tool. *McClatchy-Tribune News.* Washington, DC.

Yanak-Jonaitis, L. (2016). Clown on campus? Rumors spread as CMU police address concern. *The Morning Sun.* Retrieved from http://www.themorning-sun.com/article/MS/20161004/NEWS/161009898

Academic References

Barak, G. (2012). *Mass media and the social construction of crime: A critique and implications for the future.* Retrieved from http://www.greggbarak.com/whats_new_6.html

Baum, D. (1997). *Smoke and mirrors: The war on drugs and the politics of failure.* Boston: Little, Brown.

Berger, P. L., & Luckmann, T. (1967). *The social construction of reality.* Garden City: DoubleDay.

Bladow, K., & Raby, J. (2010). Using social media to support self-represented litigants and increase access to justice. *National Center for State Courts.* Retrieved from https://ncsc.contentdm.oclc.org/digital/collection/ctmedia/id/29/

Bladow, K., & Raby, J. (2011). *Using social media to support self-represented litigants and increase access to justice*. NCJ 243537. Retrieved from https://www.ncjrs.gov/App/Publications/abstract.aspx?id=265614

Boothe-Perry, N. (2014). Friends of justice: Does social media impact the public perception of the justice system. *Pace Law Review, 35*(1), 72–115.

Britto, S., & Noga-Styron, K. E. (2014). Media consumption and support for capital punishment. *Criminal Justice Review, 39*(1), 81–100.

Bush-Baskette, S. R. (2010). *Misguided justice: The war on drugs and the incarceration of black women*. Bloomington: iUniverse.

Chermak, S., McGarrell, E., & Gruenewald, J. (2006). Media coverage of police misconduct and attitudes toward police. *Policing: An International Journal of Police Strategies & Management, 29*(2), 261–281.

Daftary-Kapur, T., Penrod, S. D., O'Connor, M., & Wallace, B. (2014). Examining pretrial publicity in a shadow jury paradigm: Issues of slant, quantity, persistence, and generalizability. *Law & Human Behavior, 38*(5), 462–477.

Dowler, K. (2003). Media consumption and public attitudes toward crime and justice: The relationship between fear of crime, punitive attitudes, and perceived police effectiveness. *Journal of Criminal Justice and Popular Culture, 10*(2), 109–126.

Escholz, S., Blackwell, B., Gertz, M., & Chiricos, T. (2002). Race and attitudes toward the police: Assessing the effect of watching 'reality' police programs. *Journal of Criminal Justice, 30*, 327–341.

Eve, A. J. S., Burns, C., & Zuckerman, M. A. (2014). More from the #Jury Box: The latest juries and social media. *Duke Law & Technology Review, 1*(64), 61–93.

Ferrell, J., Hayward, K., & Young, J. (2008). *Cultural criminology: An invitation* (2nd ed.). London: Sage.

Fulero, S. M. (2002). Afterword: The past, present, and future of applied pretrial publicity research. *Law & Human Behavior, 26*(1), 127–133.

Gauntlett, D. (2001). *The worrying influence of 'media effects' studies*. Retrieved from http://www.theory.org.uk/tenthings.htm

Gerbner, G., Gross, L., Signorielli, N., & Morgan, M. (1980). Television violence, victimization, and power. *American Behavioral Scientist, 23*(5), 705.

Gibson, J. (2016). Social media and the electronic "new world" of judges. *International Journal for Court Administration, 7*(2), 1–9.

Greene, E., & Wade, R. (1988). Of private talk and public print: General pretrial publicity and juror decision-making. *Applied Cognitive Psychology, 2*, 123–135.

Hardaway, R., & Tumminello, D. B. (1996). Pretrial publicity in criminal cases of national notoriety: Constructing a remedy for the remediless wrong. *The American University Law Review, 46*, 39–90. Retrieved from http://amulrev. org/pdfs/46/46-1/hardaway.pdf

Harvey, C. V., McCoy, M. R., & Sneath, B. (2014, January). 10 tips for avoiding ethical lapses when using social media. *Business Law Today.* Retrieved from https://www.americanbar.org/publications/blt/2014/01/03_harvey.html

Hayes, R. M., & Levett, L. M. (2011). Jury's still out: How television and crime show viewing influences jurors' evaluations of evidence. *Applied Psychology in Criminal Justice, 7*(1), 29–46.

Hayes, R. M., & Levett, L. M. (2012). Community members' perceptions of the CSI effect. *American Journal of Criminal Justice, 38*, 216–235.

Hayes-Smith, R. M. (2009). *The CSI effect: Jurors' perceptions and trial decisions* (Unpublished Dissertation). Gainesville: University of Florida.

Houck, M. M. (2006). CSI: Reality. *Scientific American, 295*, 84–89.

Janoski-Haehlen, E. M. (2011). The courts are all a 'Twitter': The implications of social media use in courts. *Valpraiso University Law Review, 43*(1), 43–68.

Jewkes, Y. (2010). *Media & crime* (2nd ed.). London: Sage

Johnston, J., Keyzer, P., Holland, G., Pearson, M., Rodrick, S., & Wallace, A. (2011). *Juries and social media. A report prepared for the Victorian Department of Justice.* Retrieved from http://www.ncsc.org/~/media/Files/PDF/Information %20and%20Resources/juries%20and%20social%20media_Australia_ A%20Wallace.ashx

Judicial Commission of NSW, Criminal Trial Courts Bench Book (September 2011), 1–450. Retrieved from https://www.judcom.nsw.gov.au/publications/ benchbks/criminal/the_jury.html#1-450

Judicial Conference Committee on Court Administration and Case Management. (2012). Retrieved from http://www.uscourts.gov/news/2012/08/21/revised-jury-instructions-hope-deter-juror-use-social-media-during-trial

Kääriäinen, J., Isotalus, P., & Thomassen, G. (2016). Does public criticism erode trust in the police? The case of Jari Aarnio in the Finnish news media and its effects on the public's attitudes towards the police. *Journal of Scandinavian Studies in Criminology and Crime Prevention, 17*(1), 70–85.

Kerman, P. (2011). *Orange is the new black.* New York: Spiegel & Grau.

Krawitz, M. (2013). Can Australian judges keep their "friends" close and their ethical obligations closer: An analysis of the issues regarding Australian judges' use of social media. *Journal of Judicial Administration, 23*(14), 1–18.

Lab, S. P., Williams, M. R., Holcomb, J. E., Burek, M. W., King, W. R., & Buerger, M. E. (2011). *Criminal justice: The essentials.* New York: Oxford University Press.

LexisNexis. (2014). *Social media use in law enforcement.* Retrieved from https://www.lexisnexis.com/risk/downloads/whitepaper/2014-social-media-use-in-law-enforcement.pdf

Lieberman, J. D., Koetzle, D., & Sakiyama, M. (2013). Police departments' use of Facebook: Patterns and policy issues. *Police Quarterly, 16*(4), 438–462.

Lundman, R. J., & Kaufman, R. L. (2003). Driving while black: Effects of race, ethnicity, and gender on citizen self-reports of traffic stops and police actions. *Criminology, 41*(1), 195–220.

Mancini, D. E. (2013). The "CSI effect" in an actual juror sample: Why crime show genre may matter. *North American Journal of Psychology, 15*(3), 543–564.

Maricopa County. (2005, June 30). *The CSI effect and its real-life impact on justice: A study by the Maricopa County Attorney's Office.* Retrieved from http://www.maricopacountyattorney.org/Press/PDF/CSIReport.pdf

Marsh, I., & Melville, G. (2009). *Crime, justice and the media.* London: Routledge.

Newman, G. (1990). Popular culture and criminal justice: A preliminary analysis. *Journal of Criminal Justice, 18,* 261–274.

Nix, J., & Wolfe, S. E. (2017). The impact of negative publicity on police self-legitimacy. *Justice Quarterly, 34*(1), 84–108.

O'Neil, K. M. (2007, March). *Exploring the CSI effect preliminary evidence for a pro-prosecution bias.* Paper presentation at Off the Witness Stand: Using Psychology in the Practice of Justice Conference, New York.

Otto, A. L., Penrod, S. D., & Dexter, H. R. (1994). The biasing impact of pre-trial publicity on juror judgments. *Law & Human Behavior, 18*(4), 453–469.

Patry, M. W., Stinson, V., & Smith, S. M. (2008). The reality of the CSI effect. In J. Greenberg & C. Elliott (Eds.), *Communications in question: Canadian perspectives on controversial issues in communication studies.* Scarborough: Thompson-Nelson.

Podlas, K. (2006). "The CSI effect": Exposing the media myth. *Fordham Intellectual Property, Media & Entertainment Law Journal, 16,* 429–465.

Poll, E. (2012, November). The slippery slope of social media. *Law Practice Today,* Retrieved from https://www.americanbar.org/publications/law_practice_today_home/law_practice_today_archive/november12/the-slippery-ethical-slope-of-social-media.html

Powell, A. (2014, November 24–27). Pursuing justice online: Citizen participation in justice via social media. In B. West (Ed.), *Proceedings of challenging identities, institutions, and communities (TASA 2014)*, Adelaide, pp. 1–12.

Ramaswamy, C. (2016, January 11). Guilty pleasure: How *Making a Murderer* tapped our weakness for true crime. *The Guardian*. Retrieved from https://www.theguardian.com/tv-and-radio/2016/jan/11/how-making-murderer-tapped-our-weakness-true-crime-steven-avery

Radsch, C. (2016). *Cyberactivism and citizen journalism in Egypt: Digital dissidence and political change*. New York: Palgrave Macmillan.

Reardon, M. C., O'Neil, K. M., & Lawson, K. (2007, March 23–27). A new definition of the CSI effect. *Annual Meeting for the Association for Psychological Science*.

Reilly, P. (2013). Every little helps? YouTube, sousveillance and the 'anti-Tesco' riot in stokes croft. *New Media & Society, 17*(5), 755–771.

Ruva, C. L., Guenther, C. C., & Yarbrough, A. (2011). Deciphering the effects of positive and negative PTP: Examining the roles of impression formation, emotion and predecisional distortion. *Criminal Justice and Behavior, 38*, 511–534.

Salter, M. (2017). *Crime, justice and social media*. Oxon: Routledge.

Schwan, A. (2016). Postfeminist meets the women in prison genre. *Television & New Media, 17*(6), 473–490.

Seguin, P. (2011, May). The use of social media in the Superior Court of Arizona in Maricopa County. Institute for Court Management, Court Executive Development Papers.

Shelton, D. E., Kim, Y. S., & Barak, G. (2006). A study of juror expectations and demands concerning scientific evidence: Does the "CSI effect" exist? *Vanderbilt Journal of Entertainment and Technology Law, 9*, 331–368.

Sluss v. Commonwealth. (2014). 450 SW 3d 279.

Smith, S. M., Patry, M. W., & Stinson, V. (2007). But what is the CSI effect? How crime dramas influence people's beliefs about forensic evidence. *The Canadian Journal of Police & Security Services, 5*, 1–8.

Sotirovic, M. (2001). Affective and cognitive processes as mediators of media influence on crime-policy preferences. *Mass Communication & Society, 4*, 311–329.

State v. Komisarjevsky. (2011). 21 A. 3d 465.

State v. Smith. (2013, September 10). Tennessee, No. M2010-01384, 2013 WL 4804845.

Steadman, G. W. (2002). Survey of DNA Crime laboratories *Bureau of Justice Statistics*. Retrieved from https://www.bjs.gov/index.cfm?ty=pbdetail&iid=1117

Stevens, D. (2008). Forensic science, wrongful convictions, and American prosecutor discretion. *The Howard Journal of Criminal Justice, 47*(1), 31–51.

Stinson, V., Patry, M. W., & Smith, S. M. (2007). The CSI effect: Reflections from police and forensic investigators. *The Canadian Journal of Police and Security Services, 5*(3), 1–9.

Strier, F. (1992–1993). What can the American adversary system learn from an inquisitorial system of justice? *Judicature, 76,* 109–112.

Studebaker, C. A., & Penrod, S. D. (1997). Pretrial publicity: The media, the law and common sense. *Psychology, Public Policy and Law, 3,* 428–460.

Studebaker, C. A., Robbennolt, J. K., Pathak-Sharma, M. K., & Penrod, S. D. (2000). Assessing pretrial publicity effects: Integrating content analytic results. *Law & Human Behavior, 24*(3), 317–336.

Surette, R. (1998). *Media, crime, and criminal justice: Images and realities* (2nd ed.). New York: Wadsworth Publishing.

Surette, R. (2013). Pathways to copycat crime. In J. B. Helfgott (Ed.), *Criminal psychology* (pp. 251–273). Santa Barbara: Praeger.

Surette, R. (2015). *Media, crime, and criminal justice: Images, realities, and policies* (5th ed.). Stamford: Cengage Learning.

Trottier, D. (2012). Policing social media. *Canadian Review of Sociology, 49*(4), 411–425.

Tyler, T. R. (2006). Viewing CSI and the threshold of guilt: Managing truth and justice in reality and fiction. *The Yale Law Journal, 115,* 1050–1085.

United States Courts. (2014). Retrieved from http://www.uscourts.gov/news/2014/07/29/survey-finds-infrequent-social-media-use-jurors

Visco, S. D. (2016). Legality and the spectacle of murder: A review of Netflix's *Making a Murderer* (2015-). *Humanity and Society, 40*(2), 212–214.

Wall, T., & Linnemann, T. (2014). Staring down the state: Police power, visual economies, and the "war on cameras". *Crime, Media, Culture: An International Journal, 10*(2), 133–149.

Watkins, M. (2004). *Forensics in the media: Have attorneys reacted to the growing popularity of forensic crime dramas?* (Unpublished M.A.). Tallahassee: Florida State University.

Weitzer, R. (1999). Citizens' perceptions of police misconduct: Race and neighborhood context. *Justice Quarterly, 16*(4), 819–846.

Weitzer, R., & Tuch, S. A. (1999). Race, class, and perceptions of discrimination by the police. *Crime & Delinquency, 45*(4), 494–507.

Weitzer, R., & Tuch, S. A. (2004a). Race and perceptions of police misconduct. *Social Problems, 51*, 305–325.

Weitzer, R., & Tuch, S. A. (2004b). Reforming the police: Racial differences in public support for change. *Criminology, 42*, 391–416.

Weitzer, R., & Tuch, S. A. (2005). Racially biased policing: Determinants of citizen perceptions. *Social Forces, 83*(3), 1009–1030.

Wikipedia. (2016). *CSI crime scene investigation.* Retrieved from https://en.wikipedia.org/wiki/CSI:_Crime_Scene_Investigation

York, R., Evans, J., & O'Neil, K. M. (2006, March). *The CSI Effect: Presentation style, evidence quality, and a possible remedy.* Paper presented at the American Psychology-Law Society Conference, St. Petersburg.

3

#CrimingWhileWhite: Media's Construction of the Criminal

In Ferguson, Missouri, in the United States, on August 9, 2014, a white police officer, Darren Wilson, fatally shot an 18-year-old black man, Michael Brown. Michael Brown allegedly robbed a convenience store of cigarillos and Officer Wilson spotted. Michael Brown and his friend, who was also a suspect in the robbery. Officer Wilson blocked the path of the young men with his police vehicle and an altercation through the window of his vehicle occurred where they were struggling over the officer's gun until it went off. Then Michael Brown fled and the officer took chase, at which point Michael Brown turned and started going toward the officer. The officer then fired multiple shots into an unarmed Michael Brown, who eventually died. Eyewitness accounts, which some consider to be unreliable, stated that Michael Brown had his hands up. Regardless of the circumstances, the event spawned outrage regarding the police and use of force within communities of people of color. Discussion and debate surrounding this case and other similar cases continue.

Common understandings of who is a criminal and who is not a criminal are influenced by the media (Barak 2012; Surette 2015). Many people are taught whom they should fear as a potential criminal through news media, television shows, social media, and the internet. Media and society

© The Author(s) 2018
R. M. Hayes, K. Luther, *#Crime*, Palgrave Studies in Crime, Media and Culture,
https://doi.org/10.1007/978-3-319-89444-7_3

are coproducers in societal meaning making and social media is changing the manner in which we construct our society.

As discussed in Chap. 1, moral panics are created by developing and scapegoating "the other." Nowhere is this more relevant than in the construction of the criminal. The trend of who is a criminal according to legacy media accounts are immigrants, racial/ethnic minorities, and street criminals. This creates the normalized imagery of what is considered to be the most frequent crimes and who is considered to be a criminal. The imagery is steeped in sensationalism and stereotypes. Even more than stereotypes, these images of criminals have historical roots and include set archetypes such as black women as sexually aggressive or castrating matriarchs (Mogul et al. 2011), Arabs as terrorists (Shaheen 2009), or lesbians as killers (Mogul et al. 2011; Jewkes 2015). Along with continuously highlighting archetypes, media overdramatizes crime in order to capture the attention of the viewer or reader and gives a disproportionate amount of focus to violent crime (Barkan and Bryjack 2014). New media can impact the imagery of crime and criminals through reinforcement or counter rhetoric. Groups experiencing othering and marginalization are provided with a platform and voice on social media of which they often lack within legacy media.

Using contemporary examples, this chapter discusses how the media, both legacy and new media, influences who is portrayed as a criminal and societal reactions to such portrayals. In particular, this chapter will:

1. Examine the amount of crime portrayed in the media over time.
2. Explore six key myths about crime and criminals that are presented in the media.

Legacy Media and New Media: The Changing Landscape

Crime stories previously dominated local newscasts, but have been on a steady decline. In 2005, crime stories in local news accounted for 29% of coverage, and five years later this dropped to 17% (Jurkowitz et al. 2013). With younger generations not watching as much television news nor reading newspapers, their information is likely more commonly retrieved through new/social media. This means that someone's newsfeed may be filled by their own perspective on particular issues. For example, Facebook's algorithm identifies your point of view through your clicks and "likes." It then presents you with certain information (e.g. friends and news), which may or may not include objective viewpoints. Legacy media is also included in social media, but alongside individual people's views. For example, on Twitter you can find the *New York Times*, *Washington Post*, and *The Economist*. Thus, our understanding of crime is shaped by an interplay of information from legacy and new media. Although, arguably, the message might continue to be the same, just in a new format (Surette and Gardiner-Bess 2014). How we understand crime according to Jewkes (2010), is also related to whether a story is deemed to be newsworthy (see box *Newsworthiness*).

Newsworthiness In the book *Media and Crime*, Jewkes (2010) provides a discussion surrounding how media professionals chose the news stories that we hear and see everyday. They argue that there is a set of "professional criteria" which evaluate the story's *newsworthiness*. Similar, probably, to how prosecutors decide whether a case will be successfully prosecuted, these are behind-the-scenes considerations. Of course, the criteria presented here will not necessarily be exhaustive as cultural differences will provide some variations, and not all must be present in every story, but at least some will. According to Jewkes (2010), there are 12 "news structures and news values" that shape crime news in particular, and here we provide a brief explanation of each: *Threshold*—the perceived importance of an event, such as in a local context where a vandalism might be important but in a national context this story would not meet the threshold; *Predictability*—if it is a rare event, it is newsworthy; *Simplification*—even if not simple, the story needs to be easily simplified; *Individualism*—this connects *simplification* and the next news value *risk*, where the key focus is on how the offender and the victim are focused on as individuals, and not the society from whence they came. Think about the "lone wolf" characteristic that is often used in news stories; *Risk* is where it is possible that this crime might impact you, such as if an offender has yet to be caught, it makes it more newsworthy as the news narrative tends to present crime as unpredictable; *Sex*, *Celebrity*, and *Violence* are self-explanatory. If the story includes sex, a high-status person, or excessive violence, it is more newsworthy; *Proximity* is either geographical or cultural

(continued)

(continued)

closeness to the audience; Along with violence is *spectacle and graphic imagery*—the visually arresting imagery tends to support the veracity of the story in the public's mind, therefore making it more newsworthy; *Children*—a crime story including children is more newsworthy, whether they are the victim or the offender; and, finally, *conservative ideology and political diversion*, where if the story includes a getting-more-tough-on-crime discourse, it makes it more newsworthy.

The crimes that are least likely to occur are the ones that are highlighted most often in the media (Chermak 1995a, b; Surette and Gardiner-Bess 2014). According to research conducted by Pollak and Kubrin (2007), the characteristics of crime, criminals, and victims represented in the media are usually the opposite of what official crime statistics report. This is called "the backwards law" and is also demonstrated in crime entertainment and infotainment (Surette and Gardiner-Bess 2014). Infotainment (examples include COPS, Lock Up, Cold Case Files (US); GUMRAAH and CRIME PATROL (INDIA)) comprises both crime news and entertainment and impacts people's perceptions about crime more than traditional crime entertainment, because there is a belief that these shows are more representative of reality (Surette and Gardiner-Bess 2014; Surette 2015).

The news media pick up crime stories that occur least often, but because of this they stand out and are easily sensationalized. One example is the coverage of female sex offenders, where even though men are more likely to be sex offenders, there is substantial coverage when a woman is the offender (Jewkes 2015, 2010). The effect can be that individuals viewing crime news might think that a crime is more common than it is in reality. This impact is supportive of cultivation theory (described in Chap. 1), where viewing information on crime cultivates the perspective for the viewer (Shanahan and Morgan 1999). As we discussed in Chaps. 1 and 2, the more television a person views, the more their perspective of reality can be effected. The content of what is portrayed in the media is the key to understanding these perceptions when other sources are not available. These effects are also stronger when one is removed from the institution or place. For example, when one is constructing an idea of a country they have not visited, their exposure is likely to be through media images. Another example is the criminal legal system where exposure for most people is tangential so it is largely influenced by the media (Surette 2015).

Student Activity *Before taking this class (and other criminology courses), where did you receive your knowledge of criminals and the criminal legal system? What messages did you receive from these sources?*

With the majority of research cross-sectionally examining how crime and criminals are portrayed in the media, it is difficult to provide a clear picture over time. One longitudinal analysis of a sample of entertainment and news stories over a 46-year period (1945–1991), revealed how the media constructed crime in the United Kingdom (Allen et al. 1998; Livingstone et al. 2001; Reiner et al. 2000, 2003). Over this time period,

- News stories included more crime, while cinema stayed about the same.
- The content in both cinema and newspaper stories included an increase in violent crime, particularly murder.
- The most rapid increase of reports in newspapers was for terrorist offenses.

This research lends some credence to the argument that media is over-reporting violent crimes. Similarly, Pollak and Kubrin (2007) researched television and newspaper crime stories in the United States, and also found a higher prevalence of violent stories (61 out of 71 sampled) than what is found in official statistics. In the United States, public perception of crime as the most important problem in the early 1990s was attributed to the impact of network TV news (Lowry et al. 2003).

The media construction of the criminal is a bit more complicated. In Reiner's (2000) examination of entertainment and news stories from 1945 to 1991, criminals were portrayed, both fictionally and nonfictionally, as predominantly white, middle-aged or older, and male. This pattern is stable, with the exception of the representation of ethnic minority offenders beginning to increase. Surette and Gardiner-Bess (2014) also argue that the media portrayal of the criminal is often mature, white, and of high social status. Reiner et al. (2001) noted an increase in representation of ethnic minorities and further analysis of UK cinema could examine whether the trend continued beyond 1991. A great deal of the US-based research and theory argues that criminals are often portrayed as ethnic minorities in the media, for example the "black man as criminal" myth (Entman 1990; Entman and Rojecki 2000; Gilliam and Iyengar 2000; Romer et al. 1998; Russell-Brown 1998, 2009).

With new media usage continuing to rise and newspaper/television decreasing, the influence of new media's contribution to images of criminals, crime, and the criminal justice system should be examined. We venture to assert that social media may be challenging current perceptions. For example, the #BlackLivesMatter Movement introduced in Chap. 2, which in part derived from the outrage over the deaths of Trayvon Martin, Michael Brown, and Eric Garner, has led to many people questioning and challenging the criminal legal system (more on this later in the chapter). Additionally, the hashtag #crimingwhilewhite on Twitter further perpetuates the notion that crime, especially in US society, tends to be reported biasedly and the criminal legal system is also affected. One example from the 2017 Las Vegas Shooting:

@runfromphilly: I bet @BreitbartNews won't retweet this nor will they say #LasVegasShooting perp was a terrorist. **#CRIMINGWHILEWHITE** #Disgraceful

Indeed, according to Holohan (2005), the postmodern theorist Levy (2000) argued that new media would provide the potential for the enhancement of political debate and global interaction. Let's examine current perceptions and how these may be confirmed or challenged by new media.

Who Is a Criminal? Myths Versus Reality

When criminal incidents are discussed, it seems that everyone becomes an expert investigator. From "who did it" to "why did it happen," assumptions about criminal activity are everywhere. The "who is a criminal" in the United States is partially constructed by wrongfully targeting certain groups even though evidence suggests that over 90% of all Americans have committed a crime for which they could be incarcerated (Bohm 1986). The assumptions surrounding "who is a criminal" are encouraged by the media through social construction (Berger and Luckmann 1967; Surette 2015), which leads to moral panics (Critcher 2003; Jewkes 2004; Surette 2007; Carrabine 2008) that often perpetuate stereotypes. Scholars argue that this imagery not only contributes to misinformation, but can encourage harmful reactions by society (e.g. hate crimes) and in the criminal legal system (e.g. racial profiling and discriminatory policies). It may even harm individuals by becoming a self-fulfilling prophecy (Simons et al. 2003; Unnever and Gabbidon 2011). For example, the internalization of a racial stereotype such as the *criminalblackman* (Russell-Brown 1998) can influence someone to consciously or subconsciously acquiesce to the label.

Media portrayals of what is a common crime and who is the common criminal are repetitive messages. When examining the cross-sectional (and mostly content analytic) research, common themes about crime and criminals arise. Here we discuss six persistent, timely key myths (see box *Crime Myth*): (1) you should be afraid of the violent crime happening to you (Dowler 2003; Warr 1980, 1995, 2000); (2) immigrants, migrants, and refugees are criminals (Larson 2017; Tuttle 2017); (3) young men of minority racial/ethnic groups are criminals (Russell-Brown 1998, 2009); (4) women who commit violent crime are worse than men who commit violent crime (Jewkes 2015); (5) members of the LGBTQ community are hypersexual and/or sexual predators (Mogul et al. 2011); and (6) individuals with mental illness are likely to be violent (McGinty et al. 2016; U.S. Department of Health & Human Services 2017). The message that emerges from these myths about criminals is that they are the "other" and, thus, "normal" people do not need to relate to them. These representations are steeped in negative stereotypes about race, ethnicity, nationality, gender, sexuality, social class, and abelism which are not always noticeable at first glance. Additionally, these myths are interconnected, and one does not exist entirely on its own; in contrast, as we will point out, some of these myths are closely tied together.

Crime Myth By crime myth we mean the collective definition that society has applied to a crime issue. The origin is often unknown, but it is created and continued through a nonscientific telling and retelling of the exaggerated and fabricated issue. Many crime myths are extracted from a real issue, but during debate and public policy shaping the reality becomes distorted and/or contradicted (Kappeler and Potter 2005). One of the main drivers of crime myths is the media (Bohm 1986). Myths exist for a reason. The main thesis is that they serve the interests of the elite, but others argue that they have to at least serve the interests of the general public in order to persist (Bohm 1986). Think about the War on Drugs that we discussed in Chap. 1. There are drug issues in many societies, but the manner in which the issue is debated and discussed in media and politics the focus is shifted from the reality of drug issues and distorted into a huge crime issue with punitive policies that are supposed to address this issue. In reality, the policies created more harm than good as they did not target the high-level drug dealers and focused on people of color as the drug users, who were not the majority of drug users at the time.

The following sections overview and debunk common media myths about crime and criminals. This list is not an exhaustive list of media myths surrounding crime; instead, we've chosen key myths that are timely, perpetuated by both legacy and new media, and supported by academic research and ones we commonly encounter as criminologists.

Media Myth 1: You should be afraid of violent crime happening to you.
Reality: You are more likely to experience property crime victimization than violent crime victimization.

Media portrays violent crimes—murder, robbery, rape, and assault—as common events. News, television, movies, and video games all include examples of violence. According to the Media Education Foundation (2005), media violence has increased in quantity and has become more graphic, sexual, and sadistic. For instance, it is estimated that in the United States by the time a child is 18 they will have witnessed 200,000 acts of violence through the media. Media's portrayal of violence also presents us with a depiction of the criminal. Historically, one of the common images in entertainment is that of the "animalistic, irrational, and innate predators who commit violent and senseless crimes" (Surette and Gardiner-Bess 2014, p. 374). Thus, we are led to believe that violence is a fact of everyday life and we need to protect ourselves from it.

The media representation of crime is even more pronounced for urban areas, with coverage of rural areas suggesting that these places are idyllic and not criminogenic (Donnermeyer and DeKeseredy 2014). When a crime does occur in a rural community, it is covered as if it is exceptional. The focus on the "big bad city" myth has even led to criminological research lacking in rural areas (Donnermeyer and DeKeseredy 2014), and while more crime does occur in urban areas, the hyperfocus can encourage the fear of crime (especially for outsiders). Who does not have a family member or a friend from a small town that refuses to go into the city, purely based on fear?

When thinking about victimization risk, many people fear physical harm. In actuality, there is a much higher likelihood of property crime victimization. For example, according to the National Crime Victimization Survey, in 2015 in the United States there were 18.6 violent victimizations per 1000 individuals (12 years of age and older); in contrast, there were 110.7 property victimizations per 1000 individuals (Truman and Morgan 2016). Thought about in a different way, less than 1% of individuals (again, 12 years of age and older) were victimized violently in 2015, whereas over 7% of all households experienced a property crime.

As we stated, crime rates in North America are reportedly dropping; however, retrieving accurate criminal statistics is complicated. The true figure of crime is unknown. Scholars have termed this the "dark figure of crime." These are the crimes which go unreported to any entity whether formal (e.g. police) or informal (e.g. researcher). Therefore, to provide as realistic a picture of crime as possible, we present multiple sources from various countries throughout this chapter. Many countries have an official reporting mechanism, such as a law enforcement agency, where reported arrests can be used as an indicator of crime in that country or member state. In the box below, we provide a brief overview of crime trends in the United States, the EU and Australia.

Crime Statistics Across Countries

United States
The Uniform Crime Report (UCR) is the official reporting mechanism in the United States. Yearly, the UCR compiles crimes reported to law enforcement in most states. As shown in the following text, crime is generally decreasing in the United States. According to the most recent UCR (U.S. Department of Justice 2016a), here are some key findings:

- Violent crime (murder, rape, robbery, and aggravated assault)

    - Between 2006 and 2015, violent crime rates decreased by 22.3%
    - Between 2014 and 2015, violent crime rates increased by 3.1%

- Property crime (burglary, larceny-theft, motor vehicle theft, and arson):

    - Between 2006 and 2015, property crime rates decreased by 25.7%
    - Between 2014 and 2015, property crime rates decreased by 3.4%

European Union
Eurostat compiles crimes reported to the police for the EU member states. According to the Eurostat 2016 publication, between 2008 and 2014:

- Reported homicides fell by 24%
- Assaults decreased by 33.8%
- Recorded rapes increased by 37%
- For 2014, burglary (2.4%) and drug trafficking (0.3%) trended slightly downward but had been on the slow decline since 2009

Australia
There are two major crime-reporting organizations in Australia. First, the Australian Bureau of Statistics reports crime victimization throughout

(continued)

(continued)

Australia. Second, the Australian Institute of Criminology reports arrest rates through the Australian government. Here are some recent statistics on crime in Australia:

- In 2013, there were 51.47 robberies per 100,000 residents. This was a slow decline since 2001 (Australian Institute of Criminology).
- In 2013, there were 86.1 sexual assaults per 100,000 residents. Sexual assault has stayed relatively stable since 2001(Australian Institute of Criminology).
- Between 2015 and 2016, 2.4% of Australians (ages 15 years and older) experienced one physical assault. There is not a significant change from 2014 to 2015 (Australian Bureau of Statistics).

Of course, there are challenges associated with these statistics. As discussed earlier, crime that is not reported to the police will not be included in official arrest statistics. We also draw attention to three other concerns that we must be aware of when interpreting crime statistics. First, the manner in which the statistics are recorded and defined impacts our understanding of crime rates. In the United States' UCR, the *hierarchy rule* is followed when multiple crimes occur simultaneously. This rule results in only the most serious offense being counted. Another recording issue pertains to definitions of crime. According to Eurostat, when examining crime in the EU, we must remember that each member state may use different definitions. Thus, crimes that are defined differently for particular member states are combined by Eurostat and may compromise the validity of the statistics (similarly, this is also an issue in the United States because particular areas have different definitions of crimes). Additionally, crime trends in the EU may be driven by trends in particular countries. For example, robbery declined an overall 5% since 2007 (as reported in 2010) in the EU, but mainly due to the reduction in this crime as reported by Italy, Poland, England and Wales, and the Baltic States (Clarke 2013). Second, even within a country, there can be variation in crime. For instance, there are different rates of crime in metropolitan and nonmetropolitan counties in the United States (U.S. Department of Justice 2015a). Third, countries have different policies that may influence crime and make them difficult to compare. For instance, countries have different laws that may impact the commission of crime. In the United States, where gun ownership is legal, almost 72% of the 13,455 homicides committed in 2015 were committed with a firearm (U.S. Department of Justice 2015b). In contrast, in England and Wales, where ownership of handguns is prohibited (Library of Congress 2017), only 21 of the 518 homicides in 2015 were committed with a firearm (Office for National Statistics 2015).

To our knowledge, the effects of new media on the myth that you should be afraid of violent crime are yet to be studied. New media could exacerbate the myth or educate depending on the individual consumer. Legacy media controls what information is presented to the public, and social media is interactive because the individual may seek out their own information. Yet, how one chooses to interact with social media and which information one selects to consume may or may not be properly vetted or researched. A recent thesis (Hildreth 2015) attempted to examine if hours spent on social media related to fear of crime, and using bivariate statistics found there was not a significant relationship. This was a limited sample and not generalizable, but future research could include an assessment of social media usage and perceptions of crime myths and fear of crime. Future research could use a random sample of the population measuring different media usage along with fear of crime to examine whether there is a correlation. To test causality, an experiment of a real crime news event with random assignment to viewing social media, legacy media, and a control of no media could test whether there is an effect on fear of crime levels. Regardless, the fear of violent crime influences people, whether in changing their everyday activities or even fearing particular groups of people. This is where we will turn in the next myth: who is perceived as the criminal.

Myth 2: Immigrants, migrants, and refugees are criminals
Reality: Foreign-born individuals are less criminal than native born.

A common perception in many countries is that immigrants, migrants, and refugees commit more crime than the general population. As we write this chapter, this myth is being hotly discussed, debated, supported, and protested throughout the media in the United States. On January 27, 2017, President Trump of the United States issued an executive order "to protect the American people from terrorist attacks by foreign nationals admitted to the United States" (Executive Order 13769). In particular, this order stated:

I hereby proclaim that the immigrant and nonimmigrant entry into the United States of aliens from countries referred to in section 217(a)(12) of the INA, 8 U.S.C. 1187(a)(12) [Iraq, Syria, Sudan, Iran, Somalia, Libya, and Yemen], would be detrimental to the interests of the United States, and I hereby suspend entry into the United States, as immigrants and non-immigrants, of such persons for 90 days from the date of this order.

I hereby proclaim that the entry of nationals of Syria as refugees is detri-mental to the interests of the United States and thus suspend any such entry until such time as I have determined that sufficient changes have been made to the USRAP to ensure that admission of Syrian refugees is consistent with the national interest.

When the president of the United States suspends entry of refugees and immigrants "to protect the American people," there is no denying that many people in the United States view these populations as a criminal threat. Likewise, there is concern about refugees and immigrants through-out Europe whether it is a fear of terrorism or fear of losing jobs or resources (Wike et al. 2016). In addition, fear of terrorism and immigra-tion might have contributed to Brexit (Rose 2016). The framing of stay-ing in the EU was about economics; the frame of leaving was about fear of terrorism, essentially fear of the "other" (Rose 2016; Hellman 2016). This is not only in the United Kingdom, as recent research demonstrated that many Europeans tie the refugee crisis and terrorism together. This fear of the refugee/migrant as the "other" also includes fear that they will take away jobs or social benefits (Wike et al. 2016).

This is playing out all over the EU as refugees/asylum seekers are being accepted into a country, but then immediately criticized by the media. For example, in the United Kingdom the media has been accused of creat-ing moral panics by "othering" Roma migrant communities (Clark 2015). In fact, there is criticism regarding the mistreatment of Roma migrant communities across the EU. What occurs is that media stories focus on the cultural differences of the group, such as gender roles or how refugees as a collective group are refusing to do something in order to assimilate into the mainstream culture. For example, in one Belgian newspaper (*het nieuwsblad*) Lambrix (2015, Sept 24) quoted a Karolien Grosemans stating,

"We do a lot for those people. And rightly so, because we want to show solidarity. But they refuse to clean up their trash. Their culture is that it is women's work, eh." Another example in *De Staandard* is an article where they discuss how refugees declined accommodations, titled "33 Syrian Refugees Refuse Care" (Winckelmans 2015, October). In the Netherlands, the newspaper *The Post Online* (2016) posted a short piece criticizing refugees stating that they are all refusing to work. While these examples seem relatively innocuous, it is this "othering" process that aids in the creation of the "us versus you" mentality. Then when incidents occur that *do* include outsiders, such as on New Year's Eve in Cologne, Germany, where multiple women were sexually assaulted by men who were reported as of Arab or North African descent, this leads to an affirmation of the "other" as criminal. That is, the actions of these individuals (which were never confirmed as Syrian refugees) equates to the dangerousness of *ALL* refugees. Although there is no way to confirm exactly how much the sexual assaults in Germany have affected perceptions of refugees and migrants, we do see media reports on how this event has shaped discussions of immigration in Germany (see Hoffmann and Pffister 2016; Spiegel Online 2016). These discussions surround limiting immigration and include more punitive control of immigrant populations. Similar to the discussion in Chap. 1 on moral panics, refugees, migrants, and asylum seekers are scapegoated in the media and turned into criminals. Instead of being viewed as people in tragic circumstances deserving of safety and resources, they are constructed as undeserving, ungrateful, and/or potentially dangerous.

By focusing on the myth of the criminal immigrant, refugee or migrant, we ignore the risk of victimization for these groups. In Zatz and Smith's (2012) review of research on crime and victimization among immigrants in the United States, they highlight areas of victimization that affect immigrants in unique ways. In particular, they discuss: how victimization can occur as individuals enter a new country; abuse and exploitation of immigrants who work as day laborers or domestic workers; and how immigrants' experience of intimate partner violence can be shaped by various factors, including knowledge of the law and the immigration status of the perpetrator and victim. Researchers also find that being an immigrant may influence whether or not victimization is reported to the police. As Zatz and Smith (2012, p. 147) state,

> Ironically, it appears that the laws and policies enacted in response to the faulty fears that immigrants are dangerous contribute to their victimization by making immigrants, and other members of their communities, afraid to call the police or otherwise draw attention to themselves.

This quote highlights how the myth of the criminal immigrant can have consequences for victims. A specific example of this in the United States is a concept called "walking ATM's," where undocumented Latino migrants are disproportionately robbed and there is a spillover effect for documented and native Latino individuals who live in areas with higher rates of immigration (Barranco and Shihadeh 2015).

The myth of the criminal immigrant, migrant or refugee is not new. Although the myth doesn't change, the population that is targeted as the "other" has changed over time as each new racial/ethnic threat occurs. Currently, the United States is "othering" Muslims and Arabs. In the book *Reel Bad Arabs*, Shaheen (2009) presents a breakdown of more than 1000 Hollywood films where the negative representation of Arabs and Muslims is persistent and pervasive. Shaheen (2009, p. 8) argues that they are portrayed as, "public enemy number 1-brutal, heartless, uncivilized religious fanatics and money-mad cultural 'others' bent on terrorizing civilized Westerners, especially Christians and Jews." Al-Kadhi (2017), an Arab actor, recently wrote a piece in *The Independent* lamenting how he has been asked to audition for the role of terrorist at least 30 times. It is important to note that Hollywood's reach extends outside of the United States increasing the effect that these negative representations are likely having. In the United States, the rise of Islamaphobia appears to have begun immediately after 9/11 with increased hate crimes against Muslims (Hanes and Machin 2014), and, more recently, it has likely been enhanced with the terrorist acts in Paris and Brussels in 2015. Hanes and Machin (2014) found an uptick in hate crimes against Asians and Arabs in four police areas in England following the terror attack in the United States on September 11, 2001, and London in 2005. To better understand this phenomenon, Jewkes (2015) explains:

> Media representations of immigrants [and] political refugees… are frequently underpinned by powerful psychic notions of otherness which frequently find expression in a tendency to see crime perpetrated by non-white people as a product of their ethnicity, while crimes against non-whites are all too frequently constructed in ways that are tantamount to blaming the victims. (p. 132)

The impact of social media on all this, as discussed in the previous myth, could be positive or negative. Social media's influence on this myth is an empirical question that still needs to be explored. A positive effect could be where individuals dispel myths as they can expose themselves through Twitter or Facebook to people who are different than them. For example, a recent Buzzfeed article demonstrated different tweets, posts, and memes from Muslims in America and their humorous take on *being* Muslim in America (see https://www.buzzfeed.com/ikrd/59-tweets-from-muslim-twitter-that-made-people-cry-with-laug?utm_term=.xoer-GrKpm6#.ibr969PvRw). On the other hand, an individual could also find information and a network on social media that would support and reinforce their fears. Recent research regarding political communication and public policy suggests that there exists an "echo chamber" on social media, whereby individuals only engage with material that they agree (Colleoni et al. 2014; Goldie et al. 2014; Barbera et al. 2015). However, research on Twitter has suggested that online communication of nonpolitical issues (e.g. Boston Marathon Bombing) reflect a more dynamic process. Researchers found that liberals were more likely than conservatives to engage in cross-ideological discussion (Barbera et al. 2015). This suggests that crime issues may be perceived differently than political issues, even though crime has a political undertone. With that, Facebook and Twitter often change their algorithms and have received heavy criticism for the postings of fake news during the 2016 US presidential election. Researchers need to examine what role social media plays in encouraging or discouraging crime myths about groups of people that individuals have limited contact with in day-to-day life.

Regardless of the myth, the fear of foreign-born individuals is unwarranted. As we are writing this book, the American Society of Criminology's Executive Board released a statement pertaining to crime and justice issues in the United States under the Trump Administration (2017). The first main point of the statement asserts: "Immigrants do not commit the majority of crime in the United States" (1). Research continues to demonstrate that foreign-born individuals commit equal or less crime than native-born ones (Bersani 2014; Piquero et al. 2016; Larson 2017). According to Bersani (2014), foreign-born individuals over the life course have a low level of criminal involvement. Likewise, Bell and Machin (2012), in their report on migration and crime/victimization, stress that "there is virtually no evidence in any country to suggest links between migration and violent crime" (2). When it comes to property crime, the relationship is a bit more complicated, as there is a link between these crimes and migrants in areas where the labor market it is not lucrative. This suggests an economic dependency as to the reasons for crime committal.

Media Myth 3: Young men of minority racial/ethnic groups are criminals. Reality: Criminals are predominantly young and male. Differential policies and justice practices effect the racial/ethnic component within crime statistics.

The myth and fear that surround violent crime contributes to the racialized construction of the criminal "other." In many countries, the "other" are people of a marginalized race or ethnicity. In some countries, it is a complicated interplay among both race and ethnicity that aids in the creation of the "other." For example, in the Netherlands, "the other" is often black Surinamese or Dutch Caribbean Islanders (Hayes and Joosen 2015). In the United States, both black and Hispanic people have been constructed as criminal. For black males, regardless of ethnicity, their skin color profiles them as criminal. Russell-Brown (1998, 2009) points to the myth of the *criminalblackman* where largely due to media representations, young African-American/black men are the faces of crime. This myth has historic roots stemming from colonization and slavery where the myth was how hypersexualized black males raped white women (Mogul et al. 2011). We argue that this myth persists albeit as a subsection of the *criminalblackman* myth. Today, whether it is through rap music or the news, negative imagery has permeated Americans subconscious in a manner that many are still likely to overestimate how much crime black men are actually involved in (Russell-Brown 2009). Hispanic individuals also belong in this myth of excessive criminality. When they can be identified through skin color or by name recognition, they can be profiled as drug dealers/users (Gross and Barnes 2002) or illegal immigrants (Lopez et al. 2010).

From the 1990s to the present, social scientists have extensively researched the representation of racial minorities in the media. In fact, we would venture that this is probably the most researched and discussed myth presented in this chapter. From constructing Arabs in Hollywood as "brute murderers, sleazy rapists, religious fanatics, oil-rich dimwits, and abusers of women" (Shaheen 2009, p. 8) to the underrepresentation and, at times, negative depictions of African-Americans, Asian-Americans, Latinos, and Native Americans in television advertisements (Mastro and Stern 2003), we see that different racial and ethnic groups are portrayed in distinct ways.

In the 1990s and 2000s, scholars found that local news programs in the United States misrepresented crime by overrepresenting people of color as criminals (Entman 1990; Romer et al. 1998; Dixon and Linz 2000; Entman and Rojecki 2000), and they mostly focused on African-Americans/blacks. Andersen (1994) examined the depiction of drug dealers/consumers on reality-based crime shows and found that the majority of arrests were of African-American and Latino men in urban areas. Similarly, Dixon and Linz (2000) found that among local television news broadcasts in two southern California counties, blacks/African-Americans, and Latinos were significantly more likely to be portrayed as perpetrators compared with whites. However, when comparing the representation with crime statistics, it was only blacks who were overrepresented in television network news. Additionally, blacks/African-Americans and Latinos are more likely to be portrayed as perpetrators than as actors in the legal system. In a related study, Dixon et al. (2003) also found that whites, compared with blacks/African-Americans and Latinos, were overrepresented as victims and officers in TV network news. More recently, scholars are finding that media representations of criminals are changing, but still with a negative focus on racial and ethnic minority groups. In an updated analysis of Dixon and Linz (2000) in the same area in California, Dixon (2015) found that blacks were accurately depicted as perpetrators as were Latinos. Likewise, Dixon and Williams (2015), after examining 146 cable and network news programs between 2008 and 2012, found that blacks were underrepresented as perpetrators and victims. They also found that Latinos were overrepresented as undocumented immigrants and Muslims were overrepresented as terrorists on these programs.

Overall, we do find many representations of white men as criminals, but there are also many media representations of white, affluent, high–social status men who are not criminals. The earlier-mentioned research connotes how whites are overrepresented as "justice defenders" or "sympathetic victims" compared with black/African-Americans or Latinos. We may be beginning to see a more accurate representation of blacks and Latinos as perpetrators at least in the news, yet we still see an underrepresentation of them as victims or actors in the legal system. Additionally, the damage of the overrepresentation of people of color in the 1990s and 2000s likely impacted perceptions and enforcement.

One of the main effects of the "othering" in the media (and elsewhere) is the arrest of racial and ethnic minorities. This can occur even when these individuals did not commit crimes. This would be evidence of the *racial hoax* which is described as "a) when someone fabricates a crime and blames it on another person because of his race or b) when an actual crime has been committed and the perpetrator falsely blames someone because of his race" (Russell-Brown 2009, p. 100). Historically, we can see evidence of *racial hoax* within lynching laws. Currently, there is evidence of *racial hoax* when examining the Innocence Project (2017) data, according to which of the 349 DNA exonerees in the United States, 217 were African-Americans compared with 105 Caucasians, 25 Latinos, and 2 Asian-Americans. It appears that surrounding the *criminalblackman* myth, at least in the United

States, there is some sort of continuous moral panic (see Chap. 1). Just look at the reaction to US college student Olutosin Oduwole's written rap lyrics, a case where he was eventually placed on trial for and convicted of attempted terrorism (Kubrin and Nielson 2014). This student was not only black, but Nigerian, and that intersection dually placed him into a perceived role of the offender fitting into two of the crime myths.

This racial and ethnic construction of who is a criminal makes it easy for us to ignore who is actually arrested for crime. When looking at overall crime in the United States, it is found that mostly whites are arrested (U.S. Department of Justice 2016b). In the box below, we provide a brief overview of arrest in the United States, which shows that most individuals arrested for crimes are male, in their "crime prone years," and white. When examining arrest statistics in the Netherlands (Central Bureau of Statistics 2015), it is found that it is predominantly native whites who are incarcerated. What these countries have in common is that blacks are overrepresented in crime statistics compared with their proportion to the population. This aspect is often oversimplified and used by political and media personalities as justification for the myth which encourages stereotyping. The reality surrounding the overrepresentation is more complicated.

A Brief Overview of Arrests in the United States In particular, this is what we know about those arrested for crimes in the United States in 2015:

- Age (U.S. Department of Justice 2016c)
  - Individuals between the ages of 16 and 21 comprise almost 19% of arrests
  - Individuals between the ages of 22 and 29 comprise 28% of arrests
- Sex (U.S. Department of Justice 2016d)
  - Men make up 73% of all arrests and almost 80% of all arrests for violent crimes
- Race (U.S. Department of Justice 2016b)
  - Whites make up almost 70% of all arrests and 60% of all arrests for violent crimes
  - Arrests by race are complicated by the fact that the majority of individuals identifying as Hispanic or Latino are counted as white. Even so, Latinos make up only 18% of all arrests.

In the United States, even though the majority of individuals arrested for crimes are white, certain groups are disproportionately arrested. Disproportionality in the context of arrest means that even if a group makes up a certain percentage of the population, they make up an even larger percentage of those who are arrested. For example, although blacks make up 13.3% of the population (U.S. Census Bureau 2015), they make up 26.6% of those arrested for crimes overall; more specifically, blacks make up 36.4% of those arrested for violent crimes and 27.8% of those arrested for property crimes (U.S. Department of Justice 2016b). There are many explanations for disproportionate arrest, conviction, and incarceration. One of the main explanations is racial profiling. Racial profiling of black and Hispanic men in the United States has been demonstrated repeatedly within extant research (Harris 1999; Gelman et al. 2004; Weitzer and Tuch 2006; ACLU 2015; Weitzer 2015). Weitzer and Tuch (2006) argue that there is a *racial hierarchy* when it comes to policing where whites/Asians are at the top and Latinos/blacks are at the bottom. That means blacks have it the worst, but a close second are Latinos, and whites fare better than all, with Asians right behind them. Much of the research in the United States is on the stops of African-American/black and Hispanic people for drugs, which contradicts the research on drug use which demonstrates that whites use drugs at either a higher or a similar rate than African-American/black and Hispanic people (Bachman et al. 1990, 1991; Alexander 2011). Another explanation for this disproportionality is targeted policing (outside of racial profiling) that focuses on high-crime areas. This is called hot spot policing, but it targets predominantly working-class neighborhoods that are disproportionately populated with people of color. Street crime occurs often in these areas, and people with limited means are less likely to be able to relocate to another area. This, according to sociologist Elijah Anderson (1999), means that people are socialized into "street" families or "decent" families. People who live in these areas need to live within this subculture and adhere to the *code of the street*.

Some scholars would say that adherence to the *code of the street* means that part of the disproportionate levels of people of color in crime statistics is due in part to involvement in crime. We especially see this disproportionality in homicide arrests with blacks comprising approximately 51% of arrests for murder and nonnegligent manslaughter (U.S. Department of Justice 2016b). To understand the disproportionate involvement of black men in violent crime, some scholars look to structural explanations (see Sampson and Wilson 1995; Peterson and Krivo 2005). These explanations, which commonly fall under the umbrella of social disorganization theory, focus on a variety of factors including concentrated poverty, unemployment, social isolation, segregation, and residential instability. In these structurally disadvantaged communities, violent crime may be encouraged by a lack of informal social control (Sampson and Wilson 1995) or the subculture of violence (e.g. the code of the streets) (Anderson 1999). Scholars also use a variety of other theories—cultural conflict theory, strain theory, differential association theory, critical race theory, structural-cultural theory, the impact of colonialism, and conflict theory—to understand involvement in crime by racial minorities (see Gabbidon and Greene 2009; Walker et al. 2012). While scholars posit different explanations regarding the involvement in crime, crime in impoverished neighborhoods is often covered in the media in a manner that lacks a sociological understanding of structural disadvantage. In turn, we see an oversimplification of crime and criminals, and the encouragement in the narrative of "the other" and specifically the *criminalblackman*.

Another critique of this myth is that in the United States crime is usually *intraracial*, meaning that the offender and victim are of the same race. Thus, fearing another racial or ethnic group does not make rational sense. If someone is going to be afraid of violent victimization (which we are not advocating), they should be most concerned with people that look like them and that they know.

As mentioned, the myth of the minority offender is currently being challenged through social media. While Black Lives Matter Movement has used and continues to use social media as a tool to help critique the idea of the *criminalblackman*, research is needed to assess how much of an influence they actually have on public opinion. It is undeniable that the Black Lives Matter movement has a global reach as protests in solidarity have occurred in places like the United Kingdom; however, there has been some heavy criticism of the movement and we speculate even some encouragement of the myth of the *criminalblackman*. In a recent CNN article, the author writes: "Four years after its founding, BLM is still a movement without a clear meaning for many Americans. Some see it has a hate group; others as cutting-edge activism and yet others as just a step above a mob" (Blake 2016). (For more information about Black Lives Matter refer to the book *When They Call You a Terrorist: A Black Lives Memoir* by Asha Bandele and Patrisse Khan-Cullors. New York, NY: St Martins Press.) While Black Lives Matter has gained ground, another group called #SayHerName also appeared in 2015 on social media and the internet to raise awareness about police violence against black women (see: http://www.aapf.org/sayhername/). Regardless, we argue that it appears common in the United States to put forth information on new media platforms, such as memes and tweets, to educate, raise awareness, and calls to action against racialized police brutality in the United States. Future research can examine this assertion.

Myth 4: Women who commit violent crime are worse than men who commit violent crime.
Reality: Women commit a small proportion of violent crime. Prostitution and embezzlement are the only crimes where women are the majority of those arrested in the United States.

The media downplays male violence while overemphasizing female violence (Jewkes 2010; Ellis et al. 2012). Again, this is where the back-wards law (Surette and Gardiner-Bess 2014) seems to come into play—the reality is that most violent crime is committed by men but violence by women is often sensationalized and covered in the media. This seems to be the case when examining media coverage surrounding women who murder their boyfriends or husbands, which is uncommon but often covered. Just think about the recent coverage of Jodi Arias, in Arizona (United States), who murdered her ex-boyfriend. As Bonn (2015) wrote in *Psychology Today*:

She [Jodi Arias] is a convicted felon who has taken on criminal celebrity status and cultivated a massive global following due to her appearance, demeanor, and the severity of her crime, which all have been spun and stylized into a caricature by the news media. We live in an advanced technological society where countless digital and broadcast media outlets compete for stories, as well as the attention of oversaturated audiences. In this world, it often takes a story filled with violence, beauty, sex and scandal in order to break through the clutter and become a global phenomenon. Such is the story of Jodi Arias.

This largely has to do with the expectations of femininity and masculinity that are present in many cultures. Masculinity is defined by toughness and demonstrations of anger, whereas femininity is defined by submissiveness and demonstrations of sadness. Therefore, crime is constructed as an inherently masculine event, especially violent crimes. The *evil woman hypothesis* argues that when women do commit crime, they are dealt with more harshly than men by the justice system because they are going outside their gender norms (Belknap 2014). The negative imagery within the media supports this perspective.

Women who commit serious crime and are subsequently discussed in the media are usually demonized (Jewkes 2004). According to Jewkes (2004, p. 113), the media follows some standard narratives to explain women's violent criminality, which include the following:

- Sexuality and sexual deviance
- (Absence of) physical attractiveness
- Bad wives
- Bad mothers
- Mythical monsters
- Mad cows
- Evil manipulators
- Non-agents: a woman viewed as lacking agency when committing a crime; Ex: a woman who kills an intimate partner who has been abusing her

For example, we can see Jewkes' myth of the "bad mother" in the case study of the "Nanny Murder Trial" of Louise Woodward in the 1990s. Holohan (2005) discussed how the media discourse turned into how the mother of the child was to blame by not being at home with her child. The discussion of the breakdown of the family had a prominent place in the discussion of the case. We see this theme again resonating throughout the Casey Anthony trial in the late 2000s; she was accused, tried, and acquitted for the death of her two-year-old daughter Caylee Anthony. The media portrayal of Amanda Knox (see box *Amanda Knox*) also highlights many of Jewkes' narratives. In a recent documentary, *Amanda Knox* (2016), Knox states:

> The whole world knew who I had sex with: seven men! And yet I was some heinous whore: bestial, sex-obsessed, and unnatural…. And, if I'm guilty, it means I am the ultimate figure of fear.

Knox's assessment of her portrayal highlights Jewkes' narratives of sexuality and sexual deviance and mythical monsters. Interestingly, the depictions of Knox differed within each country that was covering this trial (Burleigh 2011). Knox could be used as a case study on the power of pretrial publicity (discussed in Chap. 2), wherein the media in the United States, the United Kingdom, and Italy likely led to differing conclusions formed by the public regarding Knox. In the United States, she was portrayed as a victim of a system, whereas in the United Kingdom: "Knox is the exchange-student version of Casey Anthony. She is an all-American psychopath with a pretty face masking a liar and a killer" (Burleigh 2011). In Italy, the hypersexualized version of her is most prevalent. Here we see the sexual deviant and evil manipulator narrative. The sexuality and sexual deviant narrative is often used for women as criminals and as victims. It is used to victim blame as we write about in the next chapter. This narrative, often used to demonize any women or girl who does not fit into the societal standard of a virgin, is particularly pervasive.

Amanda Knox was a 20-year-old American college student studying in Italy when she was accused of murdering her English roommate, Meredith Kercher. Knox (and her then boyfriend Raffaele Sollecito) was found guilty of murdering Kercher in 2009. Knox received a 26-year prison sentence. Two years later, her conviction was overturned and she was released. She was retried in 2013, found guilty again, and the verdict was overturned in 2015.

Student Activity *Discuss examples of female criminals portrayed in the media following each of Jewkes' other narratives.*

Continuing examples of the sexuality/sexual deviant narrative, the discussion of intersectionality is pertinent. The objectification of black female bodies throughout the media (hooks 1992) and history has led to this group's further marginalization as hypersexual. This narrative can be traced to the times of colonization and slavery, when black (African) women were framed as the jezebel archetype and viewed as "sexually aggressive, insatiable and even predatory toward white men" (Mogul et al. 2011, p. 6). As discussed, the myth of *criminalblackman* is pervasive and black women are not exempt. One example is the pervasive stereotype of black women as sexually deviant, and then viewed as sex workers, especially if they are with a white man. One recent example is *Django Unchained* actress, Daniele Watts, who was arrested in Los Angeles due to the assumption that she was a prostitute when she was simply out with her boyfriend (Boren 2014). This myth extends even further if we add in the intersection of LGBTQ, where women who are lesbian, queer, or transgender are seen as defying sexuality and/or gender norms. In 2006, a group of black lesbian friends, while walking home, were verbally assaulted by a man who harassed and then threatened to rape them. Then, depending on the version of the story you read, they assaulted him *or* he assaulted them and they fought back with two unknown men running over to help the women fight back. There was even a videotape which showed the unknown men assisting the women. During the altercation, the man was stabbed, and while the women argued it was self-defense, he argued that they attacked him and the media dubbed them "The Lesbian Wolf Pack" (Mogul et al. 2011) or called them the "Killer Lesbians" (The Public Intellectual 2011). The criminal legal system found all but one of them guilty of assault and sentenced them to prison.

Even though we are presented with stories of violent women in the media, the reality is that women commit a small proportion of violent crime. In the United States, women make up approximately 20% of those arrested for violent crimes (U.S. Department of Justice 2016d).

More specifically, women comprise 11.5% of those arrested for murder and nonnegligent manslaughter, 2.9% of those arrested for rape, and 14.4% of those arrested for robbery.

Media Myth 5: Members of the LGBTQ community are hypersexual and/or sexual predators.
Reality: Sexual assault usually occurs by someone you know, regardless of sexual orientation.

While the criminalization of queerness has a rich history in colonialism and is common and worldwide (Buist and Lenning 2015; Mogul et al. 2011), one way criminalization occurs is through focusing on hypersexuality or "othering" of LGBTQ persons as sexually deviant. When LGBTQ persons are framed as hypersexual or sexually deviant, many people assume they are also sexual predators (for other archetypes and manners of criminalization, see: Mogul et al. 2011). The criminalization of sexuality and gender identity are likely due to normalized homophobia or transphobia. One example is in the United States, where there is debate surrounding legislation regarding assigned gender and bathroom usage, which are commonly referred to as "bathroom bills" (see box *House Bill 2*). Those supporting the bills predicate their argument around sexual predators. In particular, they argue that letting transgender people use the restroom according to their gender identity (rather than their assigned biological sex) will allow male sexual predators into women's bathrooms (Steinmetz 2016). This is similar to the myth regarding homosexual men, who were believed to be waiting in bathrooms to molest children.

House Bill 2 in North Carolina, or "The Bathroom Bill," was meant to establish single-sex multiple-occupancy bathroom and changing rooms in schools. They define sex as "Biological sex. – The physical condition of being male or female, which is stated on a person's birth certificate." (For more information, read: http://www.ncleg.net/sessions/2015e2/bills/house/pdf/h2v4.pdf)

Many movies and television shows portray LGBTQ people negatively, particularly transgendered people. Participants in a recent exploratory study about media depictions of transgendered individuals overwhelmingly reported that they witnessed transphobia in the media (McInroy and Craig 2015). Researchers found that transgendered individuals are often portrayed as criminal, mentally ill, or sex workers. There are *positive* depictions of transgendered individuals in the media, more often in the movies, but the negative imagery has an impact on both transgendered individuals and the general population (McInroy and Craig 2015; Ringo 2002). Think of the movie *Ace Ventura* in which Detective Einhorn turns out to have previously been the football player Ray Finkle. They show her as deceptive and evil. Everyone in the room throws up when they find out that she used to be a he, and this is clearly an example of transphobia. Even urban dictionary has a slang called "Finkle is Einhorn," which is meant to describe when a woman turns out to also have male genitalia (http://www.urbandictionary.com/define.php?term=Finkle%20is%20Einhorn). Another more recent movie is *Albert Nobbs*, where the lead is a woman dressed as a man, but not as a transgendered individual. This movie is criticized for playing into the stereotype that people who "cross-dress" (for lack of a better term) are "posers" and are out to deceive (*The Advocate* 2011). The question is whether this kind of imagery is contributing to transphobia and, to a lesser extent, homophobia.

The existence of homophobia and transphobia is demonstrated in legislation that continues to criminalize LGBTQ persons, largely through focusing on sexual behaviors. Almost half of the countries around the globe still outlaw sex between same-sex people, and this may even be punishable by death. Historically, the policing of sexuality and gender nonconformity mainly focused on men with the use of sodomy laws (Mogul et al. 2011). According to Buist and Lenning (2015), antisodomy laws within the United States were in place as late as 2003, which is when the state of Texas decriminalized gay sex. The criminalization of LGBTQ persons is demonstrated by a few more contemporary examples (Buist and Lenning 2015):

- Being harassed or arrested for your gender presentation (*walking while trans*: assumption that one is a sex worker because of being transgender).
- In Louisiana (United States), there is a law that was prefaced on controlling prostitution, but in practice has been used to mostly arrest transgender persons and black gay men, who are then forced onto the sex offender registry.
- In the United Kingdom, there is a legislation called *rape by deception*. This is where a cisgender individual (often female) discovers that their romantic partner is transgender (often transmale) and claims that the sex was consensual only under the condition that the person was biologically what they had assumed they were.

Social media's role in perpetuating the myth of LGBTQ as sexual offenders depends on what kinds of information the consumer chooses to consume. On the positive side, social media has played a strong role in generating awareness of the rights of LGBTQ individuals, and one could argue that the recent legislation in the United States is a form of backlash. Backlash (Faludi 1991) suggests that as equality and representation progresses, there is a *backlash* from those present in the status quo. However, there is representation within social media where information about injustices is shared. When Monica Jones (see box *Monica Jones*) was arrested for *walking while trans*, one could gain access to a picture to change your Facebook profile in support of Monica Jones. The intersection of black and female transgender has similar, yet more extreme, connotations regarding sexual availability than being black and female. Other recent representations of transgender women in mainstream television shows, such as Laverne Cox in *Orange is the New Black* and Caitlyn Jenner from *Keeping up with the Kardashians*, has the potential to change societal ideas of what and who is transgender and in a sense normalizes it. However, this visibility might also heighten the fear among those who are homophobic or transphobic, and the subsequent backlash might increase hate crimes. Empirical research needs to explore how social media is affecting the way that people view LGBTQ persons.

Monica Jones is a transwoman and sex activist who was arrested in Arizona under its manifestation ordinance. The manifestation ordinance is to catch people who are attempting to "manifest" prostitution. It targets people who are engaging in conversations with people who pass by. It has been argued to unfairly target transgender women of color. Monica Jones (Strangio 2014) pled not guilty and was sentenced to 30 days in jail and a small fine.

Data on sexual assault does not indicate that offenders of sexual assault are more often from the LGBTQ community than the general population. It is quite the opposite actually; instead, it is cisgender, hetereosexual (often white) males (Greenfeld 1997) who know the victim (National Institute of Justice 2010) and who engage in sexually assaultive behavior. Even when examining child sexual abuse, which is what the transgender bathroom legislation is aimed at, the perpetrator is more likely to be a family member or close family friend (Whealin 2007; Finkelhor and Shattuck 2012). That means it is not likely to happen in a public restroom by a complete stranger. In fact, the stranger myth of sexual assault perpetration is one of the most pervasive myths about sexual assault in many societies.

Regarding who is criminal, depending on the crime, there are profiles and myths that are usually counter to the reality. When the perpetrator does not fit any of the earlier-mentioned myth categories, we commonly see another myth emerge: the criminal is mentally ill. This is where we will turn regarding our next myth.

Media Myth 6: Individuals with mental illness are likely to be violent.
Reality: Individuals with mental illness are not more violent than the general population.

Turn on your favorite crime show and chances are you'll see a suspect or an offender who is portrayed as being mentally ill. In crime-based television shows, it is more likely for characters who are mentally ill to be engaging in violent and criminal behavior than those who are not (Parrott and Parrott 2015). As we've already discussed in Chap. 1, crime-based television shows have significant viewership and, thus, have the potential to shape perceptions of individuals with mental illness.

Likewise, this connection between mental illness and crime is also present in the news media. A recent study by McGinty et al. (2016) examined the connection presented in the news media between mental health and violence. In an analysis of 400 stories from high-circulation television and print media pertaining to mental illness from 1995 to 2014, the researchers found:

- Approximately 40% portrayed a connection between perpetration of interpersonal violence and mental illness.
- Of the new stories addressing interpersonal violence, gun violence was most commonly presented.
- Coverage of individuals with mental illness committing mass shootings increased over this time period (1995–2004 vs. 2005–2014) from 9% to 22%.

Although these findings are specific to the US news media, McGinty et al. explain that the connection between the perpetration of violence and individuals with mental illness has been found in research examining news media in Spain, New Zealand, the United Kingdom, and Canada.

In direct contrast to this myth, the overwhelming majority of violent acts are not committed by mentally ill persons. According to the US Department of Health and Human Services (2017), approximately 3–5% of violent acts are committed by people with significant mental illness. Additionally, those with mental illness actually have an increased likelihood for victimization. Severely mentally ill individuals "are over 10 times more likely to be victims of violent crime than the general population" (United States Department of Health and Human Services 2017). Instead of fearing those who are mentally ill, we should be working to decrease their victimization and providing better mental health services.

Similar to the myths already presented, perceptions of those who are mentally ill are likely impacted both positively and negatively by posts and stories on social media. As discussed in Chap. 2, we are now seeing social media accounts searched after a crime is committed, and sometimes these searches confirm concerns about the mental health of the accused. In contrast, in *Psychology Today*, Lanning (2017) wrote about how vlogging about mental illness on YouTube is likely impacting the public conscious by raising awareness. The face of mental illness may be changing as people upload about their personal struggles, and not only is this potentially therapeutic to the individual but might reach others and remove the stigma (Lanning 2017). By decreasing the stigma of mental illness, we may also see a decrease in the acceptance of the myth of the mentally ill as violent. As with many of the previous myths, we still need research to empirically examine these topics in the context of social media.

Student Activity *Now that you are familiar with these common myths about crime and criminals, take some time to examine them on your favorite television or news program and see which ones you can identify. Additionally, look for examples that challenge the myths and are more in line with reality.*

Conclusion

The commonality among these myths is that the actions of a few are presumed upon an entire population of people. Are there immigrants, black men, LGBTQ persons, and/or individuals with mental illness who have committed crime? Yes, of course. We may be able to think of examples of criminal cases where the offender fits each of these particular statuses. However, these myths greatly exaggerate criminal offending by these populations. In fact, the myths tend to be presented in a manner that blames that particular characteristic for the criminality in a way that non-marginalized populations do not experience. This is part of the "othering" where only white economically privileged heterosexual males are normal and any deviation from one of these means "the other."

As we mentioned, the social locations or characteristics of people are often used to explain the reason for the criminal activity. Think about when a serial killer is a heterosexual white man; after he gets caught, people tend not to blame his whiteness, his religion (if it is Christian), and/or his heterosexuality as the reasons for his behavior. As we are writing this book, the worst mass shooting in the United States to date took place in Las Vegas, Nevada, killing 58 people. The media was consumed with the question of "why did he do it?" but throughout this discussion we were yet to hear questions about how his whiteness could have contributed to this crime. But, if a black lesbian commits a similar crime, societal blame may be placed on her sexuality or even on her blackness as reasons why she would commit the crime. These myths don't just exaggerate criminal offending; instead, they also perpetuate fear about particular populations. Many of these myths are based on fears of the "other," and through these myths, fears of the "other" as criminal grow.

The impact of media myths is that it only takes one sensationalized case to create policy. The Jeanne Clery Act, Polly Klaas Act, and the Adam Walsh Act are all examples of where one case became policy (Surette 2015). This is not to say that these policies are wrong, but it is to point out that these policies emerged in reaction to particular cases that received mass attention in the media. New media contributes to this impact, but also at times can counter it. With new media the public can decide which cases receive attention, but how will this impact the moral panic narrative? As researchers understand more about how new media is impacting people, we can harness its powers in ways to counter misinformation.

Discussion Questions

1. Watch the evening news in your community. What kinds of crime are shown to be a problem? What kinds of people are portrayed as criminals?
2. This chapter highlights six common myths about criminals perpetuated in the media. Discuss additional myths that you think are missing from this chapter.
3. Think about a high-profile crime committed by a person of privilege. How has this person's criminal behavior been explained in the media? Do these explanations follow any of the myths or not?
4. Check out mediacloud.org, which is a "platform for studying media ecosystems," developed at MIT and Harvard University. Use the tools to see how criminals and crime are framed in online media.

References

Media References

Al-Kadhi, A. (2017). I'm an Arab actor who's been asked to audition for the role of terrorist more than 30 times. If LaLa Land cleans up at the Oscars, I'm done. *Independent.* Retrieved from http://www.independent.co.uk/voices/oscars-la-la-land-moonlight-arab-muslim-actor-audition-terrorist-i-am-done-a7595261.html

Blackhurst, R., & McGinn, B. (Directors). (2016). *Amanda Knox* [Documentary]. Netflix.

Blake, J. (2016). Is black lives matter blowing it? *CNN.* Retrieved from http://www.cnn.com/2016/07/29/us/black-lives-matter-blowing-it/

Bonn, S. (2015, March 19). The media made Jodi Arias a celebrity monster. *Psychology Today.* Retrieved from https://www.psychologytoday.com/blog/wicked-deeds/201503/the-media-made-jodi-arias-celebrity-monster

Boren, Z. (2014, September 14). Daniele Watts: *Django Unchained* actress detained by Los Angeles Police after being mistaken for a prostitute. *Independent.* Retrieved from http://www.independent.co.uk/news/people/daniele-watts-arrested-django-unchained-actress-detained-in-los-angeles-after-being-mistaken-for-a-9731871.html

Burleigh, N. (2011, September 30). Why there will always be three Amanda Knoxes. *Time.* Retrieved from http://content.time.com/time/world/article/0,8599,2095586,00.html

Hoffmann, C., & Pffister, R. (2016, January 21). A feminist view of Cologne: 'The current outrage is very hypocritical'. *Spiegel Online.* Retrieved from http://www.spiegel.de/international/germany/german-feminists-debate-cologne-attacks-a-1072806.html

Lambrix, Y. (2015, September 24). Asielzoekers Weigeren OCMW-woning te Poetsen en op te Ruimen. *Het Nieuwsblad.* Retrieved from http://www.nieuwsblad.be/cnt/dmf20150924_01884362

Lanning, C. (2017, May 2). The vlogging cure. *Psychology Today.* Retrieved from https://www.psychologytoday.com/articles/201705/the-vlogging-cure?utm_source=FacebookPost&utm_medium=FBPost&utm_campaign=FBPost

Logan, L. S. (2011, July 18). The case of 'the killer lesbians'. *The Public Intellectual.* Retrieved from http://thepublicintellectual.org/2011/07/18/the-case-of-the-killer-lesbians/

Rose, R. (2016). *Fear is a double-edged sword in the EU referendum.* The UK in a Changing Europe.

Spiegel Online. (2016, January 16). Chaos and violence: How New Year's Eve in Cologne has changed Germany. *Spiegel Online.* Retrieved from http://www.spiegel.de/international/germany/cologne-attacks-trigger-raw-debate-on-immigration-in-germany-a-1071175.html

Steinmetz, K. (2016, May 2). Why LGBT advocates say bathroom 'predators' argument is a red herring. *Time.* Retrieved from http://time.com/4314896/transgender-bathroom-bill-male-predators-argument/

Strangio. (2014). Arrested for walking while trans: An interview with Monica Jones. *American Civil Liberties Union Blog.* Retrieved from https://www.aclu.org/blog/arrested-walking-while-trans-interview-monica-jones

The Advocate. (2011). *What Albert Nobbs teaches us about labels.* Retrieved from http://www.advocate.com/politics/commentary/2011/09/29/what-albert-nobbs-teaches-us-about-labels

The Post Online. (2016, November 11). Retrieved from http://nieuws.tpo.nl/2016/11/11/asielzoekers-weigeren-massaal-werk/?utm_medium=website&utm_source=nieuwskoerier.nl

The White House. (2017). Executive order protecting the nation from foreign terrorist entry into the United States. Retrieved from: https://www.whitehouse.gov/presidential-actions/executive-order-protecting-nation-foreign-terrorist-entry-united-states/

Winckelmans, W. (2015, October). 33 Syrische vluchtelingen weigeren opvang. *De Standaard.* Retrieved from http://www.standaard.be/cnt/dmf20151001_01897157

Academic References

ACLU. (2015). Stop and frisk in Chicago. *American Civil Liberties Union.* Retrieved from http://www.aclu-il.org/wp-content/uploads/2015/03/ACLU_StopandFrisk_6.pdf

Alexander, M. (2011). *The new Jim Crow: Mass incarceration in the age of colorblindness.* New York: New Press.

Allen, J., Livingstone, S., & Reiner, R. (1998). True lies': Changing images of crime in British postwar cinema. *European Journal of Communication, 13*(1), 53–75.

American Society of Criminology. (2017). *Statement of the American Society of Criminology executive board concerning the Trump administration's policies relevant to crime and justice*. Retrieved from https://www.asc41.com/

Andersen, R. (1994). 'Reality' TV and criminal justice. *The Humanist, 54*(5), 8–13.

Anderson, E. (1999). *Code of the street: Decency, violence, and the moral life of the inner city*. New York: W.W. Norton & Company, Inc.

Australian Bureau of Statistics. 2015–2016. Retrieved from http://www.abs.gov.au/Crime-and-Justice

Australian Institute of Criminology. Retrieved from http://www.aic.gov.au/statistics.html

Bachman, J. G., Wallace, J. M., Jr., Kurth, C. L., Johnston, L. D., & O'Malley, P. M. (1990). Drug use among black, white, Hispanic, native American, and Asian American high school seniors (1976–1989): Prevalence, trends and correlates. *Monitoring the Future Occasional Paper, 30*, 1–57.

Bachman, J. G., Wallace, J. M., Jr., O'Malley, P. M., Johnston, L. D., Kurth, C. L., & Neighbors, H. W. (1991). Racial/ethnic differences in smoking, drinking, and illicit drug use among American high school seniors. *American Journal of Public Health, 81*(3), 372–377.

Barak, G. (2012). *Mass media and the social construction of crime: A critique and implications for the future*. Retrieved from http://www.greggbarak.com/whats_new_6.html

Barbera, P., Jost, J. T., Nagler, J., Tucker, J. A., & Bonneau, R. (2015). Tweeting from left to right: Is online political communication more than an echo chamber? *Psychological Science, 26*(10), 1531–1542.

Barkan, S. E., & Bryjack, G. J. (2014). *Myths and realities of crime and justice: What every American should know*. Sudbury: Jones and Bartlett Publishers.

Barranco, R. E., & Shihadeh, E. S. (2015). Walking ATMs and the immigration spillover effect: The link between Latino immigration and robbery victimization. *Social Science Research, 52*, 440–450.

Belknap, J. (2014). *The invisible woman*. Belmont: Wadsworth.

Bell, B., & Machin, S. (2012). Immigration and crime. In A. Constant & K. Zimmermann (Eds.), *International handbook on the economics of migration* (pp. 353–372). London: Edward Elgar Publishing.

Berger, P. L., & Luckmann, T. (1967). *The social construction of reality*. Garden City: DoubleDay.

Bersani, B. E. (2014). An examination of first and second generation immigrant offending trajectories. *Justice Quarterly, 31*(2), 315–343.

Bohm, R. M. (1986). Crime, criminal and crime control policy myths. *Justice Quarterly, 3*(2), 193–214.

Buist, C., & Lenning, E. (2015). *Queer criminology.* New York: Routledge.

Carrabine, E. (2008). *Crime, culture and the media.* Hoboken: Wiley-Blackwell Publishing.

Central Bureau of Statistics. (2015). Retrieved from https://www.cbs.nl/en-gb

Chermak, S. M. (1995a). *Victim in the news: Crime in American news. Media.* Boulder: Westview Press.

Chermak, S. M. (1995b). Image control: How police affect the presentation of crime news. *American Journal of Police, 14*(2), 21–43.

Clark, C. (2015). Integration, exclusion and the moral 'othering' of Roma migrant communities in Britain. In V. E. Cree, G. Clapton, & M. Smith (Eds.), *Revisiting moral panics.* [E-book]. Bristol: Policy Press.

Clarke, S. (2013). *Crime trends in detail.* Retrieved from http://ec.europa.eu/ eurostat/statistics-explained/index.php/Crime_trends_in_detail

Colleoni, E., Rozza, A., & Arvidsson, A. (2014). Echo chamber or public sphere? Predicting political orientation and measuring political homophily in Twitter using big data. *Journal of Communication, 64*(2), 317–332.

Critcher, C. (2003). *Moral panics and the media.* Buckingham: Open University.

Dixon, T. L. (2015). Good guys are still always in white? Positive change and continued misrepresentation of race and crime on local television news. *Communication Research, X,* 1–18.

Dixon, T. L., & Linz, D. (2000). Overrepresentation and underrepresentation of African Americans and Latinos as lawbreakers on television news. *Journal of Communication, 50*(2), 131–154.

Dixon, T. L., & Williams, C. L. (2015). The changing misrepresentation of race and crime on network and cable news. *Journal of Communication, 65*(1), 24–39.

Dixon, T. L., Azocar, C. L., & Casas, M. (2003). The portrayal of race and crime on television network news. *Journal of Broadcasting & Electronic Media, 47*(4), 498–523.

Donnermeyer, J. F., & DeKeseredy, W. S. (2014). *Rural criminology: New directions in critical criminology.* Oxon: Routledge.

Dowler, K. (2003). Media consumption and public attitudes toward crime and justice: The relationship between fear of crime, punitive attitudes and perceived police effectiveness. *Journal of Criminal Justice and Popular Culture, 10*(2), 109–126.

Ellis, A., Sloan, J., & Wykes, M. (2012). 'Moatifs' of masculinity: The stories told about 'men' in British newspaper coverage. *Crime, Media, Culture: An International Journal, 9*(1), 3–21.

Entman, R. M. (1990). Modern racism and the images of blacks in local television news. *Critical Studies in Mass Communication, 7*, 332–346.

Entman, R. M., & Rojecki, A. (2000). *The black image in the white mind: Media and race in America*. Chicago: The University of Chicago Press.

Eurostat. (2016). *Crime and criminal justice statistics*. Retrieved from http://ec.europa.eu/eurostat/statistics-explained/index.php/Crime_and_criminal_justice_statistics

Faludi, S. (1991). *Backlash: The undeclared war against American women*. New York: Crown.

Finkelhor, D., & Shattuck, A. (2012). *Characteristics of crimes against juveniles*. Durham: Crimes against Children Research Center.

Gabbidon, S. L., & Greene, H. T. (2009). *Race and crime* (2nd ed.). Thousand Oaks: Sage.

Gelman, A., Fagan, J., & Kiss, A. (2004). An analysis of the New York City police department's "Stop-and-Frisk" policy in the context of claims of racial bias. *Journal of the American Statistical Association, 102*(479), 813–823.

Gilliam, F. D., & Iyengar, S. (2000). Prime suspects: The influence of local television news on the viewing public. *American Journal of Political Science, 44*(3), 560–573.

Goldie, D., Linick, M., Jabbar, H., & Lubienski, C. (2014). Using bibliometric and social media analyses to explore the "Echo Chamber" hypothesis. *Educational Policy, 28*(2), 281–305.

Greenfeld, L. (1997). Sex offenses and offenders. *Bureau of Justice Statistics*. Retrieved from https://bjs.gov/content/pub/pdf/SOO.PDF

Gross, S. R., & Barnes, K. Y. (2002). Road work: Racial profiling and drug interdiction on the highway. *Michigan Law Review, 101*(3), 653–754.

Hanes, E., & Machin, S. (2014). Hate crime in the wake of terror attacks: Evidence from 7/7 and 9/11. *Journal of Contemporary Criminal Justice, 30*(3), 247–267.

Harris, D. (1999). *Driving while black: Racial profiling on our nation's highways*. Retrieved from https://www.ncjrs.gov/App/Publications/abstract.aspx?ID=182825

Hayes, R. M., & Joosen, K. (2015, 25–26 June). Zwarte Piet, Judeska, and Tante Es stereotyping "the other": Crime in reality and the media. Paper presented at the meeting for the The Other: International Cultural Criminology. Amsterdam.

Hellman, M. (2016). *What's in a frame? Media framing in the 2016 'Brexit' referendum* (Published master's thesis). Lund University. Retrieved from https://lup.lub.lu.se/student-papers/search/publication/8873236

Hildreth, J. E. (2015). *Fear in the world of social media* (Published master thesis). Arlington: The University of Texas.

Holohan, S. (2005). *The search for justice in a media age: Reading Stephen Lawrence and Louise Woodward*. Burlington: Ashgate.

hooks, b. (1992). *Black looks: Race and representation*. New York: Routledge.

Innocence Project. (2017). *DNA exonerations in the United States*. Retrieved from http://www.innocenceproject.org/dna-exonerations-in-the-united-states/

Jewkes, Y. (2004). *Media & crime*. London: Sage.

Jewkes, Y. (2010). *Media & crime* (2nd ed.). London: Sage.

Jewkes, Y. (2015). *Media & crime* (3rd ed.). London: Sage.

Jurkowitz, M., Hitlin, P., Mitchell, A., Santhanam, L., Adams, S., Anderson, M., & Vogt, N. (2013). *The changing TV news landscape*. Retrieved from http://www.stateofthemedia.org/2013/special-reports-landing-page/the-changing-tv-news-landscape/

Kappeler, V. E., & Potter, G. W. (2005). *The mythology of crime and criminal justice* (4th ed.). Long Grove: Waveland Press.

Kubrin, C. E., & Nielson, E. (2014). Rap on trial. *Race and Justice, 4*(3), 185–211.

Larson, R. (2017, April 10). The immigration-crime paradox. *The Society Pages*. Retrieved from https://thesocietypages.org/trot/2017/04/10/the-immigration-crime-paradox/

Library of Congress. (2017). *Firearms-control legislation and policy: Great Britain*. Retrieved from https://www.loc.gov/law/help/firearms-control/greatbritain.php

Livingstone, S., Allen, J., & Reiner, R. (2001). Audiences for crime media 1946–91: A historical approach to reception studies. *The Communication Review, 4*(2), 165–192.

Lopez, M. H., Morin, R., & Taylor, P. (2010). *Illegal immigration backlash worries, divides Latinos*. Retrieved from http://www.pewhispanic.org/2010/10/28/illegal-immigration-backlash-worries-divides-latinos/

Lowry, D., Nio, T. C. J., & Leitner, D. W. (2003). Setting the public fear agenda: A longitudinal analysis of network TV crime reporting, public perceptions of crime, and FBI crime statistics. *Journal of Communication, 53*(1), 61–73.

Mastro, D. E., & Stern, S. R. (2003). Representations of race in television commercials: A content analysis of prime-time advertising. *Journal of Broadcasting & Electronic Media, 47*(4), 638–647.

McGinty, E., Kennedy-Hendricks, A., Choksy, S., & Barry, C. (2016). Trends in news media coverage of mental illness in the United States. *Health Affairs, 35*(6), 1121–1129.

McInroy, L. B., & Craig, S. L. (2015). Transgender representation in offline and online media: LGBTQ youth perspectives. *Journal of Human Behavior in the Social Environment, 25*(6), 606–617.

Media Education Foundation. (2005). Retrieved from http://www.mediaed. org/handouts/ChildrenMedia.pdf

Mogul, J. L., Ritchie, A. J., & Whitlock, K. (2011). *Queer (in)justice: The criminalization of LGBT people in the United States.* Boston: Beacon Press.

National Institute of Justice. (2010). Retrieved from https://www.nij.gov/topics/crime/rape-sexual-violence/Pages/victims-perpetrators.aspx

Office for National Statistics. (2015). *Homicide.* Retrieved from https://www.ons.gov.uk/peoplepopulationandcommunity/crimeandjustice/compendium/focusonviolentcrimeandsexualoffences/yearendingmarch2015/chapter2homicide#methodof-killing

Parrott, S., & Parrott, C. (2015). Law & disorder: The portrayal of mental illness in U.S. crime dramas. *Journal of Broadcasting & Electronic Media, 59*(4), 640–657.

Peterson, R., & Krivo, L. (2005). Macrostructural analyses of race, ethnicity, and violent crime: Recent lessons and new directions for research. *Annual Review of Sociology, 31*, 331–356.

Piquero, A. R., Bersani, B. E., Loughran, T. A., & Fagan, J. (2016). Longitudinal patterns of legal socialization in first-generation immigrants, second-generation immigrants, and native-born serious youthful offenders. *Crime & Delinquency, 62*(11), 1403–1425.

Pollak, J. M., & Kubrin, C. E. (2007). Crime in the news: How crimes, offenders and victims are portrayed in the media. *Journal of Criminal Justice and Popular Culture, 14*(1), 59–83.

Reiner, R. (2000). Policing and the media. In F. Leishman, B. Loveday, & S. Savage (Eds.), *Core issues in policing* (pp. 52–66). Harlow: Pearson Education.

Reiner, R., Livingstone, S., & Allen, J. (2000). No more happy endings? The media and popular concern about crime since the second world war. In T. Hope & R. Sparks (Eds.), *Crime, risk and insecurity: Law and order in everyday life and political discourse* (pp. 107–126). London: Routledge.

Reiner, R., Livingston, S., & Allen, J. (2001). Casino culture: Media and crime in a winner-loser society. In K. Stenson & R. Sullivan (Eds.), *Crime, risk, and justice: The politics of crime control in liberal democracies* (pp. 194–203). Cullompton: Willan Publishing.

Reiner, R., Livingstone, S., & Allen, J. (2003). From law and order to lynch mobs: Crime news since the second world war. In P. Mason (Ed.), *Criminal visions: Media representations of crime and justice* (pp. 13–32). Portland: Willan Publishing.

Ringo, P. (2002). Media roles in female-to-male transsexual and transgender identity formation. *International Journal of Transgenderism, 6*(3). Retrieved from: https://www.atria.nl/ezines/web/IJT/97-03/numbers/symposion/ijtvo06no03_01.htm

Romer, D., Jamieson, K. H., & de Coteau, N. J. (1998). The treatment of persons of color in local television news-ethnic blame discourse or realistic group conflict. *Communication Research, 25,* 286–305.

Russell-Brown, K. (1998). *The color of justice.* New York: New York Press.

Russell-Brown, K. (2009). *The color of justice* (2nd ed.). New York: New York Press.

Sampson, R., & Wilson, W. J. (1995). Toward a theory of race, crime, and urban inequality. In J. Hagan & R. D. Peterson (Eds.), *Crime and inequality* (pp. 37–54). Stanford: Stanford University Press.

Shaheen, J. G. (2009). *Reel bad Arabs: How Hollywood vilifies a people.* Northhampton: Olive Branch Press.

Shanahan, J., & Morgan, M. (1999). *Television and its viewers: Cultivation theory and research.* Cambridge: Cambridge University Press.

Simons, R. L., Chen, Y. F., Stewart, E. A., & Brody, G. H. (2003). Incidents of discrimination and risk for delinquency: A longitudinal test of strain theory with an African American sample. *Justice Quarterly, 20,* 827–854.

Surette, R. (2007). *Media, crime, and criminal justice: Images, realities, and policies* (1st ed.). Stamford: Cengage Learning.

Surette, R. (2015). *Media, crime, & criminal justice: Images, realities, and policies* (5th ed.). Stamford: Cengage Learning.

Surette, R., & Gardiner-Bess, R. (2014). Media, entertainment, and crime: Prospects and concerns. In B. A. Arrigo & H. Y. Bersot (Eds.), *Routledge handbook of international crime and justice studies* (pp. 373–396). Abingdon/Oxon: Routledge.

Truman, J., & Morgan, R. (2016). *Criminal victimization, 2015.* Washington, DC: U.S. Department of Justice, Bureau of Justice Statistics.

Tuttle, C. R. (2017). *Where we get our news: A multilevel analysis of the media framing of immigration and crime.* Masters Thesis University of Arkansas. Retrieved from http://search.proquest.com/openview/fae9a13dbcf39b7550 1d1590a6bfa286/1?pq-origsite=gscholar&cbl=18750&diss=y

U.S. Census Bureau. (2015). *Quick facts.* Retrieved from https://www.census.gov/quickfacts/

U.S. Department of Health and Human Services. (2017). *Mental health and facts*. Retrieved from https://www.mentalhealth.gov/basics/myths-facts/

U.S. Department of Justice, Federal Bureau of Investigation. (2015a). *Crime in the United States, 2015: Table 18*. Retrieved from https://ucr.fbi.gov/crime-in-theu.s/2015/crime-in-the-u.s.-2015/tables/table-18

U.S. Department of Justice, Federal Bureau of Investigation. (2015b). *Crime in the United States, 2015: Expanded homicide data table 7*. Retrieved from https://ucr.fbi.gov/crime-in-the-u.s/2015/crime-in-the-u.s.-2015/tables/expanded_homicide_data_table_7_murder_types_of_weapons_used_percent_distribution_by_region_2015.xls

U.S. Department of Justice, Federal Bureau of Investigation. (2016a, September). *Crime in the United States, 2015: Table 1*. Retrieved from https://ucr.fbi.gov/crime-in-the-u.s/2015/crime-in-the-u.s.-2015/tables/table-1

U.S. Department of Justice, Federal Bureau of Investigation. (2016b, September). *Crime in the United States, 2015: Table 43*. Retrieved from https://ucr.fbi.gov/crime-in-the-u.s/2015/crime-in-the-u.s.-2015/tables/table-43

U.S. Department of Justice, Federal Bureau of Investigation. (2016c, September). *Crime in the United States, 2015: Table 38*. Retrieved from https://ucr.fbi.gov/crime-in-the-u.s/2015/crime-in-the-u.s.-2015/tables/table-38

U.S. Department of Justice, Federal Bureau of Investigation. (2016d, September). *Crime in the United States, 2015: Table 42*. Retrieved from https://ucr.fbi.gov/crime-in-the-u.s/2015/crime-in-the-u.s.-2015/tables/table-42

Unnever, J. D., & Gabbidon, S. L. (2011). *A theory of African American offending: Race, racism, and crime*. London: Routledge.

Walker, S., Spohn, C., & DeLone, M. (2012). *The color of justice: Race, ethnicity, and crime in America*. Belmont: Wadsworth.

Warr, M. (1980). The accuracy of public beliefs about crime. *Social Forces, 59*, 456–470.

Warr, M. (1995). Poll trends: Public opinion on crime and punishment. *Public Opinion Quarterly, 59*, 296–310.

Weitzer, R. (2015). American policing under fire: Misconduct and reform. *Social Science and Public Policy, 52*, 475–480.

Weitzer, R., & Tuch, S. A. (2006). *Race and policing in America: Conflict and reform*. London: Cambridge University Press.

Whealin, J. (2007, May 22). *Child sexual abuse*. National Center for Post Traumatic Stress Disorder, US Department of Veterans Affairs.

Wike, R., Stokes, B., & Simmons, K. (2016, July 11). *Europeans fear wave of refugees will mean more terrorism, fewer jobs.* Retrieved from http://www.politico. eu/wp-content/uploads/2016/07/Pew-Research-Center-EU-Refugees-and-National-Identity-Report-EMBARGOED-UNTIL-1800EDT-2200GMT-July-11-2016.pdf

Zatz, M., & Smith, H. (2012). Immigration, crime, and victimization: Rhetoric and reality. *Annual Review of Law and Social Science, 8,* 141–159.

4

#Notallmen: Media and Crime Victimization

On May 23rd, 2014, a 22-year-old man, Elliot Rodger began his killing spree in California, United States, where he killed 6 people and wounded 14. After stabbing three of his male roommates to death, he shot three sorority sisters at the University of California Santa Barbara. Before going to the sorority house, he uploaded a video on YouTube in which he explained that he wanted to punish women for rejecting him and punish men for enjoying life more than him and emailed his story—"My Twisted World"—to his family and therapists, where he explained in more detail his misogyny and racism. After killing two women at the sorority house, he killed another student at a delicatessen. The killing spree ended with Elliot Rodger shooting himself (Duke 2014). After this murder/suicide with its YouTube videos and emailed manifesto, the discussion surrounding the normalization of violence against women became a media focus.

Victimization is something most of us fear and many of us actively try to prevent. We develop our ideas about our chance of victimization through the media, peers, family, friends, and even our own past experiences. Our socially constructed perception of victimization might be different than the reality of victimization. We may overestimate or underestimate our

© The Author(s) 2018
R. M. Hayes, K. Luther, *#Crime*, Palgrave Studies in Crime, Media and Culture,
https://doi.org/10.1007/978-3-319-89444-7_4

chances and we may judge other's experiences harshly, which impacts how we interact in our social world.

The media's role in this manifests largely in shaping our perceptions of the chance of victimization. After the shooting at the University of California Santa Barbara, and other mass shootings, we look at our safety differently. The media's extensive coverage of these events encourages it to be front and center in our daily lives. When shootings receive a lot of media coverage, even though they do not occur as often as other crimes, it likely increases fear of crime in the United States, aids in the overestimation of the likelihood of these events, and/or impacts judgments about the use of guns in the United States. In this chapter, we discuss how media may be influencing perceptions of victimization and what this means for the construction of victimization. Crime victims themselves within news media and even entertainment are largely marginalized. The marginalization of crime victims, however, is changing within infotainment (Surette and Gardiner-Bess 2014), and this might also be true for new media.

Media, and especially new media, can also be used to push back against victimization and perceptions of victimization. In 2014, #YesAllWomen and the counter #NotAllMen placed gendered street harassment as rape culture into the international spotlight. #YesAllWomen contains stories of how women everywhere are subjected to street harassment; this hashtag occurred in response to Elliot Rodger's killing spree. The hashtag is about how society has normalized toxic gendered behavior along with rape, and it is a part of our larger, global rape culture (Hayes and Weigand 2015). Elliot Rodger's YouTube diatribe encouraged discussions about the frequency of violence against women with #YesAllWomen, and two of the most popular favorited and retweeted tweets include:

@JessicaP_02: Because my wardrobe should not be decided by what will or will not 'provoke' or 'distract' somebody. #YesAllWomen (May 27, 2014)

@Brittany: Because I'm not an object, I don't exist to please you, and I owe you nothing. #YesAllWomen (May 27, 2014)

It is not, however, only rape where the victim's narrative is constructed; this chapter covers how the victim's narrative is socially constructed while, at the same time, being challenged by new media.

Throughout this chapter, we work to:

1. Define the "ideal" victim
2. Discuss the media construction of victims, with particular attention paid to victims of sexual assault and intimate partner violence
3. Illustrate how the ideal victim narrative is being challenged through new media

The Ideal Victim

Perceptions of victimization influence who is allowed to be a "real" victim. Take a minute and think about how these victims are viewed by larger society:

• A young man sexually assaulted by his boyfriend
• A great-grandmother whose home is burglarized
• A bank employee murdered during a robbery
• A prostitute who is raped
• An incarcerated person physically assaulted by another inmate

Which victims receive the most sympathy? Who receives the least sympathy? What factors determine how these victims are viewed? How does the victim's race/ethnicity, socioeconomic status, gender identity or sexuality shape perceptions as to their status as a "legitimate" victim?

Crimes are more newsworthy if they feature the "ideal victim" (Greer 2010), which is a socially constructed concept (Christie 1986, p. 18), and includes "a person or a category of individuals who – when hit by crime – most readily are given the complete and legitimate status of being a victim." In these cases, the person is a "hero" and completely absolved of blame in the situation. These ideal victims are therefore innocent. Christie (1986, p. 19) provides five characteristics of the ideal victim and the situation where the victimization occurred:

1. The victim is weak. Sick, old, or very young people are particularly well suited as ideal victims.
2. The victim was carrying out a respectable project—caring for her sister.
3. She was where she could not possibly be blamed for being—in the street during the daytime.

4. The offender was big and bad.
5. The offender was unknown and in no personal relationship to her.

Thinking about these attributes, ideal victims are mostly females (we'll discuss the complexity of this in cases of sexual assault at a later point in the chapter), young children (emphasis on the word young), and/or the elderly. One noteworthy example of the "ideal victim" is JonBenet Ramsey (see box *JonBenet Ramsey*). JonBenet had many characteristics of the ideal victim. She was weak, very young (only six years old) and was supposedly in her home when she was kidnapped and murdered. The offender is still unknown, but arguably "big and bad," as who would harm a defenseless little girl? The big and bad concept is where people who are victimized need to be viewed as *weaker* than the offender and have put a reasonable amount of energy into the protection of themselves (Christie 1986). In most cases, children are absolved of having to protect themselves, as they are seen as unable to do so, but adults are a different story.

JonBenet Ramsey On December 26, 1996, JonBenet Ramsey was found murdered in the basement of her family's home. JonBenet's parents had phoned her in as missing only seven hours earlier (Conrad 1999). The investigation that followed never revealed the murderer. There was a ransom note that pinned it as a kidnapping, and there was speculation that the parents committed the murder but they were cleared. Different books were written on the topic and depending on which one you read you could be led to think differently about the topic (for more read: *JonBenet: Inside the Ramsey Murder Investigation* by Steve Thomas with Don Davis, *Presumed Guilty: An Investigation Into the JonBenet Ramsey Case, the Media and the Culture of Pornograph* by Stephen Singular, or *The Other Side of Suffering: The Father of JonBenet Ramsey Tells His Story of His Journey from Grief to Grace* by John Ramsey). The media and public fascination that followed led to a lot of academic inquiry (Conrad 1999; Singular 1999; Fox et al. 2007) continues (Casarez 2016). In 2016, a mini-series aired on CBS chronicling the case yet again.

The notion of who we see as vulnerable in society plays into the ideal victim concept. Children are vulnerable. Women *can be* vulnerable. Men are not allowed to be vulnerable. This is what Walklate (2007) calls the "victimological other," and even among victimology research, men are often invisible as the victim. There is a gendered connotation to the word victim in many languages and the genealogy of the word is connected to sacrifice and this is more likely to be female (Walklate 2007). Underlying this notion of the female victim are the gendered assumptions of passivity and powerlessness. According to Christie's (1986) attributes, men can only be ideal victim if they are elderly, and women's ability to be an ideal victim is commonly compromised by knowing their offender or by their activities such as being out late at night. Underlying the attributes are societal expectations, norms, and roles that contribute to the ideal victim narrative. That is, race/ethnicity, socioeconomic status, gender, and sexuality are all key elements. In the case of JonBenet, she was very pretty, almost doll-like, white, and from an affluent family. This makes her more newsworthy (think back to the discussion of Jewkes' newsworthiness in Chap. 3). If she was black, Hispanic, or from a working-class family, her attraction as an ideal victim would likely diminish. Society has already cast these statuses as criminal (see Chap. 3), and even when it is a child, we are probably less likely to see these victims cast into the main media spotlight, such as the case with black or Hispanic victims over white victims (Liebler 2010; Min and Feaster 2010; Simmons and Woods 2015). On the opposite end of the ideal victim spectrum are the "social undesirables," such as the homeless, addicts, sex workers, and other low-status powerless people. Carrabine et al. (2004) terms it the *hierarchy of victimization* where these groups are usually controlled by the police, and so when they are victimized, they are not taken seriously.

Not only do some victims not meet the criteria of the *ideal victim* or are low on the *hierarchy of victimization*, they are blamed for their own victimization. *Victim blaming* (Eigenberg and Garland 2008) is rampant and occurs when a person is viewed as at least partially culpable for their own victimization. The location where the victimization occurred and the behavior of the victim are called into question. Like the ideal victim concept, victim blaming is also tied into societal expectations, norms, and roles surrounding gender, sexuality, race, ethnicity, and socioeconomic status. A common example of victim blaming is how we blame women for their sexual assault by judging what they were wearing at the time, how much they drank, or how late they were out. These examples, termed *rape myths* (Burt 1980), are myths mostly about the victim, but also the perpetrator, and the incidence of rape. Examples of rape myths include: "only bad girls get raped," "women ask for it," "any healthy woman can resist a rapist if she really wants to," and "rapists are sex starved, insane, or both" (Burt 1980, p. 217). Rape myths are extremely pervasive (see Edwards et al. 2011 or Suarez and Gadalla 2010 for reviews of the literature) and the media is largely responsible for the maintenance of rape culture (see box *Rape Culture*) mostly through the perpetuation of these myths (Phillips 2017). If the woman is black or Hispanic, we think it is likely that there is even less sympathy and more blame placed on the victim.

Rape Culture Rape culture occurs when within a particular culture or subculture rape is normalized, excused, and/or trivialized through the means of institutions which objectify people (usually women/girls) and blame victims' behavior while often sympathizing with the offender. As we saw with Brock Turner's father's statement during his sentencing, rape culture is alive and well. He excused and trivialized his son's crimes by blaming it on "the culture of alcohol consumption and partying" and referring to it as "20 minutes of action" (see https://heavy.com/news/2016/06/brock-turner-father-dad-dan-turner-full-letter-statement-stanford-rapist/). While the definition and the existence of "rape culture" are often contested, the term has received more popularity since 2013 (Phillips 2017). According to Phillips (2017), the term went mainstream in 2013 with the international interest of three events: (1) the Steubenville rape case in the United States, (2) the New Delhi rape case in India and, (3) the song *Blurred Lines* by Robin Thicke. (For a more thorough analysis of rape culture, read: *Beyond Blurred Lines: Rape Culture in Popular Media* by Nickie D. Phillips.) An example of rape culture—the controversy over the song *Blurred Lines* by Robin Thicke (see also Koehler 2013)—demonstrates how music mediums are believed to normalize and perpetuate violence against women, in this case sexual assault. In the song Robin Thicke sings, "You know you want it," which indicates that even if the girl/woman were to say no, Robin Thicke knows better. Even the name of the song indicates that consent is not clear-cut, in that if a girl/woman says no, then it is not clear that she means no.

Discussion Question: *Consider the intersection of a black, transgender woman who has been sexually assaulted. How might this victim be blamed?*

We see victim blaming playing out in the case of CeCe McDonald, a black transwoman in Minnesota, United States (Erdely 2014). CeCe and her friends were verbally assaulted as they walked by a group of four individuals who were yelling racist and transphobic slurs. The verbal assault turned physical and eventually CeCe was hit in the face by a glass and cut. As she was leaving the scene of the altercation, one of the individuals started following her. She stabbed him with scissors and he died. CeCe pled to second-degree manslaughter and served a 41-month term in a men's prison. Many advocates argue that her conviction was unjust—that she was only arrested, charged, and convicted for a crime because she was a black, transgender woman. As a society, black transwomen do not fit our construction of an ideal victim. Instead of viewing CeCe's behavior as self-defense, her behavior was constructed to be criminal.

Victimization: Media Construction Versus Reality

Societal perceptions of victims are partially constructed through media imagery, and the average victim is not particularly newsworthy (Surette 2015). As discussed in Chap. 3, the media focuses heavily on acts of interpersonal violence, but not necessarily from the victim's perspective. While the news tends to focus on the ideal victim, which, as indicated earlier, would be a child, there are depictions of other victims within other mediums. Within entertainment, crime victims are depicted as either "helpless fodder or as a wronged heroic avenger" (Surette 2015, p. 62), and these victims tend to be mostly white and male. However, still within both of these constructions, there is an overrepresentation of female victimization and the details surrounding their victimizations are more graphic. These graphic details likely elicit the ideal victim status more obviously, as they incite sympathy.

Therefore, in the news media, white female (especially children) victims are more likely to be represented (Gabbidon and Greene 2009; Min and Feaster 2010); in cases of missing persons, this is often termed *missing white girl syndrome*.

The social construction of victimization—both who is the victim and how it occurs—does not always represent reality. We are told to fear violent victimization of our persons or property from "stranger danger" and to protect ourselves by eyeing strangers suspiciously, carrying mace, or learning self-defense even though over half of women's violent victimizations are perpetrated by someone the victim knows (Bureau of Justice Statistics 2014). Crime is generally stable or on a decline in the United States, Europe, and Australia (see Chap. 3).

Thus, as previously mentioned, the media construction of who the *ideal victim* is relates to women, children, or the elderly, and even with these victims there are certain circumstances surrounding their victimization that need to be met in order for them to be viewed as "ideal." That is, there are multiple ways to discredit the victim and media impacts assumptions about victimization. What follows is a discussion on general crime victimization statistics that set the stage for a clearer understanding of victimization. The newest statistics from the National Crime Victimization Survey (NCVS) (Bureau of Justice Statistics 2016) in the United States found these trends in victimization:

- Sex
  - Women (21.1 per 1000) experience a higher rate of violent victimization than men (15.9 per 1000)
- Age
  - The highest rates of violent victimization are for those 12–17 years of age (31.3 per 1000) and 18–24 years of age (25.1 per 1000)
  - The lowest rate of violent victimization is for those 65 and older (5.2 per 1000)

- Socioeconomic status

  - Economically disadvantaged households (incomes $9,999 and under) have the highest rate of violent victimization (39.2 per 1000)
  - Economically advantaged households (incomes $75,000 and above) have the lowest rates of violent victimization (12.8 per 1000)

- Race and ethnicity

  - Hispanic (16.8 per 1000) and white (17.4 per 1000) individuals have lower rates of violent victimization than black individuals (22.6 per 1000) and individuals of the NCVS's broad category of American Indians, Alaska Natives, Asians, Native Hawaiians, Other Pacific Islanders, and those of two or more races (25.7 per 1000)

- Relationship to the perpetrator (Bureau of Justice Statistics 2017)

  - Over half (56%) of violent victimizations occur between an offender and victim who know each other as "intimates," "other relatives," or "well-known/casual acquaintances"

Although there are critiques of the NCVS (see Lab et al. 2011 or DeKeseredy 2016), it does paint a general picture of crime victimization in the United States for us to consider. On a grander scale, the International Crime Victimization Survey (ICVS) examines victimization internationally with survey administration taking place in 80 countries since 1989 (van Kesteren et al. 2014). In the 2000 ICVS, those living in areas with a population over 100,000 were most at risk for crime (Walklate 2007; van Kesteren et al. 2014). Houses with higher incomes were more at risk than those with lower incomes, yet when examining individual victimization as opposed to household this risk shifts. People who were under 55 were more at risk than older people. Individuals who were unmarried are also at a higher risk for victimization than married individuals. In Walklate (2007), a study was discussed that found men were 20% more at risk than women for robbery and assaults. Even when only focusing on the ICVS, there is already a more complex picture than what the ideal victim narrative would suggest. The reductionist picture of focusing only on certain characteristics, such as what is demonstrated in the ideal victim narrative, ignores the breadth and scope of victimization.

With one of the ideal victim categories focusing on women, the side effect is that we largely ignore men as victims. Most homicide victims are male, and in the United States black males make up a large proportion of this victimization rate compared to their proportion in the population (Gabbidon and Greene 2009). The amount of black male victimization is particularly notable and considered problematic as it is emblematic of how certain lives are considered more valuable than others in society, as black male victimization does not receive much media coverage comparatively to other groups. Even though our one-year snapshot demonstrates that women in 2016 had a higher victimization rate than men, the NCVS 2016 results are a reversal of previous trends—men have historically had higher rates of violent victimization than women. In the United Kingdom, young males who go out drinking two or three times a week are most likely to be victimized (Walklate 2007). Research here highlights the importance of examining victimization contextually *and* longitudinally in order to assess recurring trends.

The socially constructed victim hierarchy also encourages us to ignore the high likelihood of victimization among the homeless, drug addicts, and even sex workers. The media's construction of the ideal victim constrains our ability to see certain people as vulnerable, worthy of sympathy, and deserving of support. When thinking of homeless youth, people may envision them as the property offenders, but a systematic review demonstrated that they are also commonly victimized by having their own personal property damaged or burglarized (Heerde and Hemphill 2013), which mainstream survey research does not measure (DeKeseredy 2016). Likewise, regular drug users, who are likely to be viewed as criminals, are at high risk for victimization themselves (Koo et al. 2008; Stevens et al. 2007). Victimization is also very common among sex workers globally (Dalla et al. 2003; Deering et al. 2014).

From an overview of victimization generally, we now highlight the more specific media portrayal of victims of sexual assault and intimate partner abuse. Although there are many categories of victims we could address in this chapter, we chose to focus our discussion and analysis on sexual assault and intimate partner abuse. We chose to draw attention to these forms of victimization because the *ideal victim* narrative is extremely apparent and further complicated in the media portrayal of these victimizations.

Media Construction of Sexual Assault

The construction of the ideal victim is evident in the media coverage of many cases of sexual violence. How sexual violence is portrayed through the media encourages a rape culture that minimizes and normalizes it. Through media representations, rape myths are perpetuated and rape apologists trivialize sexual assault both of which contribute to rape culture. And of course, the intersections of social locations also impact how the victim is treated.

Regarding the framing of sexual violence, the media tends to focus on victim credibility and behavior (Belknap 2009; Franiuk et al. 2008; O'Hara 2012), which follows commonly held rape myths. During sexual assault allegations, the focus is often on the victim rather than the perpetrator. Questions about how the victim behaved, what they were wearing, and how much alcohol they consumed are common in the rhetoric that discredits the victim. The status of *ideal victim* is rarely afforded to someone who experienced sexual assault. A recent example of a media-covered sexual assault is the Delhi, India, Gang Rape case (see box *Delhi Gang Rape*). Here the victim died from the assault that occurred while she was riding the bus home at night. Riding the bus is normal behavior, but when victimized, the act is reappropriated and referenced regarding the culpability of the victim (especially women) for their assault. The media reported a story of one of the rapists stating:

> ""A decent girl won't roam around at nine o'clock at night. A girl is far more responsible for rape than a boy". He then goes on to say that, "housework and housekeeping is for girls, not roaming in discos and bars at night doing wrong things, wearing wrong clothes. About 20% of girls are good."" (BBC 2015)

While the news source in this example is not necessarily advocating this viewpoint, they are reporting commonly held rape myths. Thus, the media is one vehicle that can help to perpetuate rape myths. Interestingly, Phillips (2017) argued that the reason the Delhi, India, gang rape case garnered so much international attention is because the victim met the definition of an ideal victim for many people and she suffered severe injuries that resulted in her death, yet still there were representations that victim blame such as the example above.

Delhi Gang Rape The victim and her male friend were returning home after a movie and boarded an off-duty charter bus around 9:30 at night. There were six others on the bus, including a minor and the bus driver. The men attacked and assaulted the male friend, and he was knocked unconscious using a metal rod. The men beat and drugged the victim in the back of the bus and brutally raped her; some reports say that the rod was even used to penetrate her. After many days in the hospital and multiple surgeries, she died. Six men were arrested, and five were charged. The four adult men were found guilty of rape and murder. This case received international attention, and there were protests/marches in support of the victim (For more information watch the documentary *India's Daughter*).

Occasionally, the mainstream media openly sympathizes with accused perpetrators. In particular, the term *rape apologist* is used when media personalities lament the loss of a potential future for the accused perpetrator without mention of the impact on the victim's future. One such recent example in the United States was during the case of Brock Turner (see box *People v. Turner (2015) or The Brock Turner Case*). The media coverage *after* his conviction often referred to him as "The Stanford Swimmer" rather than "The Stanford Rapist" (LaChance 2016). The media were criticized for sympathizing with the offender and not the victim. There was widespread criticism regarding how media covered the case, which illustrates the American rape culture. Another example of a rape apologist was CNN's Poppy Harlow reporting about the promising future of the students involved in the Steubenville, Ohio (United States) rape trial. (See for example: https://www.youtube.com/watch?v=BCRt_wIM3jk.) While Poppy Harlow was called out on her comments, on social media there continues to be examples of how blame is placed on rape victims while sympathizing with offenders (Abad-Santos 2013). (See for example: http://www.theatlantic.com/national/archive/2013/03/steubenville-rape-twitter-cnn/317144/.)

People v. Turner (2015) or The Brock Turner Case This case is a sexual assault criminal case filed against Brock Turner, who at the time was a student-athlete at Stanford University. On January 18, 2015, two Swedish international students at Stanford were biking and saw Turner sexually penetrating an unconscious woman. As they approached him, he fled. The students chased, apprehended, and restrained Turner until police arrived. Turner was convicted of three counts of felony sexual assault and was sentenced to six months of incarceration and probation upon release. During Turner's sentencing, the victim, called "Emily Doe," read an impact statement about her sexual assault to the courtroom. Her victim impact statement, which was referred to by the District Attorney as "the most eloquent, powerful and compelling piece of victim advocacy that I've seen in my 20 years as a prosecutor" (Bever 2016), was posted on BuzzFeed and reportedly viewed 11 million times in the first four days (Baysinger 2016).

However, not all legacy media coverage of sexual victimization is problematic. Chancer (2005) argues that high-profile cases of victimization (read: cases given extensive media coverage) encourage people to take up social causes. For example, in the *Columbia Mattress* case in the United States, a woman who was raped while attending Columbia University carried a mattress around as part of a school project to demonstrate how she had to live with the crime. This case reached international audiences, such as in Australia (Sullivan 2016), Hungary (CPSV 2014), and the United Kingdom (Klausner 2015). This, of course, was also impacted by new media, and to what extent we do not know. We argue that the benefit of this coverage was that it added to the conversation regarding how to properly address sexual violence, including prevention to sanctions for perpetrators, on American college campuses, which continues both at the university level and at the level of the federal government. Title IX (see box *Title IX*), the legislation dealing with campus violence, was revised again and implementation of these changes is ongoing, yet not without some criticism.

Title IX Title IX is civil rights legislation to address discrimination on the basis of sex in public education in the United States, created and implemented in the early 1970s. While early focus on Title IX was on equality in sports programs in public schools, the issues of sexual harassment and violence have also been a focus. Sexual harassment and violence policies have been created and implemented on college campuses across the United States. There have been recent Title IX changes that garnered significant attention. The main outcome was the creation of mandatory reporting policies for sexual violence. Many mandatory reporting policies require faculty and staff at public universities to report to administration if a student discloses an assault. The policy is criticized by academics and practitioners as harmful to the student who has been victimized as it removes their agency. Public universities need to be in compliance with Title IX in order to continue to receive public funding.

The reality of sexual assault is that women experience this crime more often than men. In the United States, depending on the report, the exact rates range from 1 in 4 to 1 in 6 women, with women always experiencing more than men. In one study, Black et al. (2011) suggested that sexual assault for women is 1 in 5 and 1 in 71 for men. Krahe et al. (2014) examined 113 studies of sexual aggression of young people in Europe and found that lifetime prevalence rates of female sexual victimization ranged from 9% to 83%, and male rates ranged from 2% to 66%. However, girls and boys experience sexual assault at similar rates until the age of 14. The age group that experiences the most sexual assault is 16–24 (Smith and Welchans 2000). And, alcohol is the number one date rape drug (Scott-Ham and Burton 2006) with this crime most often being committed by someone the victim knows. With alcohol as the most used drug for rape, society tends to place blame on the victim for consuming and the perpetrator is viewed as less culpable due to alcohol consumption. While the *ideal victim* is often a white woman, sexual assault occurs across all racial/ethnic groups. In the United States, between 1994–1998 and 2005–2010, non-Hispanic white, black, and Hispanic females had a similar rate of sexual violence, while American Indians and Alaska Natives reported a higher rate of sexual violence during those time periods (Planty et al. 2013).

Media Construction of Intimate Partner Violence

In order to receive legacy media coverage of crime, there are aspects of a crime that makes it more newsworthy, such as the involvement of a celebrity/high-status person (Jewkes 2015), and this is evident in the coverage of intimate partner violence (in this chapter, we choose to use the term "intimate partner violence" to acknowledge that it is not only women who are victimized, even though it *is* mostly women who are victimized. There are critiques of this terminology, including: DeKeseredy 2011; DeKeseredy et al. 2017). According to Jewkes (2015), there are 12 news structures and news values that make up crime news (see Chap. 3 for an overview of Jewkes' newsworthiness), and many intimate partner violence cases only have a couple of these values. For example, an intimate partner violence situation in which a husband is controlling, emotionally abusive, and occasionally physically abuses his wife rarely makes the news. In contrast, cases of celebrities perpetrating intimate partner violence commonly receive different treatment. For example, think about the recent cases of NFL player Ray Rice's abuse of his then fiancée Janay Palmer and Oscar Pistorius' murder of his girlfriend Reeva Steenkamp; both received extensive media coverage. One recent study examined themes of intimate partner violence coverage comparing NFL players versus general population stories and found that the NFL stories were more sensationalized with a negative focus on the perpetrator (Hayes and Kwiatkowski 2015). The general population stories were brief reports with minimal context. As we discussed in Chap. 1 regarding O.J. Simpson, part of the by-product of this case is how celebrity cases are viewed differently.

The manner in which intimate partner violent stories are portrayed in the media may not represent the incidence accurately. Even when a current or intimate partner is a murder victim (called femicide when a female partner is killed), news coverage will be of the murder but will commonly ignore the abusive context or they may portray it as the perpetrator simply snapping which is a reductionist explanation (DeKeseredy et al. 2017). Gillespie et al. (2013) examined the frames of two samples of news stories wherein the femicide is framed as either domestic violence or simply a murder. Among the sample of news stories that did not define the femicide as domestic violence, the largest frame (75% of news stories) was a normalization of the event as common. The coverage of the event was "as one of many homicides or just a homicide" or "preceded by violence but not domestic violence" (Gillespie et al. 2013, p. 232).

We spoke about the media portrayal of women as victims of intimate partner violence, but men can be victims as well, although it is nowhere near as frequent as violence against women by current or former male partners. Unfortunately, media (largely through men's rights groups on the internet) has contributed to the international antifeminist backlash in opposition to violence against women initiatives, researchers, and activism, which downplays the gravity of violence against women (Dragiewicz 2008; Laidler and Mann 2008; DeKeseredy, Dragiewicz, and Schwartz 2017). There are some media (both legacy and new) which argue that gender symmetry exists in intimate partner relationships, which is simply not what research demonstrates. In the rhetoric of "but women do it too" and "women are just as bad as men" (Dragiewicz 2011; Dragiewicz and Lindgren 2009, 2011), female *and* male victims' voices get lost. Marginalized groups are even more likely to be silenced; nonwhites, immigrants, and/or LGBTQ persons are less likely to receive media coverage when they are the victims.

Socioeconomic standing, geographic location, education, and race/ethnicity are all factors that impact the likelihood of intimate partner victimization, but the most commonly researched and understood factor is sex. Regarding trends in intimate partner violence victimization, women are the majority of victims (Belknap 2009; Bureau of Justice Statistics 2014; DeKeseredy 2011), but the media representation is misleading. Sometimes the media uses the gender symmetry argument, following the controversial work of Straus and colleagues (Straus 1979, 1993), which argues that men and women are perpetrators at equal rates. This work has also been co-opted by Men's Rights Groups, and perpetuated on new media channels such as Twitter, blogs, and Tumblr (Dragiewicz and Lindgren 2009, 2011; Dragiewicz 2011). In the United States, there is also more media representation of white women as victims, while ignoring people of color (Gabiddon and Greene 2013), even though women of color experience intimate partner violence at least as high if not at higher rates than white women (Lipsky et al. 2009). Likewise, in Canada first nations women experience a higher rate of intimate partner violence than non-first nations women (Canadian Centre for Justice Statistics 2016). There is also evidence that rural compared with urban women are at a greater risk of experiencing intimate partner violence (Donnermeyer and DeKeseredy 2014). We argue that there is a focus in the media on working-class populations (with the exception of celebrities) as perpetrators and victims, but it occurs among all economic statuses. The reality of intimate partner violence is also distinguished in the manner in which it occurs, often with emotional abuse as a large defining factor. This factor is often downplayed or ignored in media representations. Context matters and media representation oversimplify and are misleading in their representations.

While we can challenge those categorizations, it is important to pay attention to the manner in which new media aids in constructing this imagery. How is social media impacting categorizations of victims? There are media representations, such as the sarcastic tweets listed in the following section, that are challenging (at least partially) the "who is the victim" category. There are also different ways that new media is not only constructing images of victimization, but is actually impacting how victimization can occur (see Chap. 5). This discussion is where we now turn.

Challenging the Ideal Victim Narrative Through New Media

While the topic of sexual assault and intimate partner violence has at times prevalent coverage within legacy media, it is possible that new media also has had an impact on the social construction of this crime. The social construction could be encouraging myths, such as victim blaming and women are as violent as men (DeKeseredy et al. 2015), but it may also challenge the current dominant narrative (Salter 2013) of the ideal victim or rape myths. Regarding encouragement of rape myths, the condescending #safetytipsforwomen occurred in 2013, to provide "safety tips" to keep women safe.

These tweets focus on women and self-defense as a means in which to combat rape and other forms of victimization. However, this feeds into the victim-blaming narrative that women (the victim) can prevent the attack if they do these things.

While we are not saying safety and precaution aren't important, it is just that focusing on the victim preventing the assault misses the point. Prevention programs should focus on the perpetrator. These tips misconstrue the reality of sexual assault and perpetuate rape myths, which suggest it is usually a stranger jumping out of the bushes and not a known assailant. The counter of #safetytipsforladies also launched in order to challenge the societal constructions of sexual assault victim blaming (Rentschler 2015). For example:

@Miss Andrist: **#safetytipsforladies** Carefully consider the increased risk of rape and sexual assault before you decide to be born a girl.

Now when looking at both of these hashtags it is difficult to discern whether it is satire or real, as they are both used by people who are pushing back against the dominant narrative.

The #YesAllWomen mentioned at the beginning of this chapter was meant to educate and challenge the dominant narrative, by demonstrating how often violence against women occurs, and even though it was challenged, the dominant message was still one in favor of the original hashtag. According to a discussion in *Slate Magazine*, the #NotAllMen hashtag was a counter to #YesAllWomen and attempted to derail the discussion with a defensive argument that not all men commit these acts (Plait 2014; DeKeseredy et al. 2015). However, favorited and retweeted tweets with the #NotAllMen hashtag were actually #YesAllWomen tweets, meaning that the conversation was still dominated by the educative discussion. For example:

Jonathon Frandzone @NotAllBhas
#YesAllWomen are tired of men finding excuses for street harassers, rapists, and murderers. Instead of saying #NotAllMen-why not prove it? (May 24, 2014)

Daniel Jakob Eager @EagerDan
So #YesAllWomen has been met with #notallmen. Kneejerk defense much fellas? Hear these Women out, they hurt and have a voice. LET THEM SPEAK. (May 25, 2014) (Hayes & Wiegand 2015)

As discussed in Chap. 3, new media such as podcasts, Netflix, and TED talks could also aid in the construction of crime and justice issues.

One such case is a TED Talk with the victim and perpetrator of a sexual assault speaking together about how the assault occurred and the aftermath where she blamed herself. This talk explains how victims and perpetrators often feel and how that can be tied into societal gender roles and expectations (see http://www.itv.com/news/2017-02-09/rape-survivor-rapist-extraordinary-ted-talk/). Another example is the Netflix mini-series *13 Reasons Why*, which demonstrates a very realistic display of sexual assault, which in our educated opinion is rarely demonstrated in media. The show, based on a book, is about a teenage girl who commits suicide and tells her story through cassette tapes that are passed onto people who are involved in her life and subsequent demise. The show, while criticized for its glamorization of suicide, demonstrates an accurate picture of rape culture in American society.

In addition to new media, such as Netflix and TED Talks, changing the dialog around sexual violence, we also see social media changing the social construction of victimization. Using three case studies—Savannah Dietrich (United States), Kim Duthie (Australia), and Georgia Grimes (United States)—Salter (2013) demonstrated how social media has provided a platform for girls and women to participate in counterpublics. According to Salter, counterpublics are a way to challenge the dominant media/social narrative regarding sexual violence. Simply put, counterpublics are places (e.g. zines and blogs) where subordinated social groups, such as women and girls, can engage in an alternative discourse on a topic. As sexual assault discussions in the public sphere surround a focus on the victim's behavior, counterpublic discussions concentrate more often on the offender's behavior or societal norms that encourage such assault (e.g. rape culture). For example, counterpublics discuss what the offender did wrong, such as pressuring the victim into drinking, or the victim describing the assault in their own words.

The difference here is that new media is not as passive as legacy media and the involvement of a subordinated group can impact public opinion. One example of this is the rape case in Steubenville, Ohio (United States), where blogger Alexandria Goddard used social media and posted screenshots of the social media posts from the assault, along with the names of the alleged perpetrators on her blog. This evidence came to the attention of the police and international media (Baker 2012). Not without controversy, however, as the parents of one of the accused filed an injunction against Goddard in *Saltsman v. Goddard*. They reached a settlement where Goddard had to post a statement that Cody Saltsman, who posted pictures and comments about the victim on the night of her assault, was sorry for what had transpired. This is but one example, and whether new media changes public opinion regularly needs to be researched. Did new media in this case impact more than just public opinion? Couldn't we argue that it impacted the outcome of the case?

Conversely, Salter's (2013) case studies highlight how, though some headway is being made to reformulate the view of victims as marginalized voices, some voices are still privileged over others. As it is in society, white, affluent, and educated voices tend to receive more attention than non-white, working-class, and less-educated voices. Even adherence to gender roles may have an impact here; a young woman who characterizes the "good girl" persona might receive more credibility than a young woman who has a "bad girl" persona. Kim Duthie, one of Salter's (2013) case studies, was an Australian 16-year-old high school student, who accused football players of sexual abuse and used new media to broadcast her story. While legacy media did pick up the story, she did not hold out as a sympathetic victim over time and there were backlash Facebook pages devoted to discrediting or disparaging her as a person. The lack of sympathy for her story could be attributed to her lack of financial resources, lack of family support, and behavior that was viewed as promiscuous.

Another sympathetic victim in the United States demonstrates how counterpublics can be a place for social and collective outrage. The sentencing of Brock Turner, discussed at the beginning of this chapter, brought on a social media hailstorm where the victim's letter was posted originally on Buzzfeed (Buzzfeed said the letter was shared with them by the victim) and reposted on numerous social media sites. The letter also received significant attention in legacy media. Most significantly, CNN anchor Ashleigh Banfield read the letter aloud on her show. This letter (see https://www.buzzfeed.com/katiejmbaker/heres-the-powerful-letter-the-stanford-victim-read-to-her-ra?utm_term=.shEOmGDL1#.hqDYQX958) had an effect, which caused people to talk about this case and the injustice of the light sentence Turner received (Baker 2016). The counterpublics of this case received national attention and raised awareness regarding the plight of sexual assault victims.

Regarding other victimization experiences, counterpublics can assist in the development and growth of a social movement. As mentioned in Chap. 3, the Black Lives Matter Movement counters the *criminalblackman* narrative, attempting to highlight the victimization of people of color particularly at the hands of law enforcement. The Black Lives Matter Movement began as a Twitter hashtag #BlackLivesMatter, created by activists in 2013 (Freelon et al. 2016). These activists, Alicia Garza, Patrisse Cullors, and Opal Tometi, created the hashtag in response to the acquittal of George Zimmerman for the murder of Trayvon Martin. It was not until the Ferguson protests in August 2014 that #BlackLivesMatter became a popular hashtag, which was later followed by the development of chapters of the Black Lives Matter organization. In their conclusion, Freelon et al. write that it is not possible to measure the exact impact of the internet on the Black Lives Matter Movement. Even with this limitation, they found that "activists used digital tools to generate alternative narratives about police violence to counter the so-called neutrality of the mainstream press. These narratives affirmed the value of unarmed Black lives" (p. 78).

The Black Lives Matter Movement draws attention to the racial hierarchy in the United States and sheds light on who is treated as a real victim. The Black Lives Matter highlights black lives, such as Trayvon Martin, Michael Brown, Sandra Bland, and Eric Garner, that have been cut short by police or vigilantes and calls for them to be viewed as victims of murder who matter. As discussed previously in this chapter, whites can be viewed as real victims, white children can be viewed as real victims, but most black or Hispanic individuals, especially men, cannot be viewed as real victims. This is representative of the *racial hierarchy* that was created in the United States and Europe during the times of slavery. During this time, media imagery and messages demonstrated whites as "civilized" and black as "savage" (Hall 2003). Hall (2003) called this the *racialized regime of representation* and was a step toward the "othering" we wrote about in Chap. 3. This "othering" was key to the creation of the *criminalblackman* (Russell-Brown 2009) as we discussed in Chap. 3, and continues to affirm understandings of who is and is not a criminal or a victim.

Conclusion

This chapter focused on the media's construction of victimization. Similar to Chap. 3, we see how perceptions that have been influenced by the media highlight who we see as an ideal victim even though the reality of victimization is far more complicated. New media is impacting perceptions of victims and at times even challenging preconceived social constructions through counterpublics.

We end this chapter by thinking about what research needs to be conducted with new media and victimization. As we wrote this chapter, we realized more research on the impact of new media on perceptions of victimization needs to occur. In particular, how impactful are counterpublics? Does #BlackLivesMatter change perceptions or does it mobilize people who already knew there was an issue with police violence against people of color? What are the negative effects of new media on perceptions of victimization? Does new media impact public opinion and does it impact the outcome of cases?

Regarding educational and challenging hashtags, we are curious about their effect. Do hashtags actually challenge the dominant narrative or is it more of an echo chamber? Regarding hashtags like #YesAllWomen or #MeToo, can it help victims feel less alone because they have a somewhat safe space where they can feel supported? As we wrapped up writing this book in the fall of 2017, #MeToo drew extensive attention to the extent of sexual harassment and assault. People shared their experiences of victimization and, in some cases, also named their perpetrator, through this hashtag. Unlike traditional media, new media provides a platform for people who experience sexual assault to speak out and tell their own truth. It is likely that multiple and diverse voices are represented on new media, whereas in legacy media they are largely ignored. Research needs to help us better understand whose voices are represented on new media and the impact of these voices.

In the next chapter, we turn to how new media impacts the perpetration of crime. New media is not only a place for victims to respond to their victimization, but it is now a platform for crime to occur. We explore new forms of criminal behavior that have emerged with developments in new media.

Discussion Questions

1. Review the list of characteristics of an ideal victim (Christie 1986) given earlier in the chapter. Do these characteristics need to be updated? If so, how?
2. What are the consequences of the social construction of the ideal victim?
3. Thinking about the social media you consume, how are ideas about victimization being challenged? How do you think #MeToo is changing the dialog around sexual assault and harassment?

References

Media References

Abad-Santos, A. (2013, March 20). The Steubenville rape apologists may make you forget you're mad at CNN. *The Atlantic*. Retrieved from http://www.theatlantic.com/national/archive/2013/03/steubenville-rape-twitter-cnn/317144

Baker, K. J. (2012, December 17). We wouldn't know about the Steubenville rape case if it wasn't for the blogger who 'complicated' things. *Jezebel*. Retrieved from http://jezebel.com/5969076/we-wouldnt-know-about-thes-teubenville-rape-case-if-it-wasnt-for-the-blogger-who-complicated-things

Baker, K. J. (2016, June). Here is the powerful letter the Stanford victim read aloud to her attacker. *BuzzFeed*. Retrieved from https://www.buzzfeed.com/katiejmbaker/heres-the-powerful-letter-the-stanford-victim-read-to-her-ra?utm_term=.shEOmGDL1#.hqDYQX958

Baysinger, T. (2016, June 7). How Buzzfeed became the outlet that made the Stanford rape victim's letter go viral. *Adweek*. Retrieved from http://www.adweek.com/digital/how-buzzfeed-became-outlet-make-stanford-rape-victims-letter-go-viral-171870/

BBC. (2015, March 3). Delphi rapists says victim shouldn't have fought back. *BBC News*. Retrieved from http://www.bbc.com/news/magazine-31698154

Bever, L. (2016, June 4). 'You took away my worth': A sexual assault victim message to her Stanford attacker. *Washington Post*. Retrieved from https://www.

washingtonpost.com/news/early-lead/wp/2016/06/04/you-took-away-my-worth-a-rape-victim-delivers-powerful-message-to-a-former-stanford-swimmer/?utm_term=.50f4b570e910

Casarez, J. (2016). The death of JonBenet: A case that's captivated the country for 20 years. *CNN*. Retrieved from http://www.cnn.com/2016/12/13/us/jonbenet-ramsey-case/

Duke, A. (2014, May 27). Timeline to 'Retribution': Isla Vista attacks planned over years. *CNN*. Retrieved from http://www.cnn.com/2014/05/26/justice/california-elliot-rodger-timeline/index.html

Erdely, S. R. (2014, July). The transgender crucible. *Rolling Stone*. Retrieved from https://www.rollingstone.com/culture/news/the-transgendercrucible-20140730

Klausner, A. (2015, May 19). Columbia student takes mattress to graduation while the student she accused of assault is forced to watch as he graduated alongside her. *Dailymail.com*. Retrieved from http://www.dailymail.co.uk/news/article-3088144/Columbia-University-student-takes-mattress-graduation-one-vowed-carry-campus-alleged-rapist-expelled-school.html

Koehler, S. (2013, September). From the mouths of rapists: The lyrics of Robin Thicke's blurred lines. *Sociological Images*. Retrieved from https://thesocietypages.org/socimages/2013/09/17/from-the-mouths-of-rapists-the-lyrics-of-robin-thickes-blurred-lines-and-real-life-rape/

LaChance, N. (2016, September 2). Media continues to refer to Brock Turner as a 'Stanford Swimmer' rather than a rapist. *The Intercept*. Retrieved from https://theintercept.com/2016/09/02/media-continues-to-refer-to-brock-turner-as-a-stanford-swimmer-rather-than-a-rapist/

Plait, P. (2014, May). Not all men: How discussing women's issues gets derailed. *Slate Blog*. Retrieved from http://www.slate.com/blogs/bad_astronomy/2014/05/27/not_all_men_how_discussing_women_s_issues_gets_derailed.html

Sullivan, R. (2016, February 22). Former and current male college students launch lawsuits against US universities over sexual assault allegations. *News.com.au*. Retrieved from http://www.news.com.au/lifestyle/real-life/true-stories/former-and-current-male-college-students-launch-lawsuits-against-us-universities-over-sexual-assault-allegations/news-story/75191d565371847e52dd93964eafc54a

Academic References

Belknap, J. (2009). *The invisible woman: Gender, crime & justice* (3rd ed.). Belmont: Thomson Wadsworth.

Black, M. C., Basile, K. C., Breiding, M. J., Smith, S. G., Walters, M. L., Merrick, M. T., & Stevens, M. R. (2011). The National Intimate Partner and Sexual Violence Survey: 2010 summary report. The Centers for Disease Control and Prevention, National Center for Injury Prevention and Control. http://www.cdc.gov/ViolencePrevention/pdf/NISVS_Report2010-a.pdf

Bureau of Justice Statistics. (2014). *Non-fatal domestic violence, 2003–2012.* Retrieved from https://www.bjs.gov/content/pub/pdf/ndv0312.pdf

Bureau of Justice Statistics. (2016). *Criminal victimization, 2015.* Retrieved from https://www.bjs.gov/content/pub/pdf/cv15.pdf

Bureau of Justice Statistics. (2017). *Percent of violent victimizations by victim-offender relationship, 2010–2015.* Generated using the NCVS Victimization Analysis Tool at www.bjs.gov.

Burt, M. (1980). Cultural myths and supports for rape. *Journal of Personality and Social Psychology, 38*, 217–230.

Canadian Centre for Justice Statistics. (2016). *Family violence in Canada: A statistical profile, 2014.* Retrieved from https://www.statcan.gc.ca/access_acces/alternative_alternatif.action?l=eng&loc=/pub/85-002-x/2016001/article/14303-eng.pdf

Carrabine, E., Iganski, P., Lee, M., Plummer, K., & South, N. (2004). *Criminology: A sociological introduction.* London: Routledge.

Chancer, L. (2005). *High profile crimes: When legal cases become social causes.* Chicago: Chicago Press.

Christie, N. (1986). Ideal victim. In E. Fattah (Ed.), *Crime policy to victim policy* (pp. 17–30). London: Palgrave Macmillan.

Conrad, J. (1999). Lost innocent and sacrificial delegate: The Jonbenet Ramsey murder. *Childhood, 6*(3), 313–351.

CPSV. (2014). https://cspv.hu/read/11/2014/uj_magyar_kozep

Dalla, R. L., Xia, Y., & Kennedy, H. (2003). You just give them what they want and pray they don't kill you: Street-level sex workers' reports of victimization, personal resources, and coping strategies. *Violence Against Women, 9*(11), 1367–1394.

Deering, K. N., Amin, A., Shoveller, J., Nesbitt, A., Garcia-Moreno, C., Duff, P., Argento, E., & Shannon, K. (2014). A systematic review of the correlates of violence against sex workers. *American Journal of Public Health, 104*(5), 42–54.

DeKeseredy, W. S. (2011). *Violence against women: Myths, facts, controversies.* Toronto: University of Toronto Press.

DeKeseredy, W. S. (2016). Using crime surveys as tools of critical insight and progressive change. In M. H. Jacobsen & S. Walklate (Eds.), *Liquid criminology: Doing imaginative criminological research* [E-book]. Oxon: Routledge.

DeKeseredy, W., Dragiewicz, M., & Schwartz, M. D. (2017). *Abusive endings: Separation and divorce violence against women.* Oakland: University of California Press.

DeKeseredy, W. S., Fabricius, A., & Hall-Sanchez, A. (2015). Fueling aggrieved entitlement: The contribution of Women Against Feminism postings. In W. S. DeKeseredy & L. Leonard (Eds.), *Crimsoc report 4: Gender, victimology & restorative justice* (pp. 1–33). Sherfield Gables: Waterside Press.

Donnermeyer, J., & DeKeseredy, W. (2014). *Rural criminology. New directions in critical criminology.* Oxon: Routledge.

Dragiewicz, M. (2008). Patriarchy reasserted: Fathers' rights and anti-VAWA activism. *Feminist Criminology, 3*(2), 121–144.

Dragiewicz, M. (2011). *Equality with a vengeance.* Boston, MA: Northeastern University Press.

Dragiewicz, M., & Lindgren, Y. (2009). The gendered nature of domestic violence: Statistical data for lawyers considering equal protection analysis. *American University Journal of Gender, Social Policy & the Law, 229*(17), 1–41.

Dragiewicz, M., & Lindgren, Y. (2011). *Equality with a vengeance.* Lebanon: Northeastern University Press.

Edwards, K. M., Turchik, J. A., Dardis, C. M., Reynolds, N., & Gidycz, C. A. (2011). Rape myths: History, individual and institutional-level presence, and implications for change. *Feminist Forum, 65,* 76–773.

Eigenberg, H., & Garland, T. (2008). Victim blaming. In L. J. Moriarty (Ed.), *Controversies in victimology* (2nd ed., pp. 21–36). Newark: Elsevier Press.

Fox, R. L., Van Sickel, R. W., & Steiger, T. L. (2007). *Tabloid justice: Criminal justice in an age of media frenzy* (2nd ed.). Boulder: Lynne Reiner Publishing.

Franiuk, R., Seefelt, J. L., & Vandello, J. A. (2008). Prevalence of rape myths in headlines and their effects on attitudes toward rape. *Sex Roles, 58*(11–12), 790–801.

Freelon, D., McIlwain, C. D., & Clark, M. D. (2016, February 29). *Beyond the hashtags: #Ferguson, #Blacklivesmatter, and the online struggle for offline justice.* Retrieved from http://cmsimpact.org/resource/beyond-hashtags-ferguson-blacklivesmatter-online-struggle-offline-justice/

Gabiddon, S. L., & Greene, H. T. (2013). *Race & crime* (3rd ed.). Thousand Oaks: Sage.

Gabbidon, S. L., & Greene, H. T. (2009). *Race and crime* (2nd ed.). Thousand Oaks: Sage.

Gillespie, L. K., Richards, T. N., Givens, E. M., & Smith, M. D. (2013). Framing deadly domestic violence: Why the media's spin matters in newspaper coverage of femicide. *Violence Against Women, 19*(2), 222–245.

Greer, C. (2010). News media criminology. In E. McLaughlin & T. Newburn (Eds.), *The Sage handbook of criminological theory* (pp. 490–513). Thousand Oaks: Sage.

Hall, S. (2003). The spectacle of the 'other. In S. Hall (Ed.), *Representation: Representations and signifying practices* (pp. 223–283). Thousand Oaks: Sage.

Hayes, R. M., & Kwiatkowski, N. (2015, November 17–22). Domestic violence, an isolated incident: How the media constructs domestic violence in the NFL. *American Society of Criminology*, Washington, DC.

Hayes, R. M., & Weigand, A. (2015, September 2–5). #notallmen, #yesallwomen: Competing discourses of male violence on Twitter. *European Society of Criminology*, Porto.

Heerde, J. A., & Hemphill, S. A. (2013). Stealing and being stolen from: Perpetration of property offenses and property victimization among homeless youth – A systematic review. *Youth & Society, 48*(2), 265–300.

Jewkes, Y. (2015). *Media & crime* (3rd ed.). London: Sage.

Koo, D. J., Chitwood, D. D., & Sanchez, J. (2008). Violent victimization and the routine activities/lifestyle of active drug users. *Journal of Drug Issues, 38*, 1105–1138.

Krahe, B., Tomaszewska, P., Kuyper, L., & Vanwesenbeeck, I. (2014). Prevalence of sexual aggression among young people in Europe: A review of the violence from 27 EU countries. *Aggression and Violent Behavior, 19*(5), 545–558.

Lab, S. P., Williams, M. R., Holcomb, J. E., Burek, M. W., King, W. R., & Buerger, M. E. (2011). *Criminal justice: The essentials* (2nd ed.). New York: Oxford University Press.

Laidler, K. J., & Mann, R. M. (2008). Anti-feminist backlash and gender relevant crime initiatives in the global contest. *Feminist Criminology, 3*(2), 79–81.

Liebler, C. M. (2010). Me(di)a culpa?: The "missing white woman syndrome" and media self-critique. *Communication, Culture & Critique, 3*(4), 549–565.

Lipsky, S., Caetano, R., & Roy-Byrne, P. (2009). Racial and ethnic disparities in police-reported intimate violence and risk of hospitalization among women. *Women's Health Issues, 19*(2): 109–118. Retrieved from https://www.ncbi.nlm.nih.gov/pmc/articles/PMC2757408/

Min, S., & Feaster, J. C. (2010). Missing children in national news coverage: Racial and gender representations of missing children cases. *Communication Research Reports, 27*(3), 207–216.

O'Hara, S. (2012). Monsters, playboys, virgins and whores: Rape myths in the news media's coverage of sexual violence. *Language and Literature, 21*(3), 247–259.

Phillips, N. D. (2017). *Beyond blurred lines: Rape culture in popular media.* Lanham: Rowan & Littlefield.

Planty, M., Langton, L., Krebs, C., Berzofsky, M., & Smiley-McDonald, H. (2013). *Female victims of sexual violence, 1994–2010.* Bureau of Justice Statistics. Retrieved from https://www.bjs.gov/content/pub/pdf/fvsv9410.pdf

Rentschler, C. (2015). Safetytipsforladies: Feminist twitter takedowns of victim blaming. *Feminist Media Studies, 15*(2), 353–356.

Russell-Brown, K. (2009). *The color of crime* (2nd ed.). New York: New York University Press.

Salter, M. (2013). Justice and revenge in online counter-publics: Emerging responses to sexual violence in the age of social media. *Crime, Media and Culture, 9*(3), 225–242.

Scott Ham, M., & Burton, F. (2006). A study of blood and urine alcohol concentrations in cases of alleged drug-facilitated sexual assault in the United Kingdom over a 3-year period. *Journal of Clinical Forensic Medicine, 13*(3), 107–111.

Simmons, C., & Woods, J. (2015). The overrepresentation of white missing children in national television news. *Communication Research Reports, 32*(3), 239–245.

Singular, S. (1999). *Presumed guilty: An investigation into the Jon Benet Ramsey case, the media, and the culture of pornography.* Beverley Hills: New Millennium Entertainment.

Smith, P., & Welchans, S. (2000). Peer education. *Violence Against Women, 6*(11), 1255–1268.

Stevens, A., Berto, D., Frick, U., Kerschl, V., McSweeney, T., Schaaf, S., Tartari, M., Turnbull, P., Trinkl, B., Uchtenhange, A., Waidner, G., & Werdenich, W. (2007). The victimization of dependent drug users: Findings from a European study, UK. *European Journal of Criminology, 4*(4), 385–408.

Straus, M. A. (1979). Measuring intrafamily conflict and violence: The conflict tactics (CT) scales. *Journal of Marriage and Family, 41*, 75–88.

Straus, M. A. (1993). Physical assaults by women: A major problem. In R. J. Gelles & D. R. Loseke (Eds.), *Current controversies on family violence* (pp. 67–87). Thousand Oaks: Sage.

Suarez, E., & Gadalla, T. M. (2010). Stop blaming the victim: A meta-analysis on rape myths. *Journal of Interpersonal Violence, 25,* 2010–2035.

Surette, R. (2015). *Media, crime, & criminal justice: Images, realities, and policies* (5th ed.). Stamford: Cengage Learning.

Surette, R., & Gardiner-Bess, R. (2014). Media entertainment, and crime: Prospects and concerns. In B. Arrigo & H. Bersot (Eds.), *The Routledge handbook of international crime and justice studies* (pp. 373–396). New York: Routledge.

van Kesteren, J., van Dijk, J., & Mayhew, P. (2014). The international crime victims' surveys: A retrospective. *International Review of Victimology, 20*(1), 49–69.

Walklate, S. (2007). *Imagining the victim of crime.* New York: Open University Press.

5

#FutureCrime: What Is Crime in the Age of New Media?

Steve Stephens killed Robert Godwin, Sr. in Cleveland, Ohio (United States), on April 16, 2017. Stephens, who is commonly referred to as the Facebook Killer, recorded the murder and posted the video on Facebook. According to reports, the video was available on his Facebook page for two hours before Facebook took the video down. This case has led to critiques of how Facebook handles criminal content (e.g. Solon 2017). Facebook founder and CEO, Mark Zuckerberg, addressed this crime by saying: "We have a lot more to do here. We're reminded of this this week by the tragedy in Cleveland. And, our hearts go out to the family and friends of Robert Godwin, Sr…. We will keep doing all we can to prevent tragedies like this from happening" (The Guardian 2017).

The commission and control of crime are changing due to new media. As we see in the Facebook Killer example, crimes are being documented online and questions are being asked about the responsibility of new media in crime control responses. In this chapter, we explore crime and victimization in the context of new media. This chapter draws on points mentioned in earlier chapters about the role of new media in crime and addresses them in more depth.

New media presents challenges for defining and controlling crime. It literally becomes a question of what is a crime? Crime is commonly defined

© The Author(s) 2018
R. M. Hayes, K. Luther, *#Crime*, Palgrave Studies in Crime, Media and Culture,
https://doi.org/10.1007/978-3-319-89444-7_5

as behavior that violates the law and results in punishment. A consensus definition of crime argues that what is defined as being illegal is a reflection of the values of mainstream society and that it is illegal because it causes harm (Siegel 2015). Based on this definition, is knowingly or unknowingly posting false information online a criminal activity? For example, after the Boston Bombing (see box *Boston Bombing*), citizens identified the wrong person as the bomber and incited harassment against his family, which brought them unnecessary pain as he was missing, but had committed suicide (Lee 2013). Should these individuals be held responsible for the harm caused to the wrongly identified person's family? Likewise, in the case of the Chibok girls, who were kidnapped in Nigeria (see box *Chibok Girls of Nigeria*), news reports that were posted and reposted on social media said that the Chibok girls were not really kidnapped and claimed the story was a fake. This is thought to have negatively impacted the humanitarian effort to rescue the girls (Busari 2017). Should those who posted claims that this human rights crisis was fake be held responsible? In both of these cases we can see the social harm that was caused—in one case, a wrongly identified suspect's family experienced harassment and, in the other case, help for kidnapped children may have been delayed. As mentioned earlier in this paragraph, the consensus definition of crime suggests that what is defined as crime is generally agreed upon. As crimes using new media are relatively new, there might not yet be agreement about this behavior as criminal. Another definition of crime, the interactionist definition, argues that behavior becomes criminal when society constructs it as criminal (Siegel 2015). With these new media examples, it may be that it will take time for society to begin to view this behavior as criminal. In the meantime, cases like these draw attention to how new media is challenging definitions of crime and the pursuit of justice.

Boston Bombing On April 15, 2013, two bombs were set off at the Boston Marathon in Boston, Massachusetts (United States) (History.com 2014). This resulted in the deaths of three people, in addition to injuries suffered by at least another 260 people. Two brothers were identified as suspects, and one was killed in a shootout with police. The second brother, Dzokhar Tsarnaev, was found guilty of 30 federal charges and is currently incarcerated in a

(continued)

(continued)

federal prison. Even though media, public, and political rhetoric tried to suggest that they were with a terrorist organization, this was not found to be the case after the investigation. What makes this case pertinent to this book on media and crime is how new media covered the case and how a person was wrongly identified (Lee 2013).

Chibok Girls of Nigeria In 2014, Boko Haram kidnapped 276 girls from school; over 100 are still missing (BBC 2017). Reportedly, the girls were going to take their exams and the motivation for the kidnapping was Boko Haram's resistance to Western education. This case began a large social media campaign called #BringBackOurGirls that was meant to raise international awareness to encourage people to send assistance.

Another way that media, and specifically new media, are changing crime is through the online behavior of groups. Some behaviors of groups gathered online for organized activities can be labeled as criminal. For example, Anonymous (see box *Anonymous*) has organized illegal activities, such as hacking, through social media sites like 4chan. Media scholars Marwick and Lewis (n.d.) argue that the alt-right/white supremacists are rising partially because of their ability to gather online and manipulate social media. Previously, people who held these beliefs would have had a more difficult time gathering because their message is not socially acceptable, and they are often isolated from each other. Through new media, such as Reddit, they can gather online and plan their physical gatherings. As legacy media also depends on social media for information and stories, the manner in which social media is structured (e.g. clickbait and algorithms) are areas ripe for manipulation where misinformation and propaganda are easily spread (Marwick and Lewis n.d.). Although these online conversations and propaganda postings are not necessarily criminal themselves, unless they specifically threaten harm, these conversations can lead to criminal behaviors.

We saw this in the wake of the Steubenville, Ohio, (United States) rape case with Deric Lostutter who is associated with Anonymous. Acting with others connected with Anonymous, Lostutter allegedly posted videos threatening the school saying that they had hacked the school's websites compromising people's emails and personal information (Kushner 2013). Lostutter was sentenced to 24 months in federal prison for "conspiring to illegally access a computer without authorization and lying to an FBI agent" (United States Department of Justice 2017).

Anonymous Originating on the page 4chan, Anonymous is a loosely affiliated group of people on the internet (Coleman 2014). This group is often termed "hacktivists" for their engagement in activities that are seen as fighting for the social good, such as the Steubenville rape case we listed in Chap. 4. Anonymous is a global entity and they have hacked into government, corporate, and religious websites and have engaged in public demonstrations commonly wearing their signature Guy Fawkes mask (Coleman 2014).

As we began to write this chapter, we were surprised by the lack of research on crime commission through new media, especially within criminology. We believe research is lagging in this area because of (1) the time that it takes academics to study and publish about new forms of crime, (2) the disconnect between criminology and media studies, (3) researchers' inability to keep up with the quick rate at which technology changes, and (4) researchers' lack of access to online communities which are vast and international. To address the problem of limited literature for a final chapter addressing new media crime, we decided to organize the chapter around four crimes utilizing new media. In each section, we begin with an example highlighting a new media crime, followed by definitions, connections to the existing scholarly literature, discussion of the prevalence of the activity, and an overview of existing legal sanctions. This allows us to highlight the limited scholarship on these new forms of crime, while also posing questions for future research.

Definitions

We begin by providing definitions to guide your reading of this chapter. As this chapter does not discuss more commonly understood and studied crimes, such as murder, robbery, or assault, we think it is necessary to spend some time clarifying these new forms of crime. Here are some terms that we will be using throughout this chapter:

4chan and *8chan*: names of the social media boards that we introduced in Chap. 1.

Cyberbullying: "willful and repeated harm inflicted through the medium of electronic text" (Patchin and Hinduja 2006, p. 152).

Cyberstalking: "refers to the crime of using the Internet, email, or other types of electronic communications to stalk, harass, or threaten another person. Cyberstalking most often involves sending harassing emails, instant or text messages, or social media posts, or creating websites for the sole purpose of tormenting the victim." (https://legaldictionary.net/cyberstalking/, 2017).

Carriage Service: means an internet service. This could be in a home or on a mobile device.

Doxxing: "publishing personal details of a victim in relation to rape threats and sexually violent content"(Powell and Henry 2016, p. 8).

Hacking: "the term hacker is defined as a person who accesses computers and information stored on computers without obtaining permission." (Prasad 2014, p. 24).

Hacktivist: a term that is attributed to Wikileaks (Lindgren and Lundstrom 2011), combines activist with hacking and is assigned to groups who appear to be accessing computers and information without permission, but in the name of a good cause or for the greater good.

Revenge Porn: The colloquial term for what academics call "image-based sexual exploitation" or "image-based sexual abuse." Revenge porn includes "the unauthorized creation and distribution of sexual images" (Henry and Powell 2015, p. 759).

Sextortion: is the act of coercing a person into a sexualized or sexual activity through some kind of pressure (Henry and Powell 2016a).

Sexting: the exchange of sexually explicit materials via cell phone, internet, or other electronic media (Mitchell et al. 2012).

Sexualized Photoshopping: "without consent, a pornographic image is superimposed onto an individual's head/body part, such that it looks as if that individual is engaged in the pornographic activity" (McGlynn et al. 2017, p. 9).

Upskirting: As part of voyeurism that is not covered in legislation is upskirting."This involves the non-consensual taking of images of an individual's pubic area underneath their outer clothing in public places" (McGlynn et al. 2017, p. 8).

Voyuerism: "is the surreptitious viewing, and/or photographing or recording of images, of sexual or 'private acts' for the purposes of sexual gratification, where the perpetrator knows the other person does not consent to being observed for sexual gratification, with perpetrators colloquially described as 'peeping toms'" (McGlynn et al. 2017, p. 7).

Swatting: contacting emergency services as a prank to get a swat team to go to an unsuspecting person's location (Barratt and Bishop 2015)

Trolling: in the most broad sense it is posting messages on a communication network with the intent to provoke, offend, or incite a negative emotional response (Bishop 2013).

Case Studies of New Media Crime

In the remaining portion of the chapter, we focus our attention on four case studies of new media crime. Each case study addresses a particular form of new media crime—trolling, revenge porn, cyberbullying, and performance crime—and examines prevalence, criminal legal response and emerging questions. Although there are ways that each of these new media crimes overlap, we choose them because we think they highlight distinct criminal behaviors.

Case Study 1: Gamergate: The Story of Trolling

Gamergate is the story of a viral hashtag that occurred after Zoe Quinn, a female game developer, was the victim of death threats and harassment targeting her sex life. The harassment occurred after she attempted to publish her game *Depression Quest* and appeared to have been instigated by her previous partner Eron Gjoni (Hathaway 2014). Trolls doxed, harassed, and threatened (including threats of death and rape) Quinn to the point that she left her home out of fear for her safety. Many of the threats were online, and some by phone. Her address was posted online, which is referred to as doxxing. While there are conflicting stories about the origins and purpose of Gamergate, the abuse of Quinn is evident. Some reports suggest that the hashtag was meant to speak out about ethics in gaming differentiating it somewhat from Quinn (Hathaway 2014), but what appears to have occurred is an all out "internet culture war" (Dewey 2014). On one side are gamemakers and critics of the gaming industry (mostly women) who are highlighting the inequality, and overt misogyny, that is present in gaming culture and advocating for change. The other side are trolls, antifeminists, "traditionalists", and the like who argue that the gaming industry is fine as is (Dewey 2014). Zoe Quinn is not the only victim of this trolling campaign, as Brianna Wu was harassed and reportedly left her home after tweeting about Gamergate. During this time, even feminist gaming scholars Chess and Shaw (2015) were subjected to harassment and criticism.

After reading this case study, it is still complicated to define trolling. An informal definition of a troll was described in Phillips' (2015, p. 1) book that we find to be helpful. When Phillips asked her brother about trolls, he said: "A troll is a person who likes to disrupt stupid conversations on the internet. They have two basic rules: nothing should be taken seriously, and if it exists, there is porn of it," meaning the Lulz. Lulz essentially means for laughs, which is considered the purpose of trolling. Cook, Schaafsma, and Antheunis' (2018) research with trolls, did not yield a unifying definition of trolling. They did find that definitions of trolling usually fit into one or more of three categories: sensation-seeking, attack, and interaction-seeking. Trolling it is often used synonymously with hacking (C. L. Cook, personal communication, December 7, 2017) even though they are distinct from one another. Hacking is the taking of information from a computer or other technology-based location without consent and is an illegal activity. Trolling, though, is not always illegal activity (e.g. repeatedly commenting on a news article and arguing with others who are commenting). Trolling can include hacking (e.g. gaining access to someone's personal information and then threatening them), and often it does, but it does not have to.

Trolling activities largely, can be defined as some type of harassment. One kind of trolling, called RIP trolling (Phillips 2011), is where trolls go onto a memorial page dedicated to a deceased person and post abusive comments (see box *RIP Trolling*). We think it is difficult for most people to find the humor in the harassment of family and friends who have just lost a loved one. Trolling can also include impersonation, cyberstalking, and even swatting. The harm caused by trolling can vary, but some of the examples, such as Gamergate listed earlier, have been quite severe. Trolling affects the victim's day-to-day life and threatens their sense of safety.

> *RIP Trolling* RIP trolling, which is also known as Memorial Trolling, occurs when "online instigators post abusive comments or images onto pages created for and dedicated to the deceased" (Phillips 2011, n.p.). In an examination of this type of trolling, Phillips argues that it is meant as a social critique of our social media posting obsessed society. Those who engage in RIP trolling see the memorial pages as disingenuous and deserving of the mean-spirited teasing.

The Gamergate case study includes cyberstalking and cybersexual harassment which was committed by many anonymous trolls. The anonymity of the trolls and the online nature of the behavior make it difficult to fit into the legal framework. Numerous people in numerous countries can be involved as both offenders and victims making prosecuting practically impossible. That is the complication with trolling; victims and offenders could be anywhere and how their behavior is defined and potentially punished depends on the country.

Student Activity *Look up your state or country's penal code definitions of stalking and harassment. Does the stalking and harassment perpetrated against Zoe Quinn fit within this particular legal code? Do you think it would be easy to prosecute a troll in your state or country based on these definitions of crime?*

When we speak of trolls, we may be speaking of one, or, as in the case study mentioned earlier, of many. Social media appears to provide the collective platform for people to create online communities, especially of the deviant nature. Trolls often connect through many social media sites (e.g. 4chan) and work together as a group. A group that is famous for the trolling activities is Anonymous (see box *Anonymous*), which grew through social media. As Trottier and Fuchs (2015, p. 34) state, regarding the growth of the Occupy Social Movement, Anonymous, or the 5* movement: "Social media are neither the causes of these phenomena nor are they entirely unimportant. Rather, they are spaces of complex manifestations of power, counter-power and power contradictions." Trolls work to take power away from others through their criminal behaviors. Some of the most well-known platforms for trolling are 4chan (Anonymous), Encyclopedia Dramatica, Something Awful, or the 5*. Groups emerge and grow within social media and are responsible for many illegal activities. Those online platforms, such as Encyclopedia Dramatica or Something Awful, provide a space where they are only disruptive online, where some of them, like 4chan, provide Anonymous a space to plan events that spill out into the streets and are demonstrative of a social movement.

As Anonymous originated in 4chan (Stryker 2011); Anonymous is the collective thus making 4chan the platform. 4chan and 8chan are where many trolls are housed, but participants of these platforms can avoid the group trolling. Lurkers or spectators usually do not engage with anyone (Coleman 2014) and instead just read the posted materials. The 4chan platform and Anonymous group, while highly visible, to our knowledge, is lacking social research. One example of Anonymous trolling is where they stated that they were to wage a cyberwar on IS (aka Daesh or ISIS) (Coleman 2014). It seems in this regard that they are more of an activist social movement that targets religious extremists than a trolling group that is just in it for the Lulz. They have also targeted people for social causes such as in support of sexual assault victims or against racism. Anonymous targeted Hal Turner, the right-wing radio personality, because they viewed him as racist (Coleman 2014). Most of these social media boards espouse to the ethos of free speech, and to attack someone on their racist speech appears to potentially run counter to this. Much of

4chan, 8chan, and Reddit are considered places where anything goes and groups can gather as all discussions are possible.

Regarding who the trolls are, Phillips (2011, 2015) argues that they are likely male, younger, and also most likely white as evidenced by the amount of misogynist and racist speech they engage in. A nonacademic evaluation of Twitter by Ross Benes, a Digiday Reporter, found that misyogynist, racist, and islamaphobic tweets are very common (Benes 2016; https://digiday.com/media/6-charts-twitters-troll-problem-numbers/); this evaluation also indicates that it is likely young, white, heterosexual males that engage in trolling behavior. Researchers have mentioned that finding female trolls is complicated, and when they do speak with them their intentions and behaviors are different than male trolls (C. L. Cook, personal communication, December 7, 2017). For example, women may be more likely to use trolling as a way to assert justice to retaliate against someone who is harassing them.

Trolling Trends

Population-based research on trolling would be difficult, and to our knowledge there is a lack of prevalence research. Therefore, we piecemealed the research together to provide a picture of the trends surrounding trolling. Using a broad definition of trolling as we do in this chapter, it would appear that trolling is possibly a fairly common behavior, and reading Phillips' (2015) book, we think that they would agree. According to Phillips (2015), Claire Hardaker, a linguist, examined the use of the word troll and argued that trolling is mainly about deception. One study conducted interviews with gaming trolls trying to assess whether the behavior was normative or deviant, with almost half of their sample (10 out of 22) indicating that it is an expected part of gaming. Some of the participants went on to indicate the YouTube channel dedicated to trolling. In YouTube, there is a channel called XboxAddictionz, which is dedicated to trolling videos in gaming and has 2.8 million subscribers. This indicates at the very least that people find viewing trolling videos entertaining. Another manner in which to assess the commonality of trolling behavior is through victimization research, which future research should address. To get a picture of what trolling looks like for women, Stevens and Aggarwal (2017) created a visual from tweets to four prominent Indian Women (See https://www.hindustantimes.com/interactives/lets-talk-about-trolls/whats-it-like-to-get-trolled-all-day-long/). While one troll could have many victims, it would highlight how widespread their reach is, and given that internet access is pretty universal, it seems that it is pretty widespread.

Although we are not aware of any large-scale representative studies examining the prevalence of harassment by trolls specifically, there are studies of the broader experience of online harassment. In a recent study, Lenhart et al. (2016) found that among a nationally representative survey of over 3000 Americans over the age of 15, 47% reported experiencing online harassment or abuse. They examined three different types of harassing behaviors: direct harassment, invasion of privacy, and denial of access. Specifically, 36% of the sample experienced direct harassment, which includes being threatened or called names. Thirty percent of respondents experienced invasion of privacy, which includes hacking, doxxing, and being tracked. Seventeen percent of participants reported denial of access, which occurs when technology is used against a person (e.g. sending lots of messages which shuts down someone's account or overwhelming a device through technical means). Lenhart et al.'s (2016) research found that men and women experience harassment at similar rates, but women experience more and harsher harassment, as do young people under 30 and sexual minorities (LGB). This study provides us with an understanding of the prevalence of online victimization, which is clearly not the same as trolling. That being said, we can speculate that some of the experiences of harassment documented in this study may be perpetrated by individuals who fit the definition of a troll.

Legal Response to Trolling

Although many people can see the harm that is caused by trolling, regulating trolling is challenging. Many of these challenges surround free speech and the limitations that can be placed on mainstream social media accounts such as Facebook, Twitter, or Instagram. The social media platforms do have some policies that prevent certain language; however, mainstream social media companies have been hesitant and, arguably, discriminant in their enforcement of the policies. The question is whether hate speech is protected, and constitutionally it is to a point by the First Amendment in the United States. There are hate speech statutes in countries such as the United Kingdom (Hare and Weinstein 2009) and France (Turley 2015). France has been leading in the laws against certain speech, and according to Turley (2015) they have gone too far.

Meanwhile in the United States, speakers who have been denied access to college campuses have argued that their freedom of speech is being violated and have been granted the right to speak. For example, White Supremacist Richard Spencer was originally denied to speak on University of Florida's campus in August 2017 (Yann 2017) and then the university reversed their decision due to issues surrounding free speech (Merelli 2017). The free speech issues are likely what prevents legislation in the United States from targeting trolling directly.

There are some attempts to regulate trolling in countries such as Australia and the United Kingdom. In Australia, "The *Criminal Code* Part 10.6 regulates internet services and some of the areas that the Part encompasses are child abuse material, child pornography, as well as using a carriage service to menace, harass or cause an offence to the reasonable person as stated in Part 10.6, Division 474.17(1)" (Findlaw.com 2017). Some states also have separate laws addressing this behavior. Findlaw (2017) suggests to seek legal advice if there is defamation of character and to report it to Australian Communications and Media Authority if the content is explicit. In the United Kingdom, according to the BBC (2016), there is legislation meant to address trolling behavior, particularly doxxing or inciting people to harass others online, but it appears vague on the standard of what is considered online harassment as it needs to be "grossly offensive." Critics argue that the legislation in reality will have little impact, and especially when you consider that trolling is often international. This means UK legislation would have no impact on a troll from the United States.

Case Study 2: The Fappening: Image-Based Sexual Abuse

Our second case study focuses on "The Fappening," which occurred in 2014 when hacked nude photos of Jennifer Lawrence and other celebrities were posted on 4chan (Williams 2017). Jennifer Lawrence reportedly felt violated, and these pictures were originally meant for her boyfriend at the time. The person responsible for the hacking was convicted and sent to a federal prison (Williams 2017). This criminal pursuit is not restricted to images of celebrities, though. In Australia in June 2015, a large amount of nude images of Australian women were posted on 8chan (Salter 2017).

Both of these are examples of *image-based sexual exploitation, image-based sexual abuse* or, *non-consensual pornography*, which are the formal terms used by scholars and are part of technology-faciliated sexual violence (box interview). Within this chapter, we chose to call it *image-based sexual abuse* (McGlynn and Rackley 2015; 2017). Commonly, this kind of behavior—posting nude photos online—is referred to as "revenge porn." This term is not only used colloquially, but it is also part of the legal definition in multiple US states (see https://www.cybercivilrights. org/revenge-porn-laws/), the United Kingdom (https://www.gov.uk/ government/uploads/system/uploads/attachment_data/file/405286/ revenge-porn-factsheet.pdf), and Australia (Lavoipierre 2017). Instead of using the term "revenge porn," scholars refer to it as *image-based sexual abuse* because it includes not only abuse by ex-partners, but also the non-consensual posting of pictures by hackers (McGlynn and Rackley 2015; 2017). Additionally, "revenge porn" is not an accurate term in that it invokes victim blaming and trivialization of the behavior. Revenge incurs at least some responsibility onto the victim as they must have done something wrong to deserve the posting of their image. Use of the word porn according to McGlynn and Rackley (2015) is designed to titillate and can distract from the behavior, and Hayes and Dragiewicz (submitted) argue that it also implies consent.

Technology-facilitated Sexual Violence: Q & A Dr Nicola Henry (RMIT University) & Dr Anastasia Powell (RMIT University)

Question: How is TFSV different from non-technologically facilitated sexual violence? How is TFSV similar to non-technologically facilitated sexual violence?

Cybercriminologists often distinguish conceptually between traditional crimes which have simply embraced technology ('technology-assisted crimes'), and the identification of new forms of criminal offending that have only become possible with advances in digital technologies. Some criminologists have concluded that there is nothing ultimately 'new' about cybercrime. For example, Peter Grabosky (2001: 243) argues that although some manifestations of virtual criminality are new, 'a great deal of crime committed with or against computers differs only in terms of the medium' and the crime is basically a 'recognizable crime committed in a completely different way'. Others, like David Wall (2001), claim that there are new forms of criminal activity in cyberspace, but use established categories of criminality such as cyber-theft, cyberbullying, virtual rape, and cyberstalking. Many criminologists make a compelling argument that although information communication technologies have enabled traditional crimes to be committed in new ways, the substantive and qualitative distinctions between offline and online criminality should not be overlooked (Burden & Palmer 2003; Capeller 2001; Furnell 2002; Pease 2001; Synder 2001; Yar 2005). Majid Yar (2005), for example, argued that new technologies at the very least act as a 'force multiplier', enabling potentially huge negative impacts on multiple victims from comparatively minimal resources or effort on the part of the offender. In an application of 'Routine Activity Theory' to cybercrime (the theory that crime just needs 'opportunity' to occur), Yar (2005) argued that there are three elements of the cyberspace environment that make possible a greater 'force' or impact of illicit activities, and thus are distinctive from traditional crime. These are: the collapse of spatial-temporal barriers (offenders can easily and more quickly target victims across a vast geographical, transnational reach); multiple connectivity (a single offender can reach thousands of targets); and the anonymity and plasticity of online identities, making deception easier, and detection and regulation a major challenge (Yar 2005). In other words, in the digital era, there are literally millions of potential targets or victims, numerous incentives for motivated offenders (both in terms of anonymity and the enormous potential reward for little expended effort), and largely an absence of capable guardianship.

As technology becomes more and more integrated into our everyday lives, the distinctions between 'traditional' and 'technology-assisted' crimes are becoming increasingly blurry. For example, GPS tracking or spyware may enable more monitoring and surveillance of victims, but yet such behaviors might be perpetrated alongside a whole set of other abusive behaviors, some of which do not involve any technology at all.

In relation to technology-facilitated sexual violence versus 'traditional' forms of sexual violence, there are similarly overlaps, distinctions, and blurred lines. While TFSV is not something fundamentally new, there are nonetheless new types of behaviors, and arguably new manifestations and impacts. On the one hand, technology may be merely a tool to enable perpetrators access to victims, for instance, perpetrators who use online dating sites to arrange to meet a victim in person and carry out a physical sexual assault. On the other hand, technology is not simply a tool in the hands of perpetrators in some acts of sexual violence, but is integral to the perpetuation of those harms. One example of this is the use of Internet sites to share nude or sexual images of a person without their consent to hundreds or thousands of others worldwide. In other words, while some acts of sexual violence will be carried out irrespective of the technology, other acts are only possible with the use of technology. Thus we argue that technology-facilitated sexual violence is better understood as an umbrella term for a set of diverse behaviours involving the use of technology to set up the act, to perpetrate the offense, and/or to cause multiple harms to victims. Although some might argue that these acts are recognizable crimes committed in new ways (see e.g. Grabosky 2001), we believe that it is imperative to understand the changing nature of sexual violence in a digital era, where technologies are not merely tools of abuse, coercion, and harassment, but are integral to perpetuating harm, suffering, and stigma to victims.

Question: What is your assessment of research on TFSV? Are scholars paying enough attention to TFSV? If not, what do you think is holding back scholarship on this topic?

With the rapid uptake of Internet-enabled devices, such as computers, laptops, mobile phones, and tablets, and online communication services, such as social media networks and social applications, it is perhaps unsurprising that digital technologies might be implicated in some way in sexually-based harms. While empirical studies have highlighted perpetrators' use of technology to facilitate domestic violence (see Burke et al., 2011; Dimond et al., 2011; Woodlock 2016), dating abuse (see Stonard et al. 2014; Zweig et al. 2013), cyberstalking (see Sheridan & Grant 2007; Spitzberg & Hoobler 2002), and the sexual exploitation of children (see Martin & Alaggia 2013; Mitchell et al. 2011; Westlake & Bouchard 2016), less research has focused on the varied nature and prevalence of TFSV more broadly against adults. Some exceptions include Thompson and Morrison's (2013) study on 'technology-based coercive behavior', which focuses on behaviors such as asking someone online for sexual information, or posting a sexually suggestive message or picture to someone's online profile. Other studies examine different behaviors; for instance, Gámez-Guadix et al. (2015: 145) define 'online victimization' as 'pressure to obtain unwanted sexual cooperation or the dissemination of a victim's sexual content through the Internet'. Similarly, Reyns et al. (2013) use Marcum et al.'s (2010) term 'cybervictimization' to refer to receiving sexually explicit images, harassment, and sexual solicitation. Our 2015 study (see Powell & Henry 2017) defines TFSV as including: technology-enabled sexual aggression (where technology is utilised to set up a rape or sexual assault); image-based sexual abuse (including the non-consensual creation, distribution, and/or threats to distribute/create, nude or sexual images); and online sexual harassment (including sexual solicitation, image-based harassment, gender-based hate speech, and online rape threats). Many existing empirical studies do not to categorize different behaviors into separate dimensions, and often 'online sexual harassment' (Barak 2005) or 'cyber harassment' (Citron 2014) serve as broad residual categories to capture a range of different digital acts of sexual aggression or harassment.

Increasingly, conceptual, practical, and legal distinctions are being made between different forms of TFSV, and empirical studies are beginning to examine these issues separately. For example, image-based violations, what some refer to as 'revenge porn', have become the focus of increasing research (see e.g. Branch et al. 2017; Gámez-Guadix et al. 2015; Garcia et al. 2015; Henry, Powell & Flynn 2017; Lenhart, Ybarra & Price-Feeney 2016; Morelli et al. 2016). To date, there have been very few qualitative studies on victim experiences of image-based sexual abuse. One exception is the study by Samantha Bates (2017) who conducted 18 in-depth semi-structured interviews with Canadian and US adult 'revenge porn' victims who had self-identified as victims or survivors. There is also a growing body of literature examining different forms of TFSV, for instance, online gender-based hate speech (see e.g. Jane 2017).

Question: Outside of academia, how do you think the general public perceives TFSV?

Just as date rape and sexual harassment have been, and continue to be, contested rather than acknowledged as forms of gendered violence, so too are digital forms of sexual violence and harassment regularly dismissed, minimized, or excused as 'normal' online behavior. Like more 'traditional' forms of sexual violence, community attitudes and beliefs contribute to underreporting, as well as low prosecution and conviction rates. In our survey on image-based sexual abuse among Australian adults aged between 16–49 (n=4,274) (see Henry, Powell & Flynn 2017), we found that while 4 out of 5 participants agreed that image-based abuse should be a crime, 70% of respondents agreed with the statement that 'People should know better than to take nude selfies in the first place, even if they never send them to anyone', and 62% agreed that 'If a person sends a nude or sexual image to someone else, then they are at least partly responsible if the image ends up online'. The problem, however, is that little research to date has explored community attitudes towards TFSV. That means we know little about how the general public perceives TFSV. Media reporting, public education campaigns, and anecdotal accounts on the different TFSV behaviors indicate that victim-blaming present obstacles to recognizing the harms associated with TFSV, and contribute to underreporting, as well as low prosecution and conviction rates (in similar ways to other forms of gendered violence).

In the qualitative component of our research into TFSV to date (see Henry & Powell 2015a; Powell & Henry 2016, 2017), many key stakeholders mentioned that victims are often turned away from police, told to turn off their computers or deactivate their social media accounts, or are treated as partly responsible for their own victimization. Part of the problem, we argue, is that physical, contact offenses continue to be treated far more seriously compared to non-physical 'forms of violence. This is further reinforced by the notion that 'cyberspace' is 'virtual' and therefore not real and as such separate from everyday life (Henry & Powell 2015b; Powell & Henry 2017). This results in a failure to capture the serious nature of technology-facilitated sexual violence.

We need more research that measures community attitudes towards TFSV, which will assist the development of public awareness campaigns, primary prevention (perpetrator and bystander) interventions, victim support activities, law reform, police training, and other measures.

Thinking about the examples at the start of this section, the first case would not be considered revenge porn per say, as the hacker had no previous relationship with Jennifer Lawrence or any of the other celebrities (as far as we know). The second case in Australia could have included ex-partners but we are unsure. Both of these cases fit the definition of image-based sexual abuse, where the prevailing notion is lack of consent for dissemination of nude imagery.

Another benefit of the term image-based sexual abuse is that it focuses on the harm to the victims, as opposed to the motives of the perpetrator, which brings attention to the non-consensual nature of the violation. This term also places it along the gamut of sexual violence legislation, meaning that sexual violence legislation might be able to be used to combat this harm. McGlynn, Rackley, and Houghton (2017) argue that image-based sexual abuse fits on the continuum with other forms of sexual violence. According to McGlynn et al. (2017), there are other behaviors that use technology and should also be included under the gamut of sexual violence. These include sexualized photoshopping, sextortion, upskirting, and voyeurism, all of which have been defined earlier in the chapter. Image-based sexual abuse is a form of online sexual harassment. Women are more likely to be the victims of online sexual harassment (Barak 2005; Henry and Powell 2016a). Henry and Powell (2016a) conducted a literature review of the empirical research on online sexual harassment and other forms of Technological Facilitated Sexual Violence (TFSV) (Box Interview with Henry and Powell). Among a German sample, 68.3% has reported experiencing online sexual harassment, with females reporting to have experienced this more often than men (Staude-Müller et al. 2012).

Another example of online sexual harassment would be receiving a picture of an unsolicited penis (aka dic pic) through a dating app such as tinder (Hayes and Dragweicz, submitted). Anedoctal evidence suggests sending dick pics is common, yet to our knowledge academic research has yet to study the phenomenon. However, the media has covered the issue; news stories, blogs, and social media posts all have coverage of sending pictures such as dick pics or posting "revenge porn."

For example, Gleeson (2016), in a story on ABC in Australia, wrote about how common and understudied sending dick pics is and how when victims that receive these pictures seek justice and turn around and "name and shame" the sender by reposting the picture could be violating revenge porn laws. Expanding beyond online sexual harassment, there is also online gender- and sexuality- based harassment and while the harassment could be of a sexual nature, there specifically are comments that are insulting to a person's gender or sexuality (examples include, but are not limited to, hate speech and impersonation) (Henry and Powell 2016a).

Image-Based Sexual Abuse Trends

According to Henry and Powell (2016a, b), there has been very little research examining image-based sexual abuse. This is complicated by conflicting definitions of image based sexual abuse, which makes it especially difficult to ascertain the scope of the problem. The research by Lenhart et al. (2016) on online victimization that we discussed earlier would also suit this category to an extent, but a recent study by Eaton et al. (2017, p. 4) attempted to address address the gap in the research on image-based sexual abuse by conducting "the first ever nationwide study to profile the rates of non-consensual pornography victimization and perpetration." It is not a representative sample, but it is large scale, and they found that 12.8% of their participants were victims or threatened of non-consensual pornography (aka image-based sexual abuse) with 5.2% of their sample reporting having been a perpetrator (Eaton et al. 2017). In other studies also, we see items that match the definition of image-based sexual abuse. A study by Gámez-Guadix et al. (2015, p. 146) about "online sexual victimization" encompasses some of this behavior. Gámez-Guadix et al. define online sexual victimization as:

> includ[ing] the experience of some of type of pressure through the Internet or mobile phones to obtain unwanted cooperation or sexual contact (e.g., share sexual information, send images with sexual content, or do something against the victim's wishes) or/and the distribution or dissemination by perpetrator of sexual images or information of the victim against his/her will.

This definition has essentially two parts with the second part being that of image-based sexual abuse. They created a ten-item instrument to measure this concept that followed the approach of the Conflict Tactics Scale (Straus et al. 1995). Overall, Gámez-Guadix et al. found that 41.6% of women and 31.9% of men had experienced online sexual victimization. The items that are specific to image-based sexual abuse include "disseminating or uploading to the internet photos or videos of you with erotic or sexual content without your consent," which had a reporting rate of 0.8% for women and 1.8% for men participants, and "disseminating information of an erotic or sexual nature about you without your consent," which had reporting rate of 2.5% for men and 3.8% for women (Gámez-Guadix et al. 2015, p. 150). The first finding regarding image-based sexual abuse is surprising, given the gendered context of this crime—Henry and Powell (2015) argue that there is inherent gender inequality and dominance in this crime. Essentially it is another crime which belongs in the violence against women continuum. The higher reporting rate by men than women may be explained by their sampling methods (this was not a population-based sample; it was a convenience sample) or the larger critiques of the Conflict Tactics Scale, which has received much criticism including that it fails to take into account context and ignores gender (DeKeseredy and Schwartz 1998). Although Gámez-Guadix et al.'s (2015) study finds that most online sexual abuse is not image-based sexual abuse, there is a need for more research using representative samples to be conducted. Another study, conducted by McAfee (2013), found from their sample of 1182 participants that one in ten ex-partners had threatened to post erotic or sexual pictures of their ex online, with 60% of these threats being carried out. Obviously, more research needs to be conducted, but from the early research there does appear to be a trend making it likely to need specific laws to address the issue.

Legal Response to Image-Based Sexual Abuse

With some countries such as the United States passing laws that criminalize image-based sexual abuse, we need to examine how often they are being used. Currently, statistics in the United States such as the Uniform

Crime Report (UCR), do not have a category for image-based sexual abuse as a crime nor does the National Crime Victimization Survey (NCVS). With the UCR recording crimes reported to the police and subsequent arrests, this would be a good way to ascertain if arrests for this crime were occurring in the United States. There are news stories that cover these crimes, and many of them focus on civil suits against the perpetrators. For example, in Michigan in 2017 a woman won a 600,000 suit against her ex-boyfriend for posting a video on Facebook without her permission (Brand-Williams 2017). There also could be legal recourse against the operators of the revenge porn sites (Franklin 2017), as in many instances they are encouraging these submissions and are acting with relative impunity. Taking down these sites would prevent the perpetrators from having a place to post them and would go a long way in preventing this crime.

Student Activity *Look up your state or country's penal code definitions of revenge porn. Do you think it would be easy to prosecute revenge porn in your state or country based on these definitions?*

Case Study 3: Cyberbullying

Our third case study moves the focus to the examination of cyberbullying. Much like our case study earlier, the crimes described in this section are aided by the availability of recording devices and the ease of social media sites for streaming. In 2010, at Rutgers University, Dharun Ravi video recorded his roommate, Tyler Clementi, having intimate relations with another person. Dharun streamed the act online and invited other students to view it. Tyler learned about the incident from his roommate's Twitter feed and shortly after the incident he took his own life (Tyler Clementi Foundation 2017). Ravi was convicted in 2012 on 15 counts, including invasion of privacy and bias intimidation, but in 2016 that ruling was overturned by the Supreme Court. He ended up pleading guilty in 2016 to a single count of attempted invasion of privacy and received time served (Gonzales 2016).

Cyberbullying, defined earlier in this chapter, is the online repetitive behavior or acts that are aggressive and target an individual. Hinduja and Patchin (2015, p. 11) include the following elements when defining cyberbullying:

Willful: the behavior has to be deliberate, not accidental.

Repeated: Bullying reflects a pattern of behavior, not just one isolated incident.

Harm: The target must perceive that harm was inflicted.

Computers, cell phones, and other electronic devices: This, of course, is what differentiates cyberbullying from traditional bullying

They argue that malicious intent is a key construct to both traditional bullying and cyberbullying, along with violence and repetition (Hinduja and Patchin 2015). Tyler Clementi's story indicates all of the above, except perhaps repetition. An example of cyberbullying that highlights Hinduja and Patchin's defining characteristics is one (or many) student(s) sending Facebook messages day after day to another student threatening violence. It can and likely includes name-calling, and, similar to in-person bullying, can include gender, sexuality, or racial epithets. When youth are involved, some of the psychosocial effects can be even more severe than for adults.

At this point, you may be thinking that cyberbullying sounds a lot like trolling. Both are focused on power and the perpetrator threatens and harasses his or her victim. We differentiate between cyberbullying and trolling because trolling tends to be subset of people, sometimes loosely organized and includes more than harassment. Cyberbullying is often an extension of in-person bullying and tends to be more localized than trolling. Often when cyberbullying is discussed socially, it includes young offenders and victims. In contrast, while trolls could be adolescents or adults, it often includes adult victims. Cook, a media scholar focused on trolls and trolling, stated that she found that when the trolls are young, the older trolls do not tolerate them and often out-troll them to get rid of them (C. L. Cook, personal communication, December 7, 2017). While cyberbullying and trolling are often used synonymously, in this section we will discuss only cyberbullying and new media's impact on that, focusing on youth. Most of the research on cyberbullying *is* with youth samples, and according to Garett, Lord, and Young (2016, p. 3), in their systematic review of cyberbullying, there is "a general consensus that cyberbullying only affects youths."

Compared with traditional bullying: the audience of cyberbullying is larger; the offender(s) does have the potential for anonymity as the victim might not know which of his or her peers are the bully; and, the victim is unable to escape the abuse. Cyberbullying varies as there are a multitude of online applications and internet programs (see list in Chap. 1) that can be used against a victim. One example was Yik Yak, which shut down in 2017. Yik Yak was based on one's location and users posted anonymously on the app based on that location. A student, or multiple students, could be in a classroom posting mean and offensive things about another student, and, if that student had the app, they could see these anonymous comments. Even gaming networks are places where cyberbullies can cause harm. Online gaming is popular among teens, and the anonymity it allows makes it easier to gang up on a player (Stopbullying.gov). Players can create avatars with alter-egos that are used to harass others.

Cyberbullying Trends

The media portrayal would certainly insist that cyberbullying is a common occurrence, but some scholars are arguing that it is an inflated issue (Hinduja and Patchin 2015) or perhaps a moral panic. As far as prevalence of cyberbullying, research has established that it does occur with some frequency, and in many countries. Early research on cyberbullying indicated that in a convenience sample of 1378 respondents under the age of 18, over 32% of the boys and over 36% of the girls had reported experiencing cyberbullying (Hinduja and Patchin 2008). Hinduja and Patchin (2015) argue that since 2007 about 25% of the students they have surveyed have indicated experiencing cyberbullying at some point. According to a recent report to the European Parliament, the 2014 EU Net Children Go Mobile Report demonstrated that 12% of 3500 children aged 9–16 experienced cyberbullying and the 2011 EU Kids Online report demonstrated that 6% of 25,142 children aged 9–16 have experienced online bullying (Pozza et al. 2016).

Legal Response to Cyberbullying

According to Hinduja and Patchin (2015), in the United States cyberbullying is prohibited by legislation more broadly prohibiting harassment. This includes the Civil Rights Act of 1974, which specifically outlawed harassment based on race, ethnicity, and religion, and the Educational Amendments of 1972 (Title IX), which included gender inequality and sexual harassment (Hinduja and Patchin 2015). For example, this could include gender-based harassment wherein a male student is harassed for acting in an effeminate manner. These acts and amendments plus the American Disabilities Act of 1990 are the legislation that encourages school administration to take action if there is behavior that is threatening students civil rights (Hinduja and Patchin 2015).

There are also court cases that set precedent to restrict student behaviors and speech on-campus, but they do not render those restrictions so freely when students set foot off campus. Response to cyberbullying done outside of school buildings after school hours on smartphones and laptops are more complicated. According to Hinduja and Patchin (2015, p. 121), the courts "will intervene in situations where off-campus speech is clearly harassing and threatening to students or staff and/or disruptive to the learning environment." However, these are not certain terms to which administrators can look to (meaning open for some interpretation). Therefore, whether administrators are *legally* allowed to intervene is unclear and differs by state. There are court cases which establish some precedents, but again these vary by state and are not always clear with guidelines as to what behaviors are punishable. While 49 states have antibullying laws, which include cyberbullying, schools still need to make sure that they do not violate the freedom of speech and expression of students.

New media is also helping to lead the charge against cyberbullying. There are new media campaigns to raise awareness and combat cyberbullying. Regarding our case study, #Upstanders is the twitter hashtag that encourages people to honor Tyler's memory and stand up to cyberbullies. Also, you may remember the It Gets Better Campaign that went viral.

Case Study 4: Performance Crimes and Terrorism

In 2015, in San Bernardino, California (United States), Syed Farook and Tashfeen Malik murdered 14 people and injured 22 people at the Inland Regional Center. Four hours after this mass murder, they were killed by police. The FBI investigated this crime as terrorism (Berman 2016). Labeling a crime as a terrorist activity is controversial in the United States as mass shooting events happen quite frequently and the term "terrorism" seems to be most likely applied if the people involved are assumed to be Muslim. In the investigation, the US Justice Department asked Apple to unlock Farook's iPhone. Due to so many unanswered questions about motivation for the crime and how they carried it out, the FBI wanted access to the iPhone in hopes that it would provide details for the investigation. Apple, in a customer letter on February 16, 2016 (https://www.apple.com/customer-letter/), wrote:

> We were shocked and outraged by the deadly act of terrorism in San Bernardino last December. We mourn the loss of life and want justice for all those whose lives were affected. The FBI asked us for help in the days following the attack, and we have worked hard to support the government's efforts to solve this horrible crime. We have no sympathy for terrorists…We have great respect for the professionals at the FBI, and we believe their intentions are good. Up to this point, we have done everything that is both within our power and within the law to help them. But now the U.S. government has asked us for something we simply do not have, and something we consider too dangerous to create. They have asked us to build a backdoor to the iPhone.

The FBI was able to access Farhook's iPhone without the help of Apple, and they dropped their court case against the company. This particular case of terrorism draws attention to the way that law enforcement investigation is restricted by policies governing the privacy of new media such as the smartphone.

After reading the previous case studies, this one may feel different because the crimes were not committed through new media. We chose this example as a case study because of other connections to new media. First, although evidence did not find that either of the shooters were formally associated with ISIS, prior to their mass murder, Malik posted a pledge from her and Farook to a terrorist leader associated with ISIS on Facebook (Berman 2016). Second, after the attacks, pictures of their apartment were taken and surfaced on propaganda by ISIS that was posted on social media (Koerner 2016). In particular, an image of their baby's crib stood out because it demonstrated how they risked everything—including their own child who is now without parents—for their cause. Last, families of the victims of this crime have filed lawsuits against Facebook, Twitter, and Google (Hamilton 2017). The families allege that these social media platforms and Google have given terrorist groups a place to share their beliefs and recruit participants. While it cannot be ascertained whether new media was the impetus for this particular instance of mass murder, we see new media playing a role in the perpetration of these crimes.

Terrorism is one of the oldest forms of performance crime (Surette 2015). Performance crimes are meant to capture the public's attention, to make a spectacle, as the acts of terrorism did in San Bernardino. Therefore, it means the intent of the criminal activity is to have an audience witness it. The audience could be immediate or after the fact, and in today's society the audience is mostly online. We also see these elements of a performance crime in the example at the start of the chapter of Steve Stephens, who used his Facebook account to document his plan and murder Robert Godwin, Sr.

The manner in which the media has previously covered performance crimes is changing. The script is being flipped so to speak, where those who commit the crime or their associates are defining the narrative through new media. According to Surette (2015), what constitutes a "crime and justice performance" (also called a performance crime) depends on how the term "performance" is defined and conceptualized in research, and new media has changed that conceptualization. Using Yar's (2012) work, Surette (2015, p. 196) argues that "the core central element of contemporary crime and justice performance is behavior created for digital distribution by either willing or unwilling performers." Performance crimes are usually recorded, shared, and distributed by the offender (Surette 2015). While our earlier-mentioned case study does not include the offenders themselves spreading news of the mass murder after the event (they could not as they were also casualties of their own violence), details and images were shared and spread through social media by terrorist groups (Koerner 2016). The spectacle of the act of terrorism was made.

Terrorism is one form of performance crime that has the ability to cause significant harm to large numbers of people. There are other forms of performance crime that utilize new media, such as "flash robs" (see box *Flash Rob*), but do not lead to the same level of harm as terrorism. Performance crimes are also tied to celebrity culture, yet unlike celebrity criminals (e.g. O. J. Simpson from Chap. 1), one *becomes* a celebrity from being a criminal (e.g. Al Capone) (Surette 2015). Think about the Elliot Rodger's case from Chap. 4, wherein after he engaged in stabbing and mass shooting (Rucker 2014), his YouTube video, *Retribution*, and his manifesto, *My Twisted World*, were located online and one can still access them. Just type his name into the Google search bar and his manifesto is at the top of the search. It is in the availability of his YouTube videos and manifesto where he provides his justifications for murder that we see how new media is impacting performance crimes (Surette 2015). Rodger is hardly the first murderer to create something to explain his criminal activity, but prior to new media, legacy media would not be able to dictate the narrative in this manner. While there are now many examples of performance crime, terrorism and political acts of protest historically were (Surette 2015) and, we argue, continue to be the main performance crimes.

> *Flash Rob* "Flash Rob," derived from the term "Flash Mob" (Zimmerman and Bustillo 2011), includes a group that runs into an establishment or attacks an individual. In August 2012, a flash rob occurred in Germantown, Maryland, involving over 30 teens who ransacked a convenience store and stole drinks, snacks, and candy. Reportedly, they gathered together to plan to commit this crime through social media (CNN 2011).

Performance Crime Trends

It is hard to estimate the prevalence of performance crimes because there are many different types of performance crimes ranging from flash robs that cause minor harm to acts of terrorism that result in a significant loss of life. Studying the prevalence of performance crimes is also made diffi-cult by how we define particular crimes. For instance, how is terrorism defined? Does the definition include both international and domestic terrorism? In the United States, international terrorism is defined as being "perpetrated by individuals and/or groups inspired by or associated with designated foreign terrorist organizations or nations (state-sponsored)" (FBI 2017). In contrast, domestic terrorism is "perpetrated by individuals and/or groups inspired by or associated with primarily U.S.-based move-ments that espouse extremist ideologies of a political, religious, social, racial, or environmental nature" (FBI 2017). And, more broadly, where do we draw the line between mass shootings and terrorism? These are all big questions that are beyond the scope of this book, but are important to consider as we think about how we study the prevalence of these par-ticular performance crimes that are aided by new media.

Keeping these concerns in mind, in the following section we highlight some of what we know about the prevalence of terrorism. There is a global terrorism database called the National Consortium for the Study of Terrorism and Responses to Terrorism (START 2017) kept through the University of Maryland (see: http://www.start.umd.edu/gtd/). Sanger-Katz (2016) reported in the *New York Times* after examining START (2017) that terrorism is up in Western societies such as North America and Western Europe, but not globally. The San Bernardino and Paris attacks did spike the numbers, but still North American and Western European countries experience low numbers of terrorism incidents comparatively to many other areas (Sanger-Katz 2016). An examination of START's (2017) global map of 1970–2015 demonstrates where the high incidences of ter-rorism are located, with many being in Central and South America, Asia, and Africa. More broadly, we can also look at research examining trends in mass shootings, which are defined by Duwe (2017b, p. 21) as "incidents that occur in the absence of other criminal activity in which guns were used to kill four or more victims at a public location" and, based on this definition, encompass acts of terrorism. Examining mass public shoot-ings in the United States from 1915 to 2013, Duwe (2017b) indicated a slight increase in mass shootings in recent years. In another article, Duwe (2017a) argues that while mass shootings are not becoming more frequent, they are becoming more deadly.

Legal Response to Performance Crimes

Most of the performance crimes we discussed earlier, such as mass public shootings defined as terrorism, are obviously already illegal and subject to punishment. What we see changing is the discussion surrounding the regulation of speech and social media content due to recruitment and dissemination of propaganda by terrorists. As there is disagreement about the regulation of new media, the United Nations (UN) has discussed their role in internet governance (Wu 2015). Although there is disagreement about whether the UN should be involved, Wu (2015) argues that the UN does have a role to play. As a start, the UN can act as a unifying agent across countries by providing a clear international definition of terrorism. As far as regulating content, this is where the complication lies with different laws by country regarding issues of speech. This, of course, resembles some of the response to the trolling activities we described earlier, in that penalizing communication brings about concerns over freedom of speech. The question as to whether it is only up to countries to regulate speech or is it also the company's role to regulate their platforms is also being debated. That is, the government does not need to be the only organization attempting to address the negative impacts of new media.

If we are as a society to address the negative impacts of new media, individuals and other organizations could get involved, even the media itself. A recommendation to legacy media is to stop covering performance crimes in detail and, more difficult and likely impossible, to encourage individuals not to view performance crimes on the interwebs or at least, not to share them. If the goal of performance crimes is to attain an audience and become famous or "internet famous," then we should not give them attention. Lankford and Madfis (2017) have argued regarding mass shootings that legacy media coverage should be limited, and the same could be proposed for coverage of other performance crimes. They propose four guidelines for the coverage of these events (Lankford and Madfis 2017, p. 6):

Do not name the perpetrator. Do not use photos or likeness of the perpetrator. Stop using the names, photos, or likenesses of past perpetrators. Report everything else about these crimes in as much detail as desired.

However, Klausen (2015) has argued that social media is "eliminating dependency" on legacy media for groups like IS. Meaning that limiting legacy media coverage might have little impact because they can spread their propaganda and recruit fighters without legacy media. The last possible (and probably least favored by many in society) recommendation is that of increased surveillance on new media sites by governmental entities or groups. Increased governmental surveillance is already occurring in public spaces, such as in the United Kingdom, where in 2013 they estimated there was 1 camera for every 11 people (Barrett 2013), but for many people, online surveillance may feel like a more significant invasion of privacy. Although an argument can be made that some of this is already occurring with Google and Facebook recording and sharing information that you post or search.

Discussion Question *Should social media be held accountable for the recruitment of criminals or crimes that are planned on their platforms? Why or why not? Discuss the challenges associated with expecting social media to police crime.*

Conclusion

These case studies highlight the complicated nature of criminal activity that utilizes new media. The crimes discussed in this chapter draw attention to timely questions of new media and crime such as: Where is the line between free speech and harassment on social media platforms? What are reasonable expectations for privacy when so much occurs on social media and smartphones are omnipresent? How do we police the internet? How do legal systems respond to crimes that happen online and in multiple countries with distinct legal codes? Can we hold social media companies responsible for criminal behavior that is planned or executed on their platforms? Although this chapter doesn't provide all of the answers to these questions, we hope that it has inspired you to think about crime and the legal responses to crime in new ways.

Discussion Questions

1. How does the definition of crime need to be expanded to include new media forms of crime?
2. How do we determine if threats on social media are criminal or simply free speech?
3. Choose one of the above case studies—trolling, image-based sexual abuse, cyberbullying, or terrorism—and discuss this question: Why does someone (or a group of people) engage in this particular behavior? What sociological or psychological factors might contribute to this behavior?
4. Choose a crime that is connected to new media that was not addressed in this chapter. Discuss how new media is helping to facilitate this crime and how it is being addressed by law enforcement.

References

Media References

Barrett, D. (2013, July 10). One surveillance camera for every 11 people in Britain says CCTV survey. *The Telegraph*. Retrieved from http://www.telegraph.co.uk/technology/10172298/One-surveillance-camera-for-every-11-people-in-Britain-says-CCTV-survey.html

BBC. (2016, October 10). Internet trolls targeted with new legal guidelines. *BBC*. Retrieved from http://www.bbc.com/news/uk-37601431

BBC. (2017, May 8). Nigeria Chibok abductions: What we know. *BBC*. Retrieved from http://www.bbc.com/news/world-africa-32299943

Benes, R. (2016, October 25). 6 charts: Twitters troll problem by the numbers. *Digiday*. Retrieved from https://digiday.com/media/6-charts-twitters-troll-problem-numbers/

Berman, M. (2016, December). One year after the San Bernandino attack, police offer a possible motive as questions still linger. *The Washington Post*. Retrieved from https://www.washingtonpost.com/news/post-nation/wp/2016/12/02/one-year-after-san-bernardino-police-offer-a-possible-motiveas-questions-still-linger/?noredirect=on&utm_term=.34cc971e6ed0

Brand-Williams, O. (2017, April 4). Woman wins 600K in Macomb County revenge porn suit. *The Detroit News.* Retrieved from http://www.detroitnews.com/story/news/local/macomb-county/2017/04/04/revenge-porn-damages-approved/100019510/

Busari, S. (2017). How fake news does real harm. *Ted.com.* Retrieved from https://www.ted.com/talks/stephanie_busari_how_fake_news_does_real_harm/discussion?languag#t-373157

CNN. (2011, August 16). 'Flash mob' robs Maryland 7-Eleven in less than a minute, police say. *CNN.* Retrieved from http://www.cnn.com/2011/CRIME/08/16/maryland.flash.mob/index.html

Dewey, C. (2014, October 14). The only guide to Gamergate that you will ever need to read. *The Washington Post.* Retrieved from https://www.washington-post.com/news/the-intersect/wp/2014/10/14/the-only-guide-to-gamergate-you-will-ever-need-to-read/?utm_term=.f4d98dbfd66a

Duwe, G. (2017a, October 4). Mass shootings are getting more deadly, not more frequent. *Politico Magazine.* Retrieved from https://www.politico.com/magazine/story/2017/10/04/mass-shootings-more-deadly-frequent-research-215678

Gleeson, H. (2016, July 8). Why do men send unsolicited dick pics? *ABC Australia.* Retrieved from http://www.abc.net.au/news/2016-07-09/why-men-send-unsolicited-dick-pics/7540904

Gonzales, R. (2016, October 27). Roommate pleads guilty in Rutgers suicide case. *NPR.* Retrieved from https://www.npr.org/sections/thetwo-way/2016/10/27/499663847/roommate-pleads-guilty-in-rutgers-suicide-case

Hamilton, M. (2017). Families of San Bernardino attack victims accuse Facebook, Google and Twitter of aiding terrorism in lawsuit. *LA Times.* Retrieved from http://www.latimes.com/local/lanow/la-me-ln-san-bernardino-tech-lawsuit-20170503-story.html

Hathaway, J. (2014, October 10). What is gamergate, and why? An explainer for non-geeks. *Gawker.* Retrieved from http://gawker.com/what-is-gamergate-and-why-an-explainer-for-non-geeks-1642909080

History.com. (2014). Boston marathon bombing. *History.com.* Retrieved from http://www.history.com/topics/boston-marathon-bombings

Koerner, B. (2016, April). Why ISIS is winning the social media war. *Wired.* Retrieved from https://www.wired.com/2016/03/isis-winning-social-media-war-heres-beat/

Kushner, D. (2013, November 27). Anonymous vs. Steubenville. *Rolling Stone.* Retrieved from https://www.rollingstone.com/culture/news/anonymous-vs-steubenville-20131127

Lavoipierre, A. (2017, November 10). New revenge porn legislation to impose fines for abusers slated this year. *ABC*. http://www.abc.net.au/news/2017-11-10/new-revenge-porn-legislation-to-impose-civil-penalties/9138040

Lee. (2013). http://www.bbc.com/news/technology-22214511

Merelli, A. (2017). The University of Florida is allowing Richard Spencer to speak because it has to. *Quartz*. Retrieved from https://qz.com/1103619/the-university-of-florida-is-allowing-richard-spencer-to-speak-because-it-has-to/

National Consortium for the Study of Terrorism and Responses to Terrorism (START). (2017). *Global Terrorism Database* [Data file]. Retrieved from https://www.start.umd.edu/gtd

Phillips, W. (2011, December 5). LOLing at tragedy: Facebook trolls, memorial pages and resistance to grief online. *First Monday*. Retrieved from http://first-monday.org/article/view/3168/3115

Rucker. (2014, May 24). Elliot Rodger's killing spree: What happened. *Washington Post*. Retrieved from: https://www.washingtonpost.com/politics/elliot-rodgers-killing-spree-what-happened/2014/05/24/207778ec-e3b2-11e3-810f-764fe508b82d_story.html?utm_term=.7192a83dcb44

Sanger-Katz, M. (2016, August 16). Is terrorism getting worse? In the West, yes. In the world, no. *New York Times*. Retrieved from https://www.nytimes.com/2016/08/16/upshot/is-terrorism-getting-worse-in-the-west-yes-in-the-world-no.html

Solon, O. (2017, April 26). Live and death. *The Guardian*. Retrieved from https://www.theguardian.com/technology/2017/apr/25/facebook-live-mark-zuckerberg-murder-video-thailand

The Guardian. (2017, April 18). Facebook's Mark Zuckerberg on video killing: "We have a lot of work to do." *The Guardian*. Retrieved from https://www.theguardian.com/technology/video/2017/apr/19/facebooks-mark-zuckerberg-on-video-killing-we-have-a-lot-of-work-to-do

Turley, J. (2015, January 8). The biggest threat to French free speech isn't terrorism. It's the government. *The Washington Post*. Retrieved from https://www.washingtonpost.com/opinions/what-it-means-to-stand-with-charlie-hebdo/2015/01/08/ab416214-96e8-11e4-aabd-d0b93ff613d5_story.html?utm_term=.9943d75b7e4b

Williams, J. (2017, November 21). Jennifer Lawrence's nude photo leak in Fappening felt like a gang bang. *Newsweek*. Retrieved from http://www.newsweek.com/jennifer-lawrence-nude-photo-leak-718172

Yann, H. (2017, April 17). White supremacist Richard Spencer denied at University of Florida. *CNN*. Retrieved from http://www.cnn.com/2017/08/16/us/richard-spencer-denied-at-university-of-florida-trnd/index.html

Zimmerman, A., & Bustillo, M. (2011, October 21). Flash Robs Vex Retailers. *The Wall Street Journal.* Retrieved from https://www.wsj.com/articles/SB100 01424052970203752604576643422390552158

Academic References

Barak, A. (2005). Sexual harassment on the Internet. *Social Science Computer Review, 23*(1), 77–92.

Barratt, J., & Bishop, J. (2015). The impacts of alcohol on e-dating activity: Increases in flame trolling corresponds with higher alcohol consumption. In J. Bishop (Ed.), *Psychological and sociological implications surrounding internet gaming addiction* (pp. 186–197). Hershey: Information Science Reference.

Bates, S. (2017). Revenge porn and mental health: A qualitative analysis of the mental health effects of revenge porn on female survivors. *Feminist Criminology, 12*(1), 22–42.

Bishop, J. (2013). *Examining the concepts, issues, and implications of internet trolling.* Hershey: IGI Global.

Branch, K., Hilinski-Rosick, C. M., Johnson, E., & Solano, G. (2017). Revenge Porn Victimization of College Students in the United States: An Exploratory Analysis. *International Journal of Cyber Criminology, 11*(1), 128–142.

Burden, K., & Palmer, C. (2003). Cyber crime: A new breed of criminal? *Computer Law & Security Report, 19,* 222–227.

Burke, S. C., Wallen, M., Vail-Smith, K., & Knox, D. (2011). Using technology to control intimate partners: An exploratory study of college undergraduates. *Computers in Human Behavior, 27*(3), 1162–1167.

Capeller, W. (2001). Not such a neat net: Some comments on virtual criminality. *Social & Legal Studies, 10,* 229–242.

Chess, S., & Shaw, A. (2015). A conspiracy of fishes, or, how we learned to stop worrying about #gamergate and embrace hegemonic masculinity. *Journal of Broadcasting & Electronic Media, 59*(1), 208–220.

Citron, D. K. (2014). *Hate crimes in cyberspace.* Cambridge, MA: Harvard University Press.

Coleman, G. (2014). *Hacker, hoaxer, whistleblower, spy: The many faces of anonymous.* Brooklyn: Verso.

Cook, C., Schaafsma, J., & Antheunis, M. L. (2018). Under the bridge: An in-depth examination of online trolling in the gaming context. *New Media & Society* [Online]. Retrieved from http://journals.sagepub.com/doi/10.1177/1461444817748578

Cyber Civil Rights. (n.d.). *38 States + DC have revenge porn laws.* Retrieved from https://www.cybercivilrights.org/revenge-porn-laws/

DeKeseredy, W., & Schwartz, M. (1998, February). *Measuring the extent of woman abuse in intimate heterosexual relationships: A critique of the conflict tactics scale.* Retrieved from http://vawnet.org/sites/default/files/materials/files/2016-09/AR_Ctscrit_0.pdf

Dimond, J., Fiesler, C., & Bruckman, A. (2011). Domestic violence and information communication technologies. *Interacting with Computers, 23*(5), 413–421.

Duwe, G. (2017b). The patterns and prevalence of mass public shootings in the United States, 1915–2013. In L. C. Wilson (Ed.), *The Wiley handbook of the psychology of mass shootings* (pp. 20–35). West Sussex: Wiley Blackwell.

Eaton, A. A., Jacobs, H., & Ruvalcaba, Y. (2017). 2017 Nationwide online study of nonconsensual porn victimization and perpetration: A summary report. *Cyber Civil Rights Initiative.* Retrieved from https://www.cybercivilrights.org/wp-content/uploads/2017/06/CCRI-2017-Research-Report.pdf

FBI. (2017). Terrorism. *Federal Bureau of Investigations.* Retrieved from https://www.fbi.gov/investigate/terrorism

Findlaw.com. (2017). *Internet trolls can be prosecuted under Australian Law.* Retrieved from http://www.findlaw.com.au/articles/4259/internet-trolls-can-be-prosecuted-under-australian.aspx

Franklin. (2017). Justice for revenge porn victims: Legal theories to overcome claims of civil immunity by operators of revenge porn websites. *California Law Review, 102*, 1303–1335.

Furnell, S. (2002). *Cybercrime: Vandalizing the information society.* London, UK: AddisonWesley.

Gámez-Guadix, M., Almendros, C., Borrajo, E., & Calvete, E. (2015). Prevalence and association of sexting and online sexual victimization among Spanish adults. *Sexuality Research and Social Policy, 12*(2), 145–154.

Garcia, A., Mirra, N., Morrell, E., Martinez, A., & Scorza, D. A. (2015). The council of youth research: Critical literacy and civic agency in the digital age. *Reading & Writing Quarterly, 31*(2), 151–167.

Garett, R., Lord, L. R., & Young, S. D. (2016). Associations between social media and cyberbullying: A review of the literature. *MHealth online.* Retrieved from http://mhealth.amegroups.com/article/view/12924/13218

Grabosky, P. (2001). Virtual criminality: Old wine in new bottles? *Social & Legal Studies, 10*, 243–249.

Hare, I., & Weinstein, J. (Eds.). (2009). *Extreme speech and democracy.* Oxford: Oxford University Press.

Hayes, R. M., & Dragewiecz, M. (submitted). Dick pics: Exhibitionism or entitlement? *Women's Studies International Forum*.

Henry, N., & Powell, A. (2015). Embodied harms: Gender, shame, and technology facilitated sexual violence. *Violence Against Women, 21*(6), 758–779.

Henry, N., & Powell, A. (2016a). Technology-facilitated sexual violence: A literature review of empirical research. *Trauma, Violence and Abuse, 19*(2), 1–14.

Henry, N., & Powell, A. (2016b). Sexual violence in the digital age: The scope and limits of criminal law. *Social & Legal Studies, 25*(4), 1–22.

Henry, N., Powell, A., & Flynn, A. (2017). *Not just 'revenge pornography': Australian's experiences of image-based abuse*. Melbourne, Australia: RMIT University. Retrieved from: https://www.rmit.edu.au/content/dam/rmit/documents/college-of-design-and-socialcontext/schools/global-urban-and-social-studies/revenge_porn_report_2017.pdf

Hinduja, S., & Patchin, J. (2008). Cyberbullying: An exploratory analysis of factors related to offending and victimization. *Deviant Behavior, 29*(2), 129–156.

Hinduja, S., & Patchin, J. W. (2015). *Bullying beyond the schoolyard: Preventing and responding to cyberbullying* (2nd ed.). Thousand Oaks: Sage.

Jane, E. A. (2017). *Misogyny online: A short (and brutish) history*. Sage Publications.

Kelly, L. (1988). *Surviving sexual violence*. Cambridge, UK: Polity Press.

Klausen, J. (2015). Tweeting the jihad. *Studies in Conflict and Terrorism, 38*(1), 1–22.

Lankford, A., & Madfis, E. (2017). Don't name them, don't show them, but report everything else: A pragmatic proposal for denying mass killers the attention they seek and deterring future offenders. *American Behavioral Scientist*. https://doi.org/10.1177/0002764217730854.

Legal Dictionary. (n.d.). *Cyberstalking*. Retrieved from https://legaldictionary.net/cyberstalking

Lenhart, A., Ybarra, M., & Price-Feeney, M. (2016). Nonconsensual image sharing: One in 25 Americans has been a victim of 'revenge porn'. LenRetrieved from https://datasociety.net/pubs/oh/Nonconsensual_Image_Sharing_2016.pdf

Lenhart, A., Ybarra, M., Zickuhr, K., & Price-Feeney, M. (2016). *Online harassment, digital abuse, and cyberstalking in America*. Data & Society Research Institute Report 11.21.16. Retrieved from https://www.datasociety.net/pubs/oh/Online_Harassment_2016.pdf

Lindgren, S., & Lundstrom, R. (2011). Pirate culture and hacktivist mobilization: The cultural and social protocols of #Wikileaks on twitter. *New Media & Society, 13*(6), 999–1018.

Marcum, C., Ricketts, M., & Higgins, G. (2010). Assessing sex experiences of online victimization: An examination of adolescent online behaviors using Routine Activity Theory'. *Criminal Justice Review, 35*(4), 412–437.

Martin, J., & Alaggia, R. (2013). Sexual abuse images in cyberspace: Expanding the ecology of the child. *Journal of Child Sexual Abuse, 22*(4), 398–415.

Marwick, A., & Lewis, R. (n.d.). *Media manipulation and disinformation online.* Retrieved from https://datasociety.net/pubs/oh/DataAndSociety_Media ManipulationAndDisinformationOnline.pdf

McAfee. (2013). *Lovers beware: Scorned exes nay share intimate data and images online.* Retrieved from http://mcafee.com/au/about/news/2013/q1/20130204-01.aspx

McGlynn, C., & Rackley, E. (2015). *Image-based sexual abuse: More than just revenge porn.* Retrieved from https://claremcglynn.files.wordpress.com/2015/10/imagebasedsexualabuse-mcglynnrackley-briefing.pdf

McGlynn, C., & Rackley, E. (2017). Image-based sexual abuse. *Oxford Journal of Legal Studies, 37*(3), 534–561.

McGlynn, C., Rackley, E., & Houghton, R. (2017). Beyond "revenge porn": The continuum of image-based sexual abuse. *SSRN.* Retrieved from https://ssrn.com/abstract=2929257

Mitchell, K. J., Jones, L. M., Finkelhor, D., & Wolak, J. (2011). Internet-facilitated commercial sexual exploitation of children: Findings from a nationally representative sample of law enforcement agencies in the United States'. *Sexual Abuse, 23*(1), 43–71.

Mitchell, K. J., Finkelhor, D., Jones, L. M., & Wolak, J. (2012). Prevalence and characteristics of youth sexting: A national study. *Pediatrics, 129*(1), 1–10.

Morelli, M., Bianchi, D., Baiocco, R., Pezzuti, L., & Chirumbolo, A. (2016). Sexting, psychological distress and dating violence among adolescents and young adults. *Psicothema, 28*(2), 137–142.

Patchin, J. W., & Hinduja, S. (2006). Bullies move beyond the schoolyard: A preliminary look at cyberbullying. *Youth Violence and Juvenile Justice, 4*(2), 148–169.

Pease, K. (2001). Crime futures and foresight: Challenging criminal behaviour in the information age. In D. Wall (Ed.), *Crime and the Internet* (pp. 18–28). London, UK: Routledge.

Phillips, W. (2015). *This is why we can't have nice things: Mapping the relationship between online trolling and mainstream culture.* Cambridge, MA: MIT Press.

Powell, A., & Henry, N. (2016). Policing technology-facilitated sexual violence against adult victims: Police and service sector perspectives. *Policing & Society, 28*(3), 1–17.

Powell, A., & Henry, N. (2017). Sexual violence and harassment in the digital era. In A. Deckert & R. Sarre (Eds.), *The Australian and New Zealand handbook of criminology, crime and justice*. Basingstoke, UK: Palgrave Macmillan.

Pozza, V., Di Pietro, A., Morel, S., & Psaila, E. (2016). *Cyberbullying among young people. European Parliament Think Tank*. Retrieved from http://www.europarl.europa.eu/thinktank/en/document.html?reference=IPOL_STU(2016)571367

Prasad, S. T. (2014). Ethical hacking and types of hackers. *International Journal of Emerging Technology in Computer Science and Electronics, 11*(2), 24–27.

Reyns, B. W., Burek, M. W., Henson, B., & Fisher, B. S. (2013). The unintended consequences of digital technology: Exploring the relationship between sexting and cybervictimization. *Journal of Crime and Justice, 36*(1), 1–17.

Salter, M. (2017). *Crime, justice & social media*. Oxon: Routledge.

Sheridan, L. P. & Grant, T. D. (2007). Is Cyberstalking Different? *Psychology, Crime and Law, 13*(6), 627–640.

Siegel, L. (2015). *Criminology: Theories, patterns, and typologies*. Boston: Cengage Learning.

Spitzberg, B.H. & Hoobler, G. (2002. Cyberstalking and the technologies of interpersonal terrorism. *New Media & Society, 4*(1), 71–92.

Staude-Müller, F., Hansen, B., & Voss, M. (2012). How stressful is online victimization? Effects of victim's personality and properties of the incident. *European Journal of Developmental Psychology, 9*(2), 260–274.

Stevens, H., & Aggarwal, P. (2017, April). What's it like to get trolled all day long. *Hindustan Times*. Retrieved from https://www.hindustantimes.com/interactives/lets-talk-about-trolls/whats-it-like-to-get-trolled-all-day-long/

Stonard K. E., Bowen E., Lawrence T. R., & Price S. A. (2014). The relevance of technology to the nature, prevalence and impact of adolescent dating violence and abuse: A research synthesis. *Aggression and Violent Behavior, 19*(4), 390–417.

Stopbullying.gov. (n.d.). *Kids on social media and gaming*. Retrieved from https://www.stopbullying.gov/cyberbullying/kids-on-social-media-and-gaming/index.html

Straus, M. A., Hamby, S. L., Boney-McCoy, S., & Sugarman, D. B. (1995). *The revised conflict tactics scales (CTS2-form A)*. Durham: Family Research Laboratory.

Stryker, C. (2011). *Epic win for anonymous: An online army conquers the web*. New York: The Overlook Press.

Surette, R. (2015). *Media, crime, & criminal justice: Images, realities, and policies* (5th ed.). Stamford: Cengage Learning.

Synder, F. (2001). Sites of criminality and sites of governance. *Social & Legal Studies, 10*, 251–256.

Thompson, M. P., & Morrison, D. J. (2013). Prospective predictors of technology-based sexual coercion by college males. *Psychology of Violence, 3*(3), 233–246.

Trottier, D., & Fuchs, C. (2015). *Social media, politics and the state: Protests, revolutions, riots, crime and policing in the age of Facebook, Twitter, and Youtube.* New York: Routledge.

Tyler Clementi Foundation. (2017). *Tyler's story.* Retrieved from https://tylerclementi.org/tylers-story/

United States Department of Justice. (2017). *Winchester man sentenced to 24 months for illegally hacking into website and lying to federal agents.* Retrieved from https://www.justice.gov/usao-edky/pr/winchester-man-sentenced-24-months-illegally-hacking-website-and-lying-federal-agents

Wall, D. (2001). *Crime and the Internet.* London: Routledge.

Westlake, B. G., & Bouchard, M. (2016). Criminal careers in cyberspace: Examining website failure within child exploitation networks. *Justice Quarterly, 33*(7), 1154–1181.

Woodlock, D. (2016). The abuse of technology in domestic violence and stalking. *Violence Against Women*, OnlineFirst.

World Health Organization (WHO) (2002). *World report on violence and health.* Geneva: World Health Organization.

World Health Organization (WHO) (2013). *Global and regional estimates of violence against women: Prevalence and health effects.*

Wu, P. (2015). Impossible to regulate: Social media, terrorists, and the role for the U.N. *Chicago Journal of International Law, 16*(1), Article 11. Retrieved from https://chicagounbound.uchicago.edu/cgi/viewcontent.cgi?article=1690&context=cjil

Yar, M. (2005). The novelty of 'cybercrime': An assessment in light of routine activity. *European Journal of Criminology, 2*, 407–427.

Yar, M. (2012). Crime, media, and the will-to-representation: Reconsidering relationships in the social media age. *Crime, Media & Culture, 8*(3), 245–260.

Zweig J., Dank M., Yahner J., Lachman P. (2013). The rate of cyber dating abuse among teens and how it relates to other forms of teen dating violence'. *Journal of Youth and Adolescence, 42*(7), 1063–1077.

6

Conclusion

As we began writing this final chapter, news broke of charges of distributing child pornography against over 1000 Danish youth (Orange 2018). Using Facebook, these individuals are accused of sharing video of two minors engaging in sexual activity. This case, the details surrounding of which are emerging as we write the chapter, reminds us that criminologists must expand their view of delinquency and crime to encompass what is occurring on new media platforms. As Ray Surette stated in his interview, in Chap. 1, "as new media comes to more define the daily 'lived' lives of people, especially youth, criminologists that ignore their existence do so at the peril of being irrelevant" (R. Surette, personal communication, July 14, 2017). This quote essentially sums up our purpose for this book: to highlight the necessity for criminologists to study new media.

In Chap. 1, we overviewed the theories that we see as central to the study of media and crime. As media studies is already an interdisciplinary field, we drew from multiple fields to theoretically frame our book. We also called for new theoretical approaches to be considered in future studies of new media and crime. Chapter 2 emphasized how media is impacting the operation of the criminal legal system and how this will continue to change with new media. We saw this play out recently as Judge Rosemarie Aquilina in Michigan (United States) allowed the victim impact

© The Author(s) 2018
R. M. Hayes, K. Luther, *#Crime*, Palgrave Studies in Crime, Media and Culture,
https://doi.org/10.1007/978-3-319-89444-7_6

statements to be livestreamed in the sentencing of Larry Nassar, who was found guilty of criminal sexual conduct against American gymnasts (Bartkowiak et al. 2018). Both Chaps. 3 and 4 unpacked how legacy and new media affect perceptions of crime and victimization. These two chapters call attention to the ways the media presents a narrative of who we should fear as a criminal and who is a legitimate victim that deserves our empathy. Drawing on ideas mentioned in previous chapters, Chap. 5 focused specifically on how crime is influenced and even carried out through new media. Using four case studies, we highlighted timely issues surrounding the perpetration and control of crime.

Throughout this volume, we draw from multiple disciplines— criminology, psychology, media studies, and sociology—to examine the ways media influences crime. Each of these disciplines provide distinct, yet related, lenses to view issues of crime and media through. We also pay close attention to race, ethnicity, gender, sexuality, and social class and the intersections of these statuses in each chapter. For example, as discussed in Chap. 4, the media impacts who we view as victims and we argue that people whose identities place them at the intersection of multiple marginalized statuses are more likely to be denied true victim status.

In the book we also suggest that new media has the potential to positively shape understandings of crime and victimization. Groups that have been stereotyped as criminals and experienced injustice in the criminal legal system are fighting back through new media such as the #BlackLivesMatter movement. Narratives of victimization are also changing with new media. Through the #MeToo campaign, victims are able to have their voices heard in social media. We believe #BlackLivesMatter, #MeToo and other social media movements may be changing the larger conversations about crime, victimization, and justice, and we encourage media criminologists to investigate the effects of these campaigns.

Future Research

Through our research for this book, we see a need for research specifically examining new media and crime. In particular, we call for research in these key areas:

- The impact of new media on law and criminal legal responses—How are laws changing to incorporate new media crimes? How is the criminal legal system responding to new media crimes?
- The influence of technology on the criminal legal system—How is technology impacting crime investigations, arrests, prosecutions, and courtroom proceedings?
- The effect of counterpublics—Are counterpublics changing public opinion on crime- and justice-related issues?
- The prevalence of technology-facilitated sexual violence—Based on representative samples, how prevalent is technology-facilitated sexual violence and how prevalent is technology-facilitated violence?
- Perceptions of trolling and motivations for trolling—Does the public perceive trolling as potentially criminal behavior? Who engages in trolling and what motivates trolling behavior?
- The role of fake news—Is fake news changing perceptions of crime and victimization?

Challenges to the Field of Media Criminology

The biggest challenge of studying new media, as we stated in Chap. 1, is the quickness with how technology and trends change. When we began writing this book in 2015, Yik Yak was being used by young people to bully (Hinduja and Patchin 2015); now in 2018, it is no longer a platform as it shut down in 2017 (Carson 2017). As we write this conclusion, snapchat is still a popular application but how it works has changed (e.g. the snaps last longer, you can create stories that last all day, and filters are increasingly popular). Researchers need to be ready to study topics in a quickly changing environment. Fast-changing technology becomes even more problematic for researchers due to the slow process of academic research and peer-reviewed publication. When researchers are collecting their own data, which is necessary when studying new topics where there are no available datasets, much time can pass between Internal Review Board approval and a peer-reviewed publication.

Another methodological challenge for researchers surrounds how particular criminal behavior is defined. As discussed in Chap. 5, many crimes related to new media are poorly defined or defined in conflicting ways, which makes conducting research or comparing findings difficult. These definitional issues become even more complicated when studying crimes that occur online by individuals in multiple countries with distinct criminal legal codes. Thus, studying new media and crime is ripe with challenges for researchers.

A broader challenge that we face in this field is combating misinformation in the media about crime. In this era of fake news, it is more important than ever that criminologists find ways to educate the public about crime and victimization from a data driven standpoint. There is a growing distrust in the mainstream media, and this could negatively impact society's understanding of crime. Although this may seem insignificant to some, we need a well-informed public to call for criminal legal reform and policies. In the classroom, professors work to overcome misinformation by teaching students how to determine the validity of news they are consuming. More broadly, the American Society of Criminology is also working to address this issue through social media. The hashtag #RealCrimeData was started in order to counter the misinformation about crime that was being shared in the media.

In conclusion, we recognize that this book asks more questions than it answers. This is a new and quickly changing field of study that is ripe for research to begin to answer these unanswered questions. Our hope is for this book to serve as a call to action for students and researchers. We encourage scholars to ask innovative questions about crime and new media and to use their research to positively impact the criminal legal system.

References

Media References

Bartkowiak, D., Haddad, K., & Monacelli, N. (2018). LIVE STREAM: Former Doctor Larry Nassar to be sentenced Wednesday after final statement. *ClickOnDetroit.com.* Retrieved from https://www.clickondetroit.com/news/live-stream-former-doctor-larry-nassar-to-be-sentenced-wednesday-after-final-statements

Carson, B. (2017). Yik Yak is officially dead. *Business Insider.* Retrieved from http://www.businessinsider.com/yik-yak-shuts-down-2017-4

Orange, R. (2018, January 27). Denmark split as row over teenage Facebook sex video widens. *The Guardian.* Retrieved from https://www.theguardian.com/technology/2018/jan/27/denmark-teenage-facebook-sex-video-row-widens

Academic Reference

Hinduja, S., & Patchin, J. W. (2015). *Bullying beyond the schoolyard: Preventing and responding to cyberbullying* (2nd ed.). Thousand Oaks: Sage.

Index

© The Author(s) 2018
R. M. Hayes, K. Luther, *#Crime*, Palgrave Studies in Crime, Media and Culture,
https://doi.org/10.1007/978-3-319-89444-7

Made in the USA
Las Vegas, NV
05 September 2021

29666024R00125